D1540292

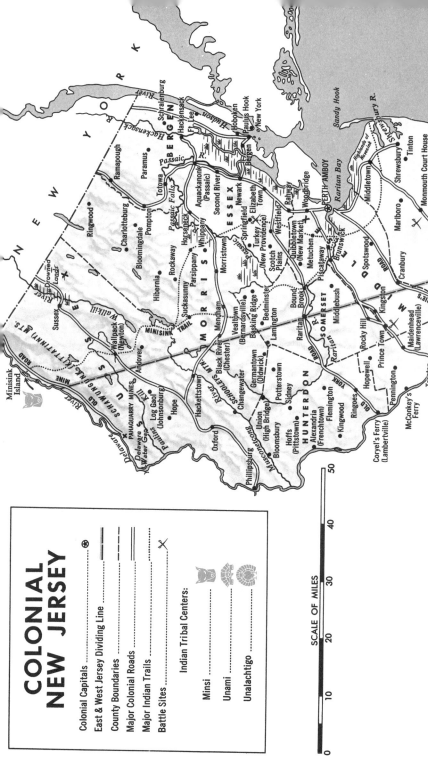

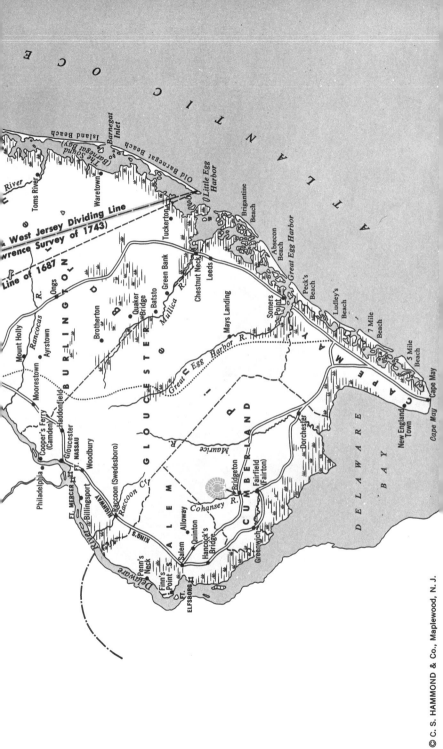

ATLANTIC OCEAN

Barnegat Inlet

Island Beach
Old Barnegat Beach
The Sound (Barnegat Bay)

Toms River
River
Waretown

West Jersey Dividing Line
Lawrence Survey of 1743
Line of 1687

Little Egg Harbor

Tuckerton
Ongs
R.

BURLINGTON

Brotherton
Ayrstown
Rancocas R.
Mount Holly

Green Bank
Quaker Bridge
Batsto
Mullica R.

Chestnut Neck
Leeds

Brigantine Beach

Absecon Beach

Great Egg Harbor

Peck's Beach

Somers Point

Ludley's Beach

Mays Landing
Great Egg Harbor R.

7 Mile Beach

GLOUCESTER

5 Mile Beach

Cape May

Moorestown
Haddonfield
Cooper's Ferry (Camden)
Gloucester
NASSAU
Woodbury
Philadelphia
FT. MERCER
Billingsport
Raccoon (Swedesboro)
Raccoon Cr.
FT. MIFFLIN
KING'S HWY.
S. KING'S
Alloway
Quinton
Salem
Hancock's Bridge
Penn's Neck
Finn's Point
FT. ELFSBORO

Delaware River

SALEM

Maurice R.

Cohansey R.

Bridgeton
Fairfield (Fairton)
Greenwich

CUMBERLAND

Dorchester

New England Town
Cape May
CAPE MAY

DELAWARE BAY

Tours of
Historic New Jersey

Sandy Hook Beacon, oldest original lighthouse still standing and in use in the United States, was built in 1764 by a group of New York merchants. See p. 89.

Photo by Adeline Pepper

Tours of
Historic New Jersey

ADELINE PEPPER

RUTGERS UNIVERSITY PRESS

New Brunswick, New Jersey

Library of Congress Cataloging in Publication Data

Pepper, Adeline.
    Tours of historic New Jersey.

    1. New Jersey—Description and travel—1951–
Guide-books. 2. New Jersey—Historic houses, etc.
I. Title.
F132.3.P4   1973   917.49'04'4   73-6889
ISBN 0-8135-0779-0 Cloth
      0-8135-0759-6 Paper

PRINTED IN THE UNITED STATES OF AMERICA BY QUINN & BODEN
COMPANY, INC., RAHWAY, NEW JERSEY

Washington's Headquarters in "the grimmest winter of the Revolution." Nearby is a federal museum, outstanding for important relics and documents of the American Revolution. See Morristown National Park, p. 47.

Photo by Adeline Pepper

Ringwood Manor, home of famous ironmasters, from "Baron" Peter Hasenclever to Peter Cooper, and also of Washington's surveyor general, Robert Erskine. See Ringwood State Park, p. 12.

HOW TO ENJOY NEW JERSEY

This is a book of ideas for whiling away some pleasant hours. But I hope these tours will also direct the traveler to an exploratory look at the vivid panorama of America's past. Today when standard values are being wrenched loose is a good time to assess our origins.

In earlier centuries New Jersey was a land of such scenic wonder that painters from France, England, Russia and Germany endured real hardships to record this beauty. Testimony to the artists' excitement abounds in paintings of Passaic Falls, Weehawken, the Delaware, the Palisades. Travelers today can still see some Jersey villages scarcely changed since the early 1800's, Monmouth battlefield with orchards and fields almost as when Washington led the troops at Freehold in 1778, meetinghouses where Quakers have gathered every "first day" since before the Revolution, mountain forests with herds of deer, windswept beaches where thousands of egrets nest. All of this, in a State which has more people per acre than any other in the Union but also produces the highest farm income per acre. Clearly, New Jersey is a State of paradoxes.

To enjoy these intriguing contrasts in full measure the first advice is: leave the expressways. Take them, to be sure, to arrive at a central goal, but from then on, travel the byways. Even a block away from Main Street, now a stereotype throughout the Nation, one finds delightful surprises from town to town in Jersey. As a sampler, explore the dogwood lanes around Far Hills, sequestered villages like charming Bloomsbury, hidden roads in the Ramapos where early English folksongs are still sung, or the Old Mine Road. Only a few squares from "strip" highways, the tourist comes upon such handsome residential parks as Ridgewood, Short Hills and Princeton, or 2000 acre preserves like South Mountain and Watchung.

One of the joys of touring New Jersey is that special gear is rarely needed. Always close at hand are restaurants and comfortable lodging. But still, one can sleep out in a lean-to under the stars, along the Appalachian Trail in Worthington, Stokes, Wawayanda and High Point State Parks.

Maps from gasoline service stations provide excellent guides for these tours. Indispensable for the Northeast is the Metropolitan New Jersey map. For intensive local exploration, county maps can be had from the Board of Chosen Freeholders at any of the 21 county seats.

As a rule, fees for parks and museums are low, and many are free. Commercial establishments operated for profit are included only if having a *bona fide* historical aspect, or as a sampling of industrial tours.

By no means is this a book just for motorists. Many great scenic and historic areas of New Jersey can be reached by plane, train, bus, motorboat, sail, canoe and foot, as described in individual tours.

At least one early map of New Jersey pictured it as the island it very nearly is. Small wonder that its 300 miles of navigable shoreline exerted, even two centuries ago, the pull of a magnetic field upon travelers. As the Jersey shore is world-famed today, this guide emphasizes some less well known but no less magnetic spots.

As this is a book of places to see, things to do, empty sites of vanished glory are usually omitted. Each tour has an historical *motif,* to set the background for an area; thus travelers can follow major battles and historic personages or trace regional industries like glassmaking or locate frontier settlements such as the Minisink valley. Trips are designed to offer variety: historic places balanced with parks, gardens, forests, beaches.

Inclusion of an historic building does not mean it is superior to any omitted. I wish I had had space to include all historic sites of New Jersey, a State with five of the major Revolutionary battlefields, with a dozen documented houses where Washington stayed, where the Revolutionary Treaty of Peace was signed, where outerspace research is expanding the universe. This guide is intended to encourage the reader's explorations, *his* help in discovery and preservation of records of stirring events. Tracking down the true story of the past can be an exciting and rewarding detective search.

A most gratifying discovery in updating *Tours of Historic New Jersey* is that the number of historic places newly opened exceeds those which have been burned, bulldozed or buried through "money malnutrition." This is scarcely cause for complacency while a great national shrine, Washington's Morristown headquarters, is being strangled by a Federal highway.

An agreeable surprise is that some new museums and salvaged historic buildings have become lively community centers. Remarkable popular support has arisen for the Miller-Corey farmhouse in residential Westfield. Visitors stand in line on Sunday afternoons to inspect antiquities and watch Colonial style pie-baking or blacksmithing. Here is a house come alive through gifts of time, creativity and funds from diverse people.

A disparate example, just as exciting, is the Morristown Museum. When I first met it during the 1964 New Jersey Tercentenary, the museum was good but small. Now fully accredited, it has become a mecca for people's avocations. "Hobbies" is too tiny a word.

Exciting too is that the James Marshall house on Lambertville's main street is restored, not flattened into a parking lot as planned in 1964. I like to think that this book had some effect in the increased life span. James Marshall was the Jerseyan who was the first person to discover gold in California, an event radically changing American history.

Sunfish, that serene lake atop the Kittatinny mountains lining the upper Delaware, has been rescued, after a struggle during which I was told this was a lost cause. Saved from becoming a drab muddy workhorse for pumped-storage electric power, ancient Sunfish Pond, well known to the Indians, was designated a United States national landmark, in lakeside ceremonies, on May 19, 1973.

In May the fireflies and the whip-poor-wills still appear at Batsto Village as they did in 1766 when the iron furnace was built there.

ADELINE PEPPER

Batsto, New Jersey
May 1973

◄§ x §►

TABLE OF CONTENTS

THE NORTHEAST

THE PALISADES AND THE
OLD DUTCH REGION

GEORGE WASHINGTON BRIDGE   1932

Renowned architect LeCorbusier called this the most beautiful bridge in the world. Although a second deck has now been added to it, the George Washington Bridge uniting Manhattan and New Jersey at the Palisades remains as magnificent as ever. For all its cobweb delicacy when viewed in a mist, the span is strong enough to carry 18,000 vehicles an hour. The cables were made by John A. Roebling's Sons of Trenton, who also made the steel strands for San Francisco's Golden Gate bridge. The designer is O. H. Ammann.

At its New Jersey terminus the bridge affords access to such main highways as Routes 46 and 80 and connections to the New Jersey Turnpike, the Garden State Parkway, and Route 17, as well as Route 9W and the Palisades Parkway north along the Hudson.

CLIFFSIDE PARK, EDGEWATER

Amidst the maze of exits, travelers sometimes search in vain for a vantage point to capture the bridge on film or paper. Here is such a spot on a flat shelf at the base of the Palisades. Just north of the bridge, this small secluded picnic ground can be reached from Palisades

Parkway *(see below)*. In spring, shad fishermen stake out their nets here as they have for nearly two centuries. One of the old-timers, Harry Lyons of Edgewater, for many years contributed fish for an annual shad bake held at the park the first Sunday after Mother's Day.

PALISADES INTERSTATE PARK   From exit of George Washington Bridge

This New Jersey–New York park strip of 50 miles preserving the unique Hudson Palisades has a scenic toll-free road providing some grand vistas of the river. Traveling the Parkway one has a triple choice: 1) to go north on one roadway and return on the other; 2) to descend the cliffs at marked intervals; 3) to explore sites on the western fringe of the park. Interesting at all seasons, the park has numerous foot trails. Points of interest: *Lookout Point,* Palisade Ave. and Parkway, affords striking panoramas of the river, Manhattan, and George Washington Bridge. *Allison Park,* a lovely spot on the crest of the Palisades; can be reached by driving up or down Hudson Terrace, under the Interstate Parkway, then east. *Henry Hudson Drive,* a road close to the river, can be reached by driving down the steep, winding route at Exit 1. *Englewood Boat Basin* here has picnic tables and outdoor grills. The beautiful Hudson Drive can be followed all the way to the *Alpine Boat Basin.* Here the *Cornwallis House* was headquarters for the British general on Nov. 18, 1776, while his army of 5000 was being ferried across the river for the cliff-climbing, surprise attack on Fort Lee, in which General Nathanael Greene just missed being captured.

GREENBROOK SANCTUARY   Rte. 9W, opp. Clinton Ave. turnoff to Tenafly

Excellent guidance in nature lore and bird-watching. Splendid views of the Hudson. By appointment only, with Palisades Nature Association, Box 203, Tenafly. $5.00 for each group of 20.

THE NEW JERSEY PALISADES ON THE HUDSON RIVER

British General Cornwallis hauled an army and ordnance up these steep cliffs for a surprise attack and capture of Fort Lee in 1766. Today a 50-mile interstate park preserves the beauty of the Palisades.

Courtesy of Rutgers University

BENJAMIN WESTERVELT HOUSE *(private)* 235 Old
   County Rd., Cresskill

Eight generations of Westervelts have lived in this
Dutch house, shown on one of Erskine's Révolutionary
maps. Especially noteworthy because modern dormers
have not been added. Other early Dutch buildings nearby
on County Rd.: Bogert Homestead, No. 35, and Samuel
Demarest House, No. 60.

TEANECK   Rte. 4 NE of George Washington Bridge

HENDRICK BRINCKERHOFF HOUSE   1728 *(private)*
   493 Teaneck Rd.

The oldest house in Teaneck and second oldest in
Bergen County this is described as the finest type of
Colonial Dutch architecture in the State.

JOHN ACKERMAN HOUSE   1734 *(private)*
   1286 River Rd.

Another Dutch house recommended by the Historic
American Buildings Survey as worthy of preservation.

Among other notable Dutch dwellings are: the Cas-
parus Westervelt House (1763), 190 Teaneck Rd.; the
Wearts Banta House (c. 1705), Lone Pine Lane; and the
Samuel Banta House (1830), 1485 Teaneck Rd.

FAIRLEIGH DICKINSON UNIVERSITY
   2 blocks S of Rte. 4.

This 50-acre campus (others at Madison and Rutherford), includes a school of dentistry, and the library on
River Road has an exhibit of old-time tooth-pullers and
related antiques. The library façade has an aluminum
sculpture by William Zorach.

HACKENSACK

BERGEN COUNTY COURT HOUSE   1912
   A domed structure designed by J. Riley Gordon.

CHURCH ON THE GREEN
The earliest building was put up in 1696, rebuilt in 1728, and, though enlarged over the years, the red sandstone structure bespeaks Colonial Dutch architecture.
From Main St., Hackensack, go N to New Bridge, then right to end of street. . .

VON STEUBEN HOUSE *(State historic site)* New Bridge Rd.
Erected in 1751, this was owned by Isaac Zabriskie, a Loyalist whose property was confiscated in the Revolution. Occupied by officers of both sides during the war, the house was later purchased by the State and presented to General von Steuben for his great services in drilling the Continentals into a disciplined army. Owning lands in upstate New York, von Steuben did not live here. An Indian dugout canoe retrieved from the Hackensack River and relics of New Jersey's famous wampum factory at Park Ridge are standouts in the large museum maintained by the Bergen County Historical Society.

PARAMUS

Jacob Epke Banta, a Dutchman who patented land in the east section in 1686, was one of the earliest recorded pioneers in Paramus. Jacob Van Saun also had a patent dated 1695 for land near here. Albert Zabriskie had property in the west portion, which was deeded to him by the Lenni Lenape in 1702. Paramus Road was an Indian trail long before it was a post road.

VAN SAUN PARK
Within this Bergen County park is a famous spring named for George Washington, as the American Army encamped near here in September of 1780 is said to have used this for water. Park has tennis courts, children's zoo, pony rides, miniature replica of an 1866 locomotive, and coaches for children's rides. Picnic tables and fireplaces.

RIDGEWOOD

OLD PARAMUS CHURCH c. 1800
   E. Glen Ave. at Rte. 17

The original cornerstone of "Peremus Kirk" was laid in 1735. In the former octagonal structure Colonel Aaron Burr and Theodosia Provost, widow of a British officer, were married in 1782. Here also the military court assembled which dismissed General Charles Lee for his retreat at the Battle of Monmouth. The blue and white interior, with charming Victorian windows and organ-pipe decorations, is one of the most interesting in New Jersey.

Adjacent is the Cornelius Bogert House *(private)*, the south section of which had a cornerstone dated 1741.

PARAMUS HISTORICAL MUSEUM 650 E. Glen Ave.

A one-room school dating from 1873, it has old-time desks, blackboard, and pot-bellied stove. Many rarities in early farm tools, firearms, Colonial kitchenware, toys, Indian relics. Wed., 2:30-4:30; Sun., 3-5. Weekday appointments for school groups. 201-445-1778.

DAVID ACKERMAN HOUSE *(private)* 415 E. Saddle
   River Road, E of Rte. 17

This is one of the few Dutch houses in Bergen County that has remained almost unchanged since c. 1692.

HARMANUS VAN DER BEEK HOUSE *(private)* W of
   Rte. 17 at triangle of Prospect St. and Maple Avenue

In early days known as the Toll House. See also the Garret Ackerman House *(private)*, 222 Doremus Ave., built by a descendant of David Ackerman about 175 years ago.

FRANKLIN LAKES

NEW JERSEY AUDUBON SOCIETY 790 Ewing Ave.,
   nr. Rte. 502

Engaged in nature conservation since 1910, the New Jersey Audubon Society through its headquarters here has ample outlet for major work because the "spread city," of which there are many in the State, is fast gobbling up green space.

As New Jersey lies beneath one of the great bird flyways of America, several sanctuaries in this strip are now supervised by the New Jersey Audubon Society: for example, the Baldwin and Lorrimer preserves described below and also the Montclair Hawk Lookout.

Membership, open to anyone, is not only a contribution to invaluable conservation work but also provides a chance to participate in field trips, such as the September Cape May weekend featuring guided tours, movies, and talks by naturalists.

Lucine L. Lorrimer Sanctuary

Marked nature study trails in 14 acres of open fields and woodlands. Inquire at New Jersey Audubon Society, 790 Ewing Ave. 9-5 Tues.-Sat. Groups by appointment.

Baldwin Wildlife Sanctuary Route 202, Mahwah

Twenty acres of Ramapo River flood plain and woodlands. Admission by key only, for $1 refundable deposit. By appointment only, with New Jersey Audubon Society, 790 Ewing Ave., Franklin Lakes. 9:30-4:30, daily; 11-4:30, weekends. Closed Thurs. and holidays.

Venturesome motorists are surprised to find how many attractive towns lie hidden behind the industrial façade of Rte. 46. Leonia is one such place, with a suburban look and a history dating from 1668.

From Rte. 46 turn off at Leonia-Fort Lee Exit. Go downhill, on Fort Lee Rd.

LEONIA

FORT LEE MEMORIAL 1916 Presbyterian Church, Fort Lee Rd. at Leonia Ave.

A bronze sculpture by Mahonri Young depicts Washington and Greene as they led the garrison down this road on Nov. 20, 1776, after abandoning newly-built Fort Lee to Cornwallis.

At Grand Ave. go left 2 blocks to Prospect St., SE corner.

BOYD-ALLAIRE-COLE HOUSE *(private)*
Earliest known owner of this Dutch fieldstone house was a Tory said to have been lynched by hanging from a tree which until recent years grew at this corner.
Reverse direction, continue on Grand to Lakeview Ave.

VREELAND HOUSE *(private)* 125 Lakeview Ave.
Its lovely doorway original, as is most of the exterior, this residence, now restored, is a choice example of Dutch architecture. The stone section dates from about 1785, the frame part, from about 1812. Interior woodwork is well preserved, and outstandingly beautiful.

RUTHERFORD

From Rte. 46, Rutherford is accessible via Rte. 17; from Manhattan, via Rte. 3.

FAIRLEIGH DICKINSON UNIVERSITY
The 15-acre Rutherford campus is the original site of the University which though established only in 1942 already has an enrollment of over 16,000. Holding seminars abroad, Fairleigh Dickinson takes special interest in foreign students. On this campus are three buildings of historic interest:
Nathaniel Kingsland House 245 Union Ave.
On his journey from Newburgh to Princeton in 1783 George Washington rested here. Its roof steeply pitched and curved, the original unit of this dwelling dates from 1670, one of the oldest in New Jersey. Remodeled for classroom use, the interior has reproductions of schoolmasters' desks. Documents, prints, and other Americana on display. Weekdays.
Richard Outwater House 1821
Adjoining the Kingsland House but quite different Dutch architecture, with gambrel roof.

The Castle   E. Passaic and Montrose Aves.

The French chateaux of Chaumont and Amboise inspired the architecture of this turreted brownstone, built at a cost of $350,000 in the 1880's.

WILLIAM CARLOS WILLIAMS HOUSE *(private)*

9 Ridge Rd. at Park Ave.

New Jersey's most noted poet, William Carlos Williams, was born in Rutherford Sept. 17, 1883, and lived in this house, still the home of his family. Long a practicing physician, Dr. Williams was the author of some forty volumes of verse and essays. He said his famous series of poems, *Paterson,* was written "to embody the whole knowable world" about him.

THE DEYS, THE RAMAPOS, AND
RINGWOOD'S IRONMASTERS

Dey Mansion
Preakness Valley Park
Pompton Lake
Shepherd's Lake State Park
The Ramapos
Ringwood Manor
Ringwood State Park
Skylands Castle
From Rte. 46 about ¼ mi. E of Rte. 23 circle, take Riverview Rd. N past Totowa Airport to Passaic Co. Golf Course; ½ mi. on Totowa Rd.

THEUNIS DEY MANSION 1740 Preakness Valley Park

It was October 2, 1780, and Major André had just been hanged as a spy by order of George Washington, and the accomplice, traitorous Benedict Arnold, had escaped to the British ship *Vulture,* lying in the Hudson. Washington and his generals, campaigning on the New Jersey side of the Hudson, began to worry about more defectors in their midst. Then came word that Sir Henry Clinton was so enraged over Major André's execution that he planned to have Washington kidnaped. It was imperative that the American commander-in-chief at once find a safe hideout.

Remembering the hospitality he had enjoyed during

July as guest of his friends Colonel and Mrs. Theunis Dey, Washington with a guard of 150 men set out for the 600-acre Dey estate tucked away in New Jersey's Watchung Hills.

The kidnap plot was no wild rumor. Some time after Washington moved in with the Deys, the Queen's Rangers, bold and ruthless cavalry led by Colonel John Simcoe, tried to crash the Continental cordon at Totowa bridge and take Washington a prisoner, but they were repulsed by alerted Americans.

In turn, Washington sent orders from here to General Harry Lee at Hawthorne for the kidnaping of Benedict Arnold. Sgt. John Champe was the soldier tapped to behave like a deserter, flee to Manhattan, stronghold of Tories, and capture Arnold. By a quirk of fate, the plot failed. For years, Champe was wrongly branded a deserter.

In 1780 the wide boards of beautiful Dey Mansion were trod by nearly everybody loyal to the Continental side. And one who wasn't, for in July Benedict Arnold had been here, in his head the plans to turn West Point over to the enemy.

One of the great Colonial houses of the Northeast, Dey Mansion in the green setting of 367-acre Preakness Valley Park, seems scarcely changed from the 18th century, even to the herb garden, so expertly has it been restored. Most of the interior woodwork and paneling is original. Authentic furnishings are in room settings, with choice delftware, elegant fourposters, Colonel Dey's musket, pewter plates given by the Deys to Washington, rare chests and tables. Young girls in Colonial costume are on hand the second and fourth Saturday afternoon of each month to demonstrate spinning, lace-making, soap-making, baking, and candle-dipping. Guided tours, 40 minutes. Children with adults only. Groups, advance reservations. Tues., Wed., Fri. 1-5; Sat., Sun. 10-5. 25¢.

Return to Rte. 23, go N to Riverdale and Hamburg Tpke.

POWDER HORNE MILL INN   1726

Hamburg Tpke., Riverdale

The brook that turned the wheel to make flour for Washington and the army encamped around Totowa in 1780 still flows past the Powder Horne Mill, now a restaurant. Hundreds of acres here belonged to a prominent Dutch family of ironmasters, the Ryersons *(see Ringwood)*, thought to have built the large white house *(private)* opposite the mill. The latter is said to have been run by a Negro living in slave quarters still at the rear of the house. 201-038-0777.

POMPTON LAKES

Created by damming the Pompton River, Pompton Lakes, now lined by private cottages, are well stocked with trout and boat liveries are handy. The countryside was settled by Dutch in the 1680's and still to be seen are their low cozy houses that seem as strongly rooted as trees.

POMPTON-RAMAPO RIVER

Starting as "white water" above the New York line near Tuxedo, the Ramapo broadens below Oakland to become the Pompton. This winding stream with the brooding Ramapo Mountains to the west is a favorite with canoeists and trout fishermen. Seasoned paddlers often start their trip just below Suffern and continue on down to the Passaic River, but newcomers are advised to explore the waterway first by car from Route 202, a tree-shaded road between Oakland and Route 17.

For Ringwood State Park take Rte. 511 N past Wanaque Reservoir. Alternate route: From Pompton Lakes, go NE to Rte. 202, then NE to Oakland; at rear of Oakland postoffice take Skyline Drive NW to Erskine and Rte. 511.

WANAQUE RESERVOIR

A beautiful mountain lake, one of New Jersey's largest, man-made and reserved as a pure-water source for the Newark district. *No visitors,* except by guided tour: write Commissioners, Wanaque Reservoir, Wanaque, N.J.

From Route 511 follow park signs to . . .

RINGWOOD MANOR STATE PARK

In the tradition of ironmasters, "Baron" Peter Hasenclever rode around these wild hills in coach-and-four and had a brass band play for him every evening. That he dined from gold plates as reputed is doubtful but he may have felt entitled to such luxury for his amazing development of an iron-making village here in 1765 which won him high praise from his sponsors, the English "Ringwood Company."

Some will find Peter Cooper the more fascinating ironmaster, a New Yorker who began life so poor that he made his own shoes but when he died had left a great endowment for the Cooper Union whereby penniless boys could be educated.

Most mysterious was Robert Erskine, Scottish engineer who threw in his lot with the Revolutionists and decades later was found to be Washington's secret surveyor-general. For Erskine, of whom there is no known portrait, was map-maker *par excellence* to George Washington, the surveys accurate even by today's standards. After the strain of the Pompton Mutiny, as a result of which Washington had ordered two Americans to be shot, the commander-in-chief came here for Erskine's solace and hospitality, one of several visits. Erskine is buried here, and the miners of Abram S. Hewitt's day were fearful that his ghost walked.

Another ironmaster John Jacob Faesch received highest praise from Revolutionary General Knox who said Faesch's shells were "almost perfect." Martin Ryerson, a mighty ironmaster descended from an early Dutch family in this region, furnished shot for the War of 1812.

Ringwood's rambling chateau is an exciting accretion of 78 rooms, many open and containing the original furnishings of the Coopers and the Hewitts who gave the richly historic park to the State. The gun and trophy room, the Ryerson parlors, Peter Cooper's bedroom, the early English dining room, and the music room with hand-painted seascapes are among many tastefully furnished rooms. Open May 1-Oct. 31, Tues.-Sun., 10-4.

The grounds of Ringwood's 579 acres, which include a formal garden, are also replete with history. A prized item is an enormous iron chain, its links two feet long, such as was made at Ringwood for the Continentals as a barrier against British ships sailing up the Hudson.

One of New Jersey's major historic sites, though not widely known, Ringwood can be especially rewarding to those who do some advance reading about it. A first-hand account is *Those Were the Days* by Edward Ringwood Hewitt. $1.00 per car, 25¢ per person; see also Skylands, in Supplement.

From Ringwood Park Exit turn left and go N on Ringwood-Sloatsburg Rd. for 2 mi. then follow park signs to . . .

SHEPHERD'S LAKE STATE PARK

More varied types of recreation are available than at any other New Jersey State park in these 400 wooded acres atop Eagle Mountain, formerly a private club. A sparkling natural lake of 75 acres offers such summertime enjoyment as a sand beach, picnic groves, good fishing, and boating. In addition the park has a ski slope leading onto the lake, and ice skating is another winter feature. Other major attractions are 4 skeet fields and 3 trap-shooting fields, as well as a practice range with an instructor in charge. Guns can be rented. Range open Tues., Thurs., 6-10; Wed., Fri., 1-10; Sat., Sun., 10-6. The clubhouse, open year 'round, has an inviting restaurant-bar overlooking Shepherd's Lake. Restaurant open daily in summer; Wed.-Sun. in other seasons. A reminder of former owners is a stone chapel built by the Prince family on a wooded hillside. Religious services and weddings can be arranged for in the chapel, through Ringwood State Park.

> *Optional route: Continue N to Sloatsburg, N.Y., then via Rte. 17 to Suffern, N.Y. for connections with N.Y. Thruway.*
>
> *Or return to New Jersey from Suffern via Rte. 17S to Rte. 4 and George Washington Bridge. See also Palisades Interstate Park.*

THE PATERSON SUBMARINE AND LAMBERT CASTLE

PATERSON
WEST PATERSON

The Great Falls of the Passaic affected people in various ways. Dutch missionaries to the Jerseys in 1678 marveled over the 70-foot cascade of foam. In time the Falls became a fashionable watering place. Washington Irving as a frequent visitor to Cockloft Hall on the Passaic near Newark was inspired in 1807 to write a poem, "The Falls of the Passaic." But when Sam Patch, a spinner in a Paterson cotton mill, saw the new Clinton Bridge here at Passaic Falls in 1827, his impulse was to jump, and jump he did, before a crowd. The applause, when Sam surfaced, was such sweet music that he made a career of jumping, even surviving Niagara. On Friday the 13th, 1829, handbills given out at Genesee Falls advertised "Sam Patch's Last Leap." It was.

During the Revolution when Alexander Hamilton saw the Great Falls *his* thought was to harness its ceaseless power, which he did in 1791 by helping to establish here the Society for Useful Manufactures, a plan to make Paterson a "federal city" where everything the young nation needed would be produced. As a manufacturer, the Society failed but through a generous charter covering 700 acres around the Falls, the stockholders controlled lucrative water rights until as recently as 1946. Hydroelectric power from the Great Falls attracted scores of industries, and Paterson became in turn "the cotton town," "the silk city," "the locomotive center." Headlong industrialization brought labor strife: the first strike in the nation when women and child millworkers in 1828 demanded a 12-hour day; and one of the grimmest strikes and lockouts, in 1913. But in the 1940's with nation-wide improvement in labor relations, Paterson entered a new and happier phase. In 1971 a 19th century industrial area of 89 acres, mainly around Spruce and Market Sts., was named the Great Falls Historic District. Buildings not opened.

PATERSON CITY MUSEUM   268 Summer St., at Broadway

A former carriage house holds a collection of minerals that ranks with more famous ones at the Smithsonian Institution and Harvard University. Rotating exhibits of massive specimens, world-wide in scope, and fluorescent minerals shown under "black light," now labeled and displayed by professionals, will appeal not just to "rock hounds" but to any who are intrigued by semi-precious stones. Jewel-like too are myriads of Central American insects collected by Thomas Hallinan, an electrical engineer who helped build the Panama Canal.

The largest assemblage of Lenni Lenape artifacts in the State is here, mostly from the Paterson area, for the Great Falls was a magnet attracting Indian encampments.

A popular feature of the museum is geologic excursions, led by qualified instructors, to such points as Bound Brook and Summit quarries for rock collecting, Garret Mountain, Little Falls, Stokes State Forest, and the Franklin mines. Lists can be obtained by mail.

Deserving a room of its own is a 14-foot iron submarine built in 1878 at Samuel Colt's Old Gun Mill Yard (see p. 16) by John P. Holland, Irish patriot and Paterson schoolmaster, and William Dunkerley, an engineer. Though it promptly sank at its launching in the Passaic, the iron tub managed to submerge for 24 hours in a later trial. Again proving recalcitrant it was abandoned until a half century later when some Paterson boys found it buried in mud. Mon.-Fri., 1-5. Sat., 10-5. Free.

Take Broadway NW to Prospect, turn left, then right to Van Houten St.

OLD GUN MILL 1836 *(not open)* NW cor. Mill and Van Houten Sts.

The first repeating revolver was made here in 1836 by Samuel Colt who wasted six years and all his money trying to convince the government and his backers that his invention was more than a novelty. At a demonstration on the Capitol steps in Washington, Colt's guns fired as predicted. But the horses of President Van Buren's carriage bolted and the driver was killed. After more such setbacks, Colt sold all his machinery, even his last revolver. Then came the Mexican War. With it, Sam Walker of the Texas Rangers remembered the excellent Colt revolver. No longer having a model, Colt made a new one, asked Eli Whitney of Whitneyville, Conn., to make more. Within two years the inventor had his own mill; he lived to be a multimillionaire. The first silk spinning in Paterson was done in the Old Gun Mill by Christopher Colt, Sam's brother.

PASSAIC FALLS McBride Ave. near bridge.

Except in spring thaws or after heavy rains, most of the falls is diverted by a dam for power. Over the years much of the steep gorge has been cut away by man, for this brownstone has made building blocks not only for countless structures in New Jersey but also for Trinity Church in Manhattan.

Cross to W side of Passaic River.

WESTSIDE PARK Totowa and Preakness Aves.

On view here is John P. Holland's first successful submarine, the *Fenian Ram,* named for the Irish patriotic society which helped finance him. In 1881 the *Ram* stayed under water for an hour but, lacking a periscope, collided with a Weehawken ferry and sank. A contemporary of Holland, Simon Lake, Jr., of Ocean City patented the first periscope. As early as the 1880's an English clergyman, G. W. Garrett, was selling steam submarines to foreign governments.

> *From Grand St., turn right at Main St. At Barclay St. turn right, up hill and continue into Valley Rd. First right turn after light is entrance to Garret Mountain Reservation and . . .*

LAMBERT CASTLE   1892 *(museum)*

Working for 32 cents a week in an English cotton mill of 1844, a boy of ten heard about America, land of opportunity. Seven years later the boy, Catholina Lambert, was in Boston earning $4.00 a week. Three years later Lambert was a member of the firm, makers of silk ribbons. The company soon expanded to the "Silk City," and Catholina Lambert became one of its richest residents. Recalling Warwick Castle he modeled his home after it and placed the mansion on this rocky escarpment surveying all Paterson. The interior he furnished with a mélange of *objets d'art*. To show off his gallery of over 350 paintings he once invited 800 people, brought by private trains from New York, to a munificent evening party.

But with the silk strike of 1913, Lambert was forced to sell his collections to satisfy creditors. Auction receipts were a third of the real value of the paintings. The collections which had been promised to the city included Renoirs, Monets, and Constables.

Now county-owned, the castle still has a gold-leaf ceiling in the dining room, hand-stenciled walls, hand-carved oak woodwork—an elaborate décor somewhat obscured by many accessions of the Passaic County Historical Society. Prang lithographs of the Civil War, silk "pictures" made with Jacquard looms, powder horns, and antique machinery are among unusual items. Because of the profusion of unlabeled objects, the free

guide service is recommended. Wed., Thurs., Fri., 1-4:45.
Weekends, 11-4:45. Free.

> *From Lambert Castle Exit go right to fork. Take
> diagonal right road for 1 mi. to entrance, from
> Weaseldrift Rd., of . . .*

GARRET MOUNTAIN RESERVATION

From the 75-foot observation tower one gets a maplike
view of the Passaic Valley and its industrial development. The 575-acre mountain tract is surprisingly wild
considering its proximity to a congested city. Picnic
groves, playing fields, shelter houses, and a scenic drive
leading to Barbours Pond. Bathing here.

> *Continue forward on Weaseldrift Rd., turn left at
> Old Rifle Camp Rd. For connection with Rte. 23,
> take Pellington Blvd. W (see Dey Mansion and
> Ringwood Tour).*
>
> *For Montclair Tour, return to Valley Rd. (which
> passes Lambert Castle), but go* south.

HIKERS' MOUNTAINS—
FISHERMEN'S BROOKS

Boonton	West Milford
Silas Condit Park	Greenwood Lake
Butler	Hewitt State Forest
Norvin Green State Forest	Upper Greenwood Lake
Wanaque Reservoir	Bearfort Mountain
	Newfoundland

"New Jersey's Last Frontier" might be a proper phrase
for some of this country in the Bearfort Range, its
rugged hills dotted with lakes, 80 square miles of them
in West Milford Township alone. Although beloved of
hikers and iron-furnace or Indian buffs, this watershed
region with scenic drives appeals to motorists as well.
Fishing is excellent, especially in the Pequannock. None
of the State forests or parks mentioned is developed
and so visitors should ˌnot expect facilities there, but
eating places are close at hand. The New York–New

Jersey Trail Conference has performed a notable service in laying out over 60 miles of hiking trails in the Wyanokie Hills of Norvin Green State Forest and on Beaufort Mountain *(see Hiking Trails).*

Boonton is accessible from Rtes. 46, 287, 80, or 202.

BOONTON

Hilly Boonton rests on the edge of the precipitous gorge of the Rockaway River, once vital power for early mills and forges. From the hilltops one can see the pretty lake which is Parsippany Reservoir. Beneath it lies Old Boone Town, an iron-making community flooded in 1902 to provide a water supply for Jersey City.

From Main St. continue to W. Main St. and cross bridge. Take first left road up hill to Reserve St.

PUDDING STONE INN 1 Reserve St.

Once an eyrie for the mansion of an ironmaster, the grounds of this hotel afford bird's-eye views of Parsippany Reservoir. An inn for over 60 years, Pudding Stone numbered President Theodore Roosevelt and Joyce Kilmer among its many famous visitors.

Return to Main St. and proceed N to Powerville Rd. At Riverside Hospital turn left to . . .

THE TOURNE   Morris County Park

The top of this rocky wooded cone, its altitude 875 feet, is a lookout with sweeping views in almost a full circle. On a clear day one can see the Manhattan skyline. From the second parking lot in this 225-acre preserve, it is about a 20-minute hike to the summit of the Tourne. In a valley below, along a rushing brook, is a shadowy wildflower trail with rich profusion of blooms and ferns, labeled for botany tours. Picnic groves, fireplaces, ball field. Free.

Return to Powerville Rd., go left and continue on this winding lane, which becomes Kinnelon Rd., for about 12 mi. At Ricker Rd. turn left to . . .

SILAS CONDIT PARK   Morris County Park

A speakeasy hideaway in Prohibition times has been transformed into a pleasing 200-acre hillside park with a small spring-fed lake. With a few changes, a dine-and-dance bungalow, an interesting bit of 1920's architecture with stained glass windows, has become an attractive lakeside pavilion. In spring, trails lead through thick blooms of laurel. Boating and bass fishing, but no swimming. Free.

Return to highway and go left to Rte. 23. (At this intersection travelers may want to continue just across Rte. 23 to Butler, a nice hill-and-dale town. From here a road leads northwest to Norvin Green State Forest, 2260 unspoiled acres, for hikers and hunters.) On Rte. 23 about 5 mi. W of Butler take Echo Lake Rd. N.

SIDE TRIP TO WANAQUE RESERVOIR

At Upper Macopin, take Westbrook Rd. E across reservoir.

An early Indian trail, Westbrook Road runs east, then down through Stonetown, with several early houses along the way. Across the bridge of Wanaque Reservoir the scene rivals that of the Thousand Islands in the St. Lawrence River, according to some travelers. A high crag on the mountain was an Indian council site: *Wikadoma* or "Black Rock." From the east shore of Wanaque Reservoir, Route 511 goes north to Ringwood Manor State Park, a major State historic site.

At Macopin Road the route east across Wanaque Reservoir has some of the most striking scenery in New Jersey, with vistas reminiscent of Montana lakes in the Rockies. The views are especially beautiful at sunset. Wanaque Reservoir is not open for public use, however.

To West Milford continue north on Macopin Rd.

WEST MILFORD

As the hills west of Route 513 are the hikers' mountain, Bearfort, visitors may want to use West Milford as a base for trips in the area. A helpful map of the many secondary roads can be obtained from the township offices of West Milford. Fronting on Pinecliff Lake, West Milford has also spread to Greenwood Lake. Several spots for swimming and picnicking near Macopin Road. The nicely proportioned Presbyterian Church was built in 1817.

GREENWOOD LAKE

A true mountain lake, Greenwood has steep, forested shores, some as high as 700 feet, and extends for about 7 miles, across the New York border, with fine prospects from shore drives. No bathhouses, but boats can be rented. Iceboat races are the big excitement, and skating is good but there are no public accommodations. The west shore at Lakeside had early Indian encampments.

Follow Greenwood Lake Tpke. E to Hewitt . . .

HEWITT

All about are signs of the fabulous Ringwood iron mines, estimated to have produced 2½ million long tons of ore since 1765, chiefly during the ownership of Peter Cooper and Abram S. Hewitt *(see Ringwood Tour)*. The old country store here served the mine for many years. Hiking clubs often use Hewitt as a rendezvous, and a sign here marks the start of the West Milford Historical tour.

From West Milford take Union Valley Rd. to . . .

ABRAM S. HEWITT STATE FOREST

Lying between the two Greenwood lakes, this rugged tract of 1890 forested acres is undeveloped but has great appeal to hunters. No public accommodations. Surprise

Lake, accessible from West Milford, is a jaunt for seasoned hikers.

UPPER GREENWOOD LAKE

A beautiful lake with islands and irregular shore line, the name of one of its roads, Longhouse Drive, suggests that the Indians, too, favored this body of water. Moe Mountain lies along the south shore, and in early times the Mountain Laurel Inn was called Moe's Tavern.

Take scenic Clinton Rd. S to Newfoundland.

BEARFORT RIDGE   E of Clinton Rd.

The highest range in Passaic County, this is a beautiful woodland watershed that has created major reservoirs serving cities of New Jersey's northeast.

CLINTON RESERVOIR   W of Clinton Rd.

Across the road from Clinton Dam is Clinton Furnace which opened in 1837 and smelted iron for a few years. It has been largely restored by the Newark Watershed Administration. Several lovely waterfalls tumble down the brook near the furnace.

ROCK COLLECTORS' HEAVEN AND A WILDERNESS PARK

Andover Furnace	Hamburg
Andover Playhouse	Lake Wawayanda State
Huntsville	Forest
Wolverton Tavern	Picatinny Arsenal
Franklin Mineral Dump	Upper Greenwood Lake

From Rte. 46 W, at Netcong take Rte. 206 N to Andover.

ANDOVER

Andover iron was better suited than any other American ore for making steel, said William Livingston, New

Jersey's Governor during the Revolution. The problem was to lay hands on that iron, as Andover Furnace and its forge were owned by Loyalists who had been quietly parceling out this rich mine and 11,000 acres to friends and relations. As persuasion didn't work, the American Board of War finally cracked down and sent Colonel Thomas Maybury to run the blast furnace, soon smelting exclusively for the Revolutionists.

ANDOVER PLAYHOUSE
This large fieldstone building in the center of town dates from the time of William Allen and Joseph Turner, Philadelphians who started Andover Furnace in 1760. The generous scale of the adjacent fieldstone mill, now an antiques shop, suggests the affluence of this Colonial iron village. Slaves were used in some early north Jersey mines, as witness this notice for Andover in 1770: "The owners have six Negroe Slaves to hire out or sell, who are good Foremen, and understand the making and drawing of Iron well."

OLD STONE HOUSE *(private)* Rte. 206
Opposite the playhouse, on the left bank of 206N this substantial building was the ironmaster's house, no doubt the one mentioned in a 1770 advertisement as "an elegant Stone Dwelling."
(See Morris Canal Tour, for the restored, historic village of Waterloo, site of Andover Forge. Proceed S on Rte. 206; 3 mi. S of Cranberry Lake turn W on county road.)

Take county road W of Andover to . . .
HUNTSVILLE

A picturesque little hamlet on the trout-loving Pequest River and Brighton Lake. About 75 feet above the bridge is the former Wolverton Tavern, now a buff stucco residence *(private)* right of the road. Early court sessions in present Sussex County were held here prior to 1765 when the courthouse was moved to Newton. This rolling peaceful country has dozens of inviting roads, many seemingly little changed since the 18th century.

Return to Andover, take Rte. 517 NE to Franklin via Sparta and Ogdensburg. Lake Mohawk near Sparta is a sparkling body of water but most of the shore line is privately owned by year-round residents.

FRANKLIN

This was the site of one of the largest zinc deposits in the world. In geologic ages past, metamorphic processes altered ancient zinc beds, producing a wide variety of new minerals. The result is a mineralogists' heaven. Over 190 different minerals have been found at Franklin, 30 of them (such as franklinite), nowhere else in the world.

No less than 25 different fluorescent rocks occur here—rocks that glow sulphuric yellow, "poison" green, luminous pink, lavender, and vivid rose when "black light"—ultraviolet radiation—is turned on them. The dump of the old Buckwheat Mine of the New Jersey Zinc Company is now the property of Franklin Borough and is open to the public. Bit by bit, rock collectors have already carted away a couple of small mountains. For a one-dollar fee amateur prospectors may not only collect samples but also use the ultraviolet light equipment set up in "sentry boxes" to test their rock finds.

As early as 1640 the Dutch were prospecting here and before the Revolution Lord Stirling, the American peer, hopefully sent several tons of rock to England. Before the discovery of zinc, Franklin Furnace in the 1830's was a pig-iron center with a smelter and two forges. The New Jersey Zinc Company was founded in 1848 but four years went by before zinc could be unlocked from the ore body. In some peak years half a million tons of zinc were obtained here, but now the ore body is depleted, and Franklin is notable as a picture of earlier mining times. At the mineral dump one can see a mock zinc mine, replica of the original, a lighted display of fluorescents, and a collection of 257 different minerals. Tues.-Sat. 9-5; Sun., 1-6; permits from borough clerk or attending policeman. Reservations for groups. *Gerstmann Museum,* 14 Walsh Rd., privately owned, is open free on weekends.

From Rte. 23 in Franklin, turn left at shopping center; ¼ mi. to diggings.

Continue N on Rte. 23 to Hamburg.

HAMBURG

Daniel Haines, Governor of New Jersey in 1843 and again in 1848, made his home in Hamburg and died here in 1877. Best known for pioneering to improve teacher-training he was also a leader in the care of the mentally disordered and in prison reform.

Take Rte. 94 NE to Vernon, then Rte 515 S for about ½ mi. to winding county road on left. Cross Wawayanda Mountain to village of Highland Lakes. Go right for 1 mi. to Wawayanda Rd. on left, continuing into park . . .

WAWAYANDA STATE FOREST

"One of the last great natural treasures of undeveloped recreation land in the State." Thus former Governor Richard J. Hughes described this 4400-acre forested plateau recently acquired under New Jersey's Green Acres program. Beautiful Lake Wawayanda covering 255 acres has an irregular wooded shoreline and is dotted with islands. Rowboats can be rented, and a closed-off road forms an easy foot-trail for exploring part of the park. A fascinating ruin is a beautifully constructed iron-furnace stack dating from 1845, and nearby is a photogenic mule-barn. Although these structures are off-limits to the public, they are interesting to see in their unreconstructed state. Laurel Pond edged by pines, laurel, and rhododendron is unmarred by a single picnic table.

Wawayanda Park will not be developed for multiple use for some time; there are *no facilities* such as bathhouses, but hikers, fishermen, and hunters who are self-sufficient in the woods will enjoy the park. A ranger is on duty.

Return to Rte. 515 S to Stockholm on Rte. 23.

Alternate scenic route: *Return to Highland Lakes at Rte. 94; turn right (N.E.) and proceed to Warwick Tpke. (at shopping center); follow this road to right for 4.5 mi. to Upper Greenwood Lake. Go 1 mi. to Clinton Rd. and continue S on it through Newark Watershed which ends with Clinton Reservoir near Rte. 23. This 10-mile uninhabited stretch where trees meet overhead and brooks flow alongside is one of the loveliest in New Jersey.*

From Rte. 23 the motorist has a choice of several scenic roads leading south to the vicinity of Dover: Rte. 513 or Oak Ridge Rd. or the Berkshire Valley Rd.

PICATINNY ARSENAL   Rte. 15, 1 mi. N of Dover

A 6500-acre U.S. Army installation. Guided tours of museum only, containing some 11,000 types of ordnance ammunition. Special events on Armed Forces Day. Reservations, *by mail only,* for persons of high school age or over.

THE WATCHUNGS:
WASHINGTON'S STRONGHOLD

NEWARK IN CHERRY BLOSSOM TIME

NEWARK

New Jersey Tpke. Exit 14 or Rte. 22, exit to Rte. 21 and McCarter Hwy., then one block left to Broad St.

Puritans who came to New England seeking religious freedom were not always tolerant of religious sects other than their own. But from earliest days of American settlement "Jarsey" was known as a refuge for the persecuted. Newark was settled, in 1666, by such a group, a band of 30 Congregationalist families, headed by Captain Robert Treat, who felt forced to leave New Haven, Conn.

WASHINGTON PARK

Site of a market set up by Newark's founders, the spot is commemorated by Gutzon Borglum's sculpture of a Puritan and an Indian. The "Original People," as the Lenni Lenape Indians called themselves, were not cordial to late-comers until Captain Treat and his followers agreed to pay for a tract of land extending from the Passaic River west to the Watchung Mountains. Payment was mainly wampum and 32 gallons of whisky.

"OLD FIRST" PRESBYTERIAN CHURCH   1787

820 Broad St., S of Market St.

In spite of feuds among Newark's founding fathers, during which the shepherd of the flock, Rev. Abraham

Pierson, Jr., went back to New Haven in a huff (and later became first president of Yale College), the Congregationalists by 1719 had become Presbyterians. By 1791 they had dedicated this splendid Georgian church which they had built from freestone quarried near what is now Bloomfield Avenue.

TRINITY EPISCOPAL CHURCH   Broad St. near Central Ave.

Should a field of grain be harvested on Sunday if rain threatened to destroy the crop? Col. Josiah Ogden, wrestling with his conscience, decided that the Lord would not want people to go hungry, and so the sheaves were brought in. But later such a storm whirled about Col. Ogden that he quit his church and helped found Trinity, about 1733. The only New Jersey church in a public park, Trinity was built on the colonists' military training ground, long called Lower Common and today known as Military Park, a small triangle of land on Broad Street. In the park is a Gutzon Borglum sculpture of 42 bronze figures, a soldiers' memorial. A statue of Major General Philip Kearny pays tribute to the brash and heroic commander of the New Jersey volunteers in the Civil War.

ESSEX COUNTY COURTHOUSE 1906
Market St. W to Springfield Ave.

Stealing the scene from the imposing Renaissance building by architect Cass Gilbert is Gutzon Borglum's warmly appealing bronze of Abraham Lincoln. When asked why he placed the Civil War President at one end of the bench, the sculptor replied that Lincoln was the kind of person who would make room for another.

Inside the courthouse is Howard Pyle's painting of the *Landing of Philip Carteret*. The grand jury room holds Frank D. Millet's conception of a famous courtroom scene, when a jury foreman in 1774 rebuked New Jersey's Provincial Chief Justice for charging that the Colonists' complaints against George III were trifles.

SETH BOYDEN STATUE   1890
Broad St., Washington Park

Karl Gebhardt's bronze depicts Seth Boyden as many persons of his time remembered him, wearing a blacksmith's leather apron and standing beside an anvil. Blacksmith he was, but more than that, one of America's greatest inventors. His discoveries, said Thomas A. Edison, "have been the basis of great industries which have spread over the entire world."

His greatest triumph perhaps was in producing cast iron that could be hammered without breaking. He developed "patent" or baked leather, without ever patenting it, earned a few thousand from the invention and lived to see others profitably invest six million dollars in the process, in Newark alone.

Although Boyden had never built a locomotive, when the Morris & Essex Railroad needed one that could climb the steep grade in the Oranges, he produced the hill-climber *Orange*. Boyden built the first camera in the United States, made the first daguerreotype here, invented machines for making nails, brads, and files, helped Samuel F. B. Morse with the telegraph. Each time as he seemed about to reap a fortune he sold out for trifling sums. Ceaselessly inventive, he developed a cheap process for making sheet iron, then sold the method at a bargain to Newark manufacturers. Boyden's only patent, for making hat bodies, was contested in the courts; they sustained his right to work in the hat factory for wages of $50 a month. Still poor at 67, Boyden retired to a house (now standing in Maplewood) given to him by some industrialists who had grown rich through his inventions. Instead of retiring, the inventor turned to horticulture and produced the Boyden strawberry, so large that it took only 15 of them to equal a pound. A few months before his death at 81, Seth Boyden said he still had enough ideas for inventions to fill two more lifetimes.

NEWARK MUSEUM AND PLANETARIUM   43 Washington St., opp. Washington Park

Rated among the best in the nation, the Newark Museum, sparked by the ideas of its founder John Cotton Dana, emphasizes community service. Year 'round, the museum features major, themed shows. Workshops in painting, sculpture, ceramics, and weaving have greatly stimulated the creative arts in New Jersey.

Art Collections

A Tibetan collection with over 2000 articles, one of the two finest in the nation, includes a silver Wheel of the Law, described as "The most glorious Buddhist emblem in America." Exceptional also are Chinese and Japanese art objects. American paintings and sculpture are of outstanding quality and number, and in the decorative arts the museum likewise excels. New Jersey pottery and glass, British and American silver, antique clocks, coins, English ceramics, ancient Mediterranean glass, African objects, and early American quilts and textiles are a few of the specialties.

Open weekdays 12 noon to 5:00; Sun. and holidays, 1-5. Sunday afternoon science demonstrations. Group tours (minimum of 10), 10-2 weekdays. Sunday films, gallery talks, concerts, science programs. Free. Calendar of events available.

Planetarium

New astronomy programs every two months, Sept. through June, on weekends and holidays at 2:00 and 3:00. Also Mon., Wed., in July and Aug. at 12:15 P.M. 25¢ and 50¢. Reservations for groups larger than 10.

Science Museum

Of such diversity as birds, fossils, seashells, 10,000 minerals, the Otto Goetzke gem collection, insects, and botanicals; unusual assemblage of working models in the physical sciences.

Junior Museum

One dime buys a "life" membership through high school, with the chance to take part in exciting art and science workshops.

Newark's Oldest Schoolhouse

Built in 1784 on Chancellor Avenue, it was moved stone by stone in 1938 by WPA workers to the museum's garden. Summer weekday noon programs here, including jazz concerts at 12:30 Thurs.

Newark Fire Museum in Marcus Ward carriage house

An 1853 handpumper "Neptune," and two motorized fire trucks, often with real firemen present, are stars. Scale models, rare pictures of fire-fighting, other memorabilia. Mon., Wed., Fri. 12-3; Tues., Thurs., Sat. 12-4; Sun. 1-4:30.

NEWARK PUBLIC LIBRARY   5 Washington St.

Another product, like the Newark Museum, of the zeal of John Cotton Dana, librarian from 1902 to 1929, and of his skill in making such institutions forces in community progress. Thousands of volumes on general and historical subjects; one of the largest collections on business topics. Changing exhibits of prints, photos, books. Mid-day movie shorts; occasional film programs for children; evening movies and concerts for adults. Free. Calendar of events on request.

JOHN PLUME HOUSE   c. 1710   *(private)*   407 Broad St., at RR overpass

Now in a most unflattering milieu the oldest building in Newark, the rectory of the House of Prayer, still has much appeal. The house might well be every photographer's mecca for it was here that flexible film was first created, by the Rev. Hannibal Goodwin who was seeking—and found—a substitute for breakable glass stereopticon slides of Bible stories. The clergyman in 1887 applied for a patent on his film, wound on a spool for use in a camera, but the patent was not granted until two years before his death in 1900. Meantime, a chemist employed by Eastman Kodak Company applied for a patent on similar film. The courts at long last awarded a judgment to Goodwin's widow in 1914, only shortly before her death.

Continue N on Broad to Broadway; as downhill traffic here is one-way, go forward on Broad a few blocks before turning left.

NEW JERSEY HISTORICAL SOCIETY   *(museum)*
230 Broadway nr. Taylor St.

Antill-Ross Parlor

The classic beauty of this paneled parlor is all that remains to suggest the splendor of Ross Hall, a mansion which stood on the bank of the Raritan opposite New Brunswick. Built about 1740 by Edward Antill, a Tory who a year earlier had married the daughter of New Jersey's Governor Lewis Morris, Ross Hall under a later owner was headquarters for Washington and his officers in July, 1778. There they celebrated the second anniversary of Independence, in this very room toasting their hostess Sarah Ross, "a pretty Widdow," whose husband acquired the estate about 1772.

Two floors contain professionally arranged exhibits of such Jerseyana as early prints, blown glass, guns, portraits, jewelry, railroads, steamboats, and special shows. Large library, with manuscript collections of State history. Free. 10-4:30 Tues.-Sat. Closed July and August.

Continue S on Broadway, toward Newark ctr. Turn sharp right into Bloomfield Ave., to Branch Brook Park.

BRANCH BROOK PARK   Clifton Ave.

Spring's first great floral spectacle in the Northeast—cherry blossom time in New Jersey—fills Essex County parks with pink and white flowers by the billions during mid-April. Branch Brook Park and other Newark parks offer a larger and more varied display of Oriental flowering cherry trees than that at Washington's Tidal Basin. Blossoms range from deep pink to pure white, with one variety of yellow hue. Every evening until 11 P.M. the floral pageant is flood-lighted, giving a totally new effect. Over 5000 flowering cherry trees have been set out in Essex County parks, with a major planting in South Mountain Reservation. The Newark trees are mainly in the northeast section of Branch Brook, the first county park in the nation, designed by Frederick Law Olmsted.

Ice-skating both on an artificial rink and natural ponds; rink open daily from mid-October to mid-March, with professional instruction offered. Season tickets available. Nearly 500 acres, the park also has tennis and bocce courts, ball fields and two small lakes for fishing and rowing.

From Bloomfield Ave., turn right, into High St.; turn right at Clinton for 1 block. Take diagonal Elizabeth Ave. to Weequahic Park. Enter ½ block to left, from Frelinghuysen Ave.

WEEQUAHIC PARK

An 18-hole golf course, bridle paths, tennis courts, ball fields and basketball courts are in the east section. Here too is an 85-acre spring-fed lake stocked with fish. Weequahic's 300 acres have flowering trees, a rose garden, and picnic areas.

NEWARK INTERNATIONAL AIRPORT   Rtes. 1 and 9, at N. J. Tpke., exit 14

Lindbergh's solo transatlantic flight in 1927 so inspired Newark officials that in 1928 they opened a 68-acre airport which by 1972 covered 2300 acres and served over 6,000,000 passengers a year with an air cargo center that was second largest in the world. With additions made in 1973 and projected enlargement the airport will by 1980 serve 19,000,000 passengers a year, a quarter of them on overseas flights. With a federally operated control tower that is a maze of electronic marvels, Newark Airport has pioneered in many aviation advances, among them the bi-directional runway which obviates circling approaches. First used here also were instruments to measure ceiling and visibility and to transmit such data automatically.

The Airport is a facility of the Port Authority of New York and New Jersey. Tours are not offered at this time but there are excellent accommodations for visitors, including the famous Newarker Restaurant.

SPRINGFIELD BATTLES, WATCHUNG RESERVATION AND GREAT SWAMP

Elizabeth
Boudinot House
Belcher-Ogden House
Warinanco Park
Springfield
Cannonball House
Presbyterian Church

Watchung Reservation
Great Swamp Nature
  Center
Drew University
Fairleigh Dickinson
  University
College of St. Elizabeth

ELIZABETH

With 4 log huts in 1664, this was the first English settlement in New Jersey (established as the Elizabethtown Associates) under grant from Col. Richard Nicolls. The grantees received half a million acres by paying the Indians 20 fathoms of cloth, two guns, two kettles, 400 fathoms of white wampum, and a few other trifles. No bargain as it turned out, for the Duke of York almost simultaneously, on June 23, 1664, gave all of East Jersey, including this same land, to Sir George Carteret. The ensuing confusion brought a century of bickering, riots, and rebellion. In 1668, after arrival of Philip Carteret as Governor of East Jersey, Elizabeth became New Jersey's first capital, an honor not held for long, as by 1682 "Amboy Perth" was the seat of government, alternating with Burlington.

If, as has been said, Elizabeth was the cradle of Princeton University, the founding father was the Rev. Jonathan Dickinson, for 40 years pastor of the Presbyterian Church in Elizabeth, who served as first President of the College of New Jersey.

PRESBYTERIAN CHURCH   1786
Broad St., S of Caldwell Pl.

One of several inspiring churches to rise phoenix-like from the ashes left by British-Hessian raids from Staten Island in 1780, the prior building here was burned on Jan. 25, in revenge for the militant actions of the pastor, the Rev. James Caldwell. Marked for extinction by the enemy, he had often preached with loaded pistols beside him in the pulpit. When his church was destroyed he moved his wife and children to Connecticut Farms (now Union), and he became chaplain of the New Jersey troops and deputy quartermaster. A moving speaker, beloved by his congregation, idolized by the soldiery, and a powerful force in the rebellion, Parson Caldwell had but a short time to live. In 1781 he was shot at Elizabethtown wharf by an American sentry later hanged on evidence that he had been bribed to do the deed. The Caldwells are buried in this churchyard and their family Bible is in the vestibule.

Few congregations produced more towering leaders of the Revolution than did the Presbyterians at Elizabeth, among them: William Livingston who was elected the first Governor of New Jersey after the Tory head of state, William Franklin, was deposed; Colonel Aaron Ogden, Elias Boudinot, General Elias Dayton, and Abraham Clarke, a Signer of the Declaration of Independence.

BOUDINOT HOUSE *(State historic site)* c. 1750
 1073 E. Jersey St.
"Boxwood Hall" was the home of Elias Boudinot who as head of the Continental Congress was actually first president of the 13 colonies. With the Revolution won, he signed the treaty of peace with Britain. It was Boudinot who in 1789 introduced a resolution in Congress to establish a national day of thanksgiving, which was followed by President Washington's proclamation of Thursday, November 26, as the day. From the steps of Boxwood Hall, Boudinot delivered an impassioned oration over the body of Parson James Caldwell who had survived the British assault on Springfield in 1780, only to be killed by a sentry at Elizabethtown wharf on November 24, 1781. Boudinot adopted one of the Caldwell sons, who later became a successful judge.

Remarkable for fine interior paneling, the house,

which was built by Samuel Woodruff, now holds collections of toys, dolls, and miniature furniture, as well as historical items of Elizabeth. 25¢.

BELCHER-OGDEN MANSION *(Elizabeth Historical Society Foundation)* 1046 E. Jersey St.

Its story connected with famous personages of the Colonies and the Revolution this "Flemish bond" brick house, now restored, ranks as one of the most important historic shrines of the Northeast. Research appears to reveal that the east half was the homestead of John Ogden, Jr., one of the four founders of Elizabeth, and his descendants lived here until 1751 when Jonathan Belcher moved in as Royal Governor of New Jersey, to stay until he died in 1757. As he left an inventory of furnishings (the latter destroyed in a foiled British attempt to kidnap Elisha Boudinot in 1780), the mansion has been restored with rare antiques to approximate the Belcher list. Woodwork, mantels, and cupboards by Samuel Woodruff are of exceptional beauty.

By 1797 Col. Aaron Ogden, a beloved hero of the Monmouth and Yorktown battles, and a descendant of the Elizabeth founder, had bought the house, the parlor of which is furnished in memory of him. In 1812 Col. Ogden became Governor of New Jersey, and 12 years later he entertained his friend Lafayette in this house. In 1901 the great-grandson of the French marquis was a guest here. Weds. 9:30-11. Groups: 201-355-4391.

BONNELL HOUSE *(Elizabeth Historical Society Foundation)* 1045 E. Jersey St.

SONS OF THE AMERICAN REVOLUTION, STATE HDQ.

Oldest house in Elizabeth, this was built by Nathaniel Bonnell I about 1682. He had been allotted a 6-acre homestead in the original grant creating Elizabeth. Exterior and interior restored but furnished as an office.

ADMIRAL HALSEY BIRTHPLACE *(restaurant)*   134 W. Jersey St.

A famous commander of U.S. Naval Forces in the South Pacific in World War II, Fleet Admiral William F. Halsey, Jr., was born here on October 30, 1882. Among his victorious exploits was the great sea fight against the Japanese in the Solomon Islands, in which 23 enemy ships were sunk.

ST. JOHN'S EPISCOPAL RECTORY   1696
   633 Pearl Street, nr. hospital
Oldest brick building in Elizabeth, now being restored.

CAVALIER JOUET HOUSE   *(nursing home)*   408 Rahway Ave.

Once known as the Old Chateau this was the main building on the estate of Cavalier Jouet, which was confiscated because the Cavalier remained loyal to the English for offering haven to exiled Huguenots.

ELIZABETH DAILY JOURNAL   295 N. Broad St.

The State's oldest daily newspaper, its lineage goes back to the Jersey *Journal,* first printed in 1785 at 39 Broad Street by Shepard Kollock, who as early as 1779 was publishing an anti-royalist sheet at Chatham.

From Elizabeth ctr., S on Rahway Ave. to . . .

WARINANCO PARK   St. Georges Ave., Roselle

A Union County park that is much in demand for sports, Warinanco has tennis courts, ball fields, ice rinks, a lake for fishing and boating. The Chatfield Gardens have a continuing show of annual flowers, and in spring the azalea plantings are lovely.

From Elizabeth, take Rte. 24 W to . . .

UNION

Two weeks before the Battle of Springfield the enemy annihilated the village of Connecticut Farms here. Rev. Caldwell's wife was shot twice as she and two of her children huddled in a parsonage bedroom. Miraculously the baby in her arms survived. With premeditated vengeance soldiers carried the body of Mrs. Caldwell outside, then burned the house to ashes.

LIBERTY HALL   1772 *(private)*   Morris Ave. at North Ave.

Many feel that this mansion was the capital of liberty in New Jersey for this was the house built by William Livingston, first elected Governor of the State, who, for his patriotic devotion, was returned to this office for 14 consecutive years until his death in 1790. During the Revolution the enemy had a price on Livingston's head and several times searched the house for him. In 1774 his daughter Sarah was married in the great hall to John Jay, later the first Chief Justice of the United States. Young Alexander Hamilton stayed with the Livingstons while attending Francis Barber's Academy. George and Martha Washington head the list of the many famous people who have slept at Liberty Hall. Since a niece of Governor Livingston bought the property to make a home for her son Peter Kean, seven generations of that family have lived here.

PRESBYTERIAN CHURCH   1784
Stuyvesant Ave. at Chestnut St.

With the war's end the congregation, although impoverished, at once rebuilt their church. Hessian soldiers killed at Connecticut Farms are buried in the churchyard.

Continue on Rte. 24 (road of the British-Hessian advance on Springfield)

SPRINGFIELD

The British and the Hessians put the torch to Springfield on June 23, 1780 and burned all but four buildings to the ground. Yet despite such fury the enemy were defeated in their objective: to capture Morristown. Upwards of 10,000 men fought in the Springfield struggle, and after the 2-day battle was over, the British retreated to Staten Island and never again invaded New Jersey.

PRESBYTERIAN CHURCH 1791
Rte. 24 at Springfield Ctr.

The church that was on this corner in the Revolution was burned to the ground as another of the rebel Presbyterian parishes. While the church still stood, the Americans ran out of paper wads to fire their guns. In the thick of the fray, the fighting parson James Caldwell dashed into the church and came out with armfuls of Watts' hymnals, which he tore up as he shouted "Give 'em Watts, boys—give 'em Watts!" Inspired by the "high priest of the Revolution," as the British spoke of Caldwell, the New Jersey militia were said to have fought as never before.

THE OLD MANSE *(rectory)* Morris Ave. at Church Mall

In trying to burn the Old Manse the British tossed a sofa into the flames but this put out the fire and spared Rev. Van Arsdale's home, which had been Washington's headquarters in June of 1780. In 1844 a top story was added to the attractive house.

REVOLUTIONARY WAR CEMETERY *(near rectory)*

Seventy-six identified American soldiers of the Revolution lie buried here; as well as enemy Hessians killed at the battle of Connecticut Farms (Union), June 7, 1780.

CANNONBALL HOUSE c. 1750 *(museum)*
126 Morris Ave.

A cannonball embedded in the west wall gave this house its name and is now on display as part of the excellent museum of the Springfield Historical Society. The Abraham Hutchings homestead, this was one of four buildings that survived the furious fight for Springfield. Home of Gen. Jonathan Dayton after the war. Sun., 2-4, Sept. 1 to July 1.

ANTHONY SWAIM HOMESTEAD 1744 *(private)*
31 S. Springfield Ave.

Because it was filled with Hessian wounded, this house escaped burning by the British during the struggle for Springfield.

*Continue on Rte. 24 past Five Points at Millburn
and Morris Aves. Take left fork "Broad St. Summit."
Over bridge, turn left on Middle Ave., to Briant's Pond.*

SUMMIT

BRIANT'S POND AND PARK   Springfield   Ave.   and
   Briant Pkwy.

The tavern of Jacob Briant, a patriot for whom this
small park is named, was George Washington's headquarters from June 7 to June 22, 1780, when the Americans were braced for the enemy assault on Springfield. A
map drawn by Robert Erskine, Washington's surveyor-
general, shows the tavern to have been just within the
triangle made by Broad Street and Springfield Avenue,
behind which were grouped General Greene's troops.

SITE OF BEACON AND ALARM GUN   Marker at 226
   Hobart Ave., just off Rte. 24 at traffic light.

A dense pine forest on a hill slashed by ravines, that
was Summit in the Revolution, but the unfriendly terrain helped keep the enemy from capturing the military
capital at Morristown. Even more vital for defense was
the system of 23 flaming beacons devised by Washington,
which alerted the back country by a chain of lookouts
extending north through Boonton even across the New
York border. Beacon No. 10 was set up on this hill under
Washington's own direction and was the only one known
to have had an alarm gun as well. The first of these
cannon, the famous "Old Sow," has been found to be
the gun now on the Princeton campus at Nassau Hall.
A second cannon, the "Crown Prince," captured at the
Battle of Springfield, replaced the original one and now
is in the National Historical Museum at Morristown.
Summit yearns to have it returned to Beacon Hill. Mod-
ern paintings of the Summit beacon can be seen in the
National State Bank and the Summit Trust Company.

From Summit: on Morris Ave., just below Overlook Hospital, take Baltusrol Rd., then Glenside Ave. for 2 mi. From Rte. 22: enter at New Providence Rd. . . .

WATCHUNG RESERVATION

A 2000-acre forested tract in the Watchung Hills, this Union County park offers year-round recreation. Through efforts of Dr. Harold N. Moldenke, formerly chief naturalist at Trailside Museum, it is a center for free instruction in nature craft. Hiking trails and bridle paths encourage exploration of an area rich in Indian lore, a terminal moraine of the Great Glacier, remnants of a Revolutionary settlement, and wildlife. Picnic spots close to lovely groves of dogwood. Watchung stables adjacent. *Seeley's Pond and Falls* provide a photogenic scene. Green Brook is especially favored by trout fishermen.

LAKE SURPRISE

This pond was created in pre-Civil War times when David Felt built a dam here for a papermill. Some buildings of his deserted village, Feltville, remain. Ice skating.

TRAILSIDE MUSEUM

A large exhibit of live and mounted animals and birds, as well as teaching displays of flora. Sunday afternoon travelogues and nature lectures. Demonstrations and talks on weekday mornings except Fridays to school classes or adults; advance reservations to Trailside Museum, Mountainside, N.J. Courses in natural history for adults, every Wednesday at 4 P.M. for 10 months each year. Museum open Mon., Tues., Wed., Thurs., 3-5; weekends and holidays, 1-5. Free.

From Summit, take Morris Ave. NW to Watchung Ave., go left, across Passaic River, which is Summit-Chatham border.

CHATHAM

In Bonnell Town, early name for Chatham, the boast was that no British troops had ever set foot in the village, which was crowded with American brigades during the Revolution. Markers and numerous early houses on Main Street.

BONNELL HOUSE   c. 1750   32 Watchung Ave.

Built by Nathaniel Bonnell IV, this dwelling was continuously lived in by Bonnells until 1916 when the family was "daughtered out." On Washington's march to Yorktown, a number of his soldiers slept here, some on the kitchen floor. Mrs. Bonnell, whose husband owned the nearby gristmill on the Passaic River, spent the night baking bread for the men and had to step over their sleeping forms as she tended the oven. The oven is still there. Pottery-making. Mon.-Sat., 9-5. Free.

From the Shunpike (Watchung Ave.) follow Noe Ave. SW 0.6 mi. to its end at Southern Blvd.; go left on Southern ½ mi. to Jay Rd., opp. Chatham Twp. High School. Jay Rd. to parking lot . . .

GREAT SWAMP WILDLIFE REFUGE
FISH AND WILDLIFE SERVICE, U.S. DEPT. OF INTERIOR

The *Great Swamp Nature Center,* a rustic one-story building on 30 acres of land owned by the Morris County Park Commission provides ingress to this 5600-acre tract which hundreds of persons have discovered to be much more attractive than its name indicates. Once part of a prehistoric lake, and virtually undisturbed for centuries, the swamp was the center of public furor in the early 1960's when the Port of New York Authority announced plans for a jetport here. Citizens for miles around rallied—not over the plight of a few muskrats but the threatened loss of a greenbelt way of life—in a whole series of suburbs and exurbs from Bernardsville to Morristown, from Basking Ridge to Short Hills. By public subscription over a million dollars was raised and given to the North American Wildlife Foundation of Morristown for purchase of the above acreage which was then turned over to the Federal Government. The Great Swamp is already proving its worth as a botanical laboratory, with over 80 species of flowering plants and shrubs, 40 varieties of trees, and 150 species of birds. Occasionally deer, fox, and mink are seen in the swamp, which is far from being all marshland. The nature center is open Mon. through Fri., 8-4:30. 201-647-1222.

MADISON

Known in Colonial times as Battle Hill or Bottle Hill, Madison in the winter of 1777 had an encampment of Continental soldiers in Loantaka Valley, and officers were billeted among such early local families as the Tuttles, Elys, Kitchells, and Thompsons. Many houses of Colonial ancestry remain, their histories obscure, on such streets as Ridgedale Avenue. On Madison's Main Street are the campuses of three leading educational institutions: Drew University, a branch of Fairleigh Dickinson University, and the College of St. Elizabeth. First commuter in Madison was Judge Francis Lathrop who in 1841 paid $100 for the privilege of riding the rails between Madison and Newark for a year.

D. WILLIS JAMES MEMORIAL LIBRARY   1900
Museum of Early Trades and Crafts
Main St. and Green Village Rd.
A tiny building but a gem in Gothic style, the rosy limestone quarried at Boonton, the tile roof from Holland. Inside, when sunlight streams through the hand-blown leaded glass windows set with unique Tiffany medallions of ships, pastoral scenes, and heraldry, the effect is like a jewel-box. Almost the entire interior is hand crafted, from forged bronze chandeliers and railings to stenciled walls and ceiling. Exhibits of primitive tools. Weekdays, 10-5; Sun. 2-5. July through Labor Day: closed Sun. and Mon.

MADISON BOROUGH HALL   1935   Opp. R. R. Station, King's Rd.

The granite edifice topped by a cupola is the million-dollar gift of Mrs. Marcellus Hartley Dodge, daughter of William Rockefeller. Doors of the building are solid bronze, the stair rails of polished brass, and the walls of colored marble. In the Council chamber, hung with silver chandeliers, are tapestries and paintings and a desk used by Abraham Lincoln as a congressman.

BOTTLE HILL TAVERN   c. 1804   117 Main St.

A posthouse, known as the Waverly, soon after the Morris-Elizabeth toll road opened in 1804, this inn was the scene in 1825 of a fete for Lafayette, who was welcomed by young girls in white and "roses and evergreens." Now housing a restaurant, the building has been preserved by the Madison Historical Society.

Go W on Main St.; at fork take right road (Park St.) for one block; right on Ridgedale.

SAYRE HOMESTEAD   c. 1745   *(private)*   31 Ridgedale Rd.

When "Fighting Parson" James Caldwell was shot at Elizabethtown wharf, after his wife had been murdered by a Redcoat, hospitable Deacon Ephraim Sayre found room for half a dozen of the orphaned Caldwell children in this appealing small house set close to the street. The deacon was also host to General Anthony Wayne when his brigade was encamped in Loantaka Valley during the bitter winter of 1777.

LUKE MILLER HOUSE   1730   *(private)*   105 Ridgedale Rd.

Maj. Luke Miller, a young officer with the Americans encamped in Bottle Hill in 1777, was born here. Sometimes opened on request for adult tours.

WINDEYER HOUSE   1795   *(private)*   47 Madison Ave.

David Howell, one of Madison's early residents, built the pillared house at another location. In 1812 it was bought by Durest Blanchet, a founder of St. Vincent's

Church, who was one of the French emigrés who fled here from the West Indies to escape the excesses of the French Revolution. Owned by Blanchet descendants.

DREW UNIVERSITY   1866   36 Madison Ave.

A full-fledged university with graduate school, the institution was founded for the education of Methodist ministers through pledges—only partially fulfilled—by Daniel Drew, unscrupulous stock manipulator who, with Cornelius Vanderbilt and Jay Gould, wrecked the treasury of the Erie Railroad in the 1860's.

On a beautiful and historic campus Drew University, covering 130 acres, annually graduates some 1800 men and women.

Mead Hall   1830-1836

Set in a grove of soaring oaks, this expansive red brick hall with magnificent portico of Corinthian columns seems the archetype of a university building. Actually, it was the home of William Gibbons, who inherited the millions of his father Thomas, a Georgian planter, Loyalist, lawyer, banker, slaveholder, and duelist who settled in Elizabeth about 1800 and became famous through the Supreme Court case of *Gibbons* v. *Ogden* of 1824, which broke the Livingston-Fulton steamboat monopoly on the Hudson River. The elder Gibbons gave Cornelius Vanderbilt his first job of any consequence, as captain of a Raritan River steamboat, and later the two men organized a steamboat-stage line between New York and Philadelphia. Selling his father's vessels, William Gibbons took to horse-and-cattle breeding at Elizabeth. In 1830 he began building the estate known as "The Forest," of which Mead Hall became the heart, a splendid example of Mississippi Delta architecture in Yankeeland. Squares of black and white marble form the floor in the entrance of Mead Hall which still shows its former grandeur: double staircases, elaborate cornices, double fireplaces, and carved woodwork. In the great hall are portraits of Daniel Drew and Roxanna Mead Drew, his wife. Gibbons' estate cost him $300,000 but possibly just one of his race horses helped pay expenses. The horse was *"Fashion,"* still rated as "Queen of the American Turf." *Asbury Hall*

This red brick building with classic pediment was the Gibbons carriagehouse for 23 horses and vehicles. *Embury Hall*, another imposing structure, was the Gibbons granary. *Rose Memorial Library* has over 400,000 volumes. In the Tipple Room are first editions and items of prime rarity associated with John and Charles Wesley, founders of Methodism. Also the 10,000-volume library of Walter Koehler, noted church historian of Heidelberg. The *Graduate Center* has a display of Biblical archeology.

FAIRLEIGH DICKINSON UNIVERSITY   1942   Rte. 24

A portion of Hampton Court, the palace built for Cardinal Wolsey on the Thames in 1526, was the model for the central unit of the Florham-Madison campus of Fairleigh Dickinson University. Designed by Stanford White, the palatial structure, restrained in design, was the former residence of Florence Vanderbilt Twombly, granddaughter of Cornelius Vanderbilt. The latter was a crony of Thomas Gibbons and at one time an implacable enemy of Daniel Drew *(see Drew University above)*. The 187-acre landscaped campus has many rare trees and shrubs. A coeducational, accredited university, Fairleigh Dickinson has campuses at Teaneck and Rutherford; enrollment at the Madison campus is about 4000.

COLLEGE OF ST. ELIZABETH   1899   Convent Station, Rte. 24

The oldest college for women in the State and one of the first Catholic institutions in the nation to award degrees to women, the College of St. Elizabeth is on a 440-acre campus overlooking the Passaic Valley. A Shakespearean garden here has a setting of ancient trees. The college has won a reputation for its Greek plays presented in an outdoor theater.

GRIMMEST WINTER OF THE REVOLUTION

MORRISTOWN

FORD MANSION AND HISTORICAL MUSEUM
Morristown National Historic Park

The mansion of Col. Jacob Ford, Jr., in Morristown where George Washington spent the winters of 1777 and 1779-1780 is one of America's great historic shrines, for here crucial decisions were made and here Revolutionary leaders gathered. Morristown was a stronghold which the enemy never penetrated—try as they might at the great Battle of Springfield. But here in 1779 the enemy of Washington's army, encamped at Jockey Hollow, was winter, the coldest of that century.

The National Park consists not only of the stately mansion, refurbished in 1964, but the finest Washington museum in the country, and a 1238-acre forest preserve with historic sites at Jockey Hollow.

Among the prized furnishings of Ford Mansion is a desk at which Washington penned some of the most important papers of his career. The historical museum holds large collections of Colonial and Revolutionary arms, costumes, and household furnishings. Dioramas illustrate the Jockey Hollow scene. Free maps provide for a self-guided tour of the two major centers. "Morristown, a Military Capital of the American Revolution," a booklet sold at the Mansion, tells the story with such clarity that it is indispensable.

The Mansion is about a 5-minute walk from the Erie-Lackawanna Railroad Station. Daily, 10-5; 50¢ admission. Jockey Hollow open year 'round; free.

From Ford Mansion, 1/4 mi. W on Morris St., first right turn before overpass to . . .

SCHUYLER-HAMILTON HOUSE   5 Olyphant Dr.

To this house in 1780 a courier brought a love letter so warm that the recipient, young Betsy Schuyler, still wore it in a tiny silk purse around her neck as she lay dying at the age of 97. The ardent suitor, later her husband, had long since died, felled by Aaron Burr in a duel on the Weehawken Palisades. This letter was but one dashed off by 23-year-old Alexander Hamilton while scribe to Washington at Morristown.

The house belonged to Dr. Jabez Campfield, senior surgeon for the American Army, and billeted here in 1780 was Dr. John Cochran, then surgeon-general, as well as uncle to Betsy who came to visit in Morristown. In spring the fiery young Hamilton had proposed to his "little nut-brown maid" and by December he, whose ancestry was beclouded, had married General Philip Schuyler's daughter, descendant of rich Dutch patroons.

Originally at the corner below, Dr. Campfield's house was saved from destruction by the Morristown D.A.R. The rooms are furnished in authentic antiques of the period, including Dr. Campfield's portrait and Betsy Schuyler's embroidered cap. Fri.-Sun., 1-4. Groups: 201-267-4039. Free.

From Morris St., turn left after overpass; continue to Macculloch Ave.

MACCULLOCH HALL   1806   45 Macculloch Ave.

This manor house was built for George Macculloch, originator and chief engineer of the Morris Canal project which, in 1831, linked the Delaware and Hudson rivers by a man-made waterway from Phillipsburg to Newark Bay. Restored, the mansion has lavish collections of fine porcelain, silver, furniture, and portraits in room-settings of various periods. Open only to organized groups for meetings.

THOMAS NAST HOUSE *(private)*   MacCulloch Ave. at Miller Rd.

From 1872 to 1902 this was the home of Thomas Nast, one of the most famous American political cartoonists, who created the symbols of the Democratic donkey and the Republican elephant. When the corrupt Tweed Ring came into power in 1868 and began looting the New York City treasury of millions of dollars, Nast's biting cartoons exposed "Boss" Tweed and his gang but failed to stem a financial panic in the city.

SEATON HACKNEY FARM PARK   South St., 1 mi. S of
  Morristown ctr.
A Morris County Park for the horsey set features individual and group riding lessons, for a fee. A few
horses for hire without instructions. Bridle trails in Loantaka Brook Reservation. Frequent horse shows in ring.
Daily except holidays.

MORRIS COUNTY COURT HOUSE   1827
  Washington at Western Ave.
An outstanding example of Greek Revival architecture.

BURNHAM PARK   Washington St. (Rte. 24) at edge of
  town
In the terrible winter of 1779-1780 this was the Park
of Artillery, commanded by General Henry Knox. Snow
was so deep that one regiment sent to harass the British
on Staten Island transported the cannon on sleds.
Throughout the Revolution Morristown was an army
hospital center, and here in this city park is a reproduction of one of the log hospital huts. Nearby is a
statue of Tom Paine.
  3 mi. W of Morristown Green on Rte. 24 is . . .

LEWIS MORRIS PARK   Mendham Rd.
  Adjoining Jockey Hollow Forest Preserve on the northwest, Lewis Morris Park can also be entered from its
opposite end, at Tempe Wick Road. This section at
Leddell's Pond has day and night camps for organized
groups. Picnic areas and overlooks in this scenic 500-acre
tract are close to Route 24. Park is wild enough for deer,
fox and raccoon. Trail maps from Morris County Park
Commission.
  *From Morristown Green, 2 mi. on Speedwell Ave.,
at bridge . . .*

SPEEDWELL LAKE AND IRONWORKS SITE
  Jacob Arnold's ironworks here in the Revolution was
one of several in the region which the enemy sought to
destroy but never got close to. Longest associated with
Speedwell Iron Works was Judge Stephen Vail who soon

after 1814 converted it to a foundry. Here under Vail's direction the main drive shaft was made for the S. S. *Savannah,* first steam vessel to cross an ocean, the pioneer ship for which James P. Allaire cast the cylinder and Daniel Dod of Elizabethtown made the boiler.

Some picturesque stone walls and bridge supports of historic Speedwell Iron Works are preserved here at Speedwell Lake, created by W.P.A. workers during the Depression.

ALFRED VAIL MILL AND VILLAGE   333   Speedwell Ave., beyond bridge. See Supplement.

Restored in 1973, this frame mill, once part of Speedwell Iron Works, is one of the most historic buildings in New Jersey. Townsfolk assembled here on Jan. 6, 1838 and heard the first electromagnetic telegraph message sent by the inventors Alfred Vail and Samuel F. B. Morse. Carried by 3 miles of wire looped around this building, the first message was, "A patient waiter is no loser," no doubt intended for Stephen Vail who had financed the experiments of his son and Morse.

From Village Green at Washington St. turn at court house on Western Ave. Take first left and follow signs to top of steep short hill to . . .

FORT NONSENSE

Site only of a fort that General Washington built in 1777 as "a safe retreat in case of Necessity." Reconstructions of 1937 now destroyed.

Follow Western Ave. and signs for 3.3 mi. to . . .

JOCKEY HOLLOW

Now a national forest preserve containing historic sites, Jockey Hollow in the terrible winter of 1779-1780 was the campground of the main Continental army, up to 10,000 men. All but 3 units of the military campsites are within the present park, the locations well marked. The camp hospital here was reconstructed from documents of Dr. James Tilton, surgeon at Morristown in its grimmest winter.

Wick Farmhouse c. 1750

Surrounded by rail fences, a farm garden, and a weathered barn, Henry Wick's shingled farmhouse makes an idyllic picture today, but in 1780 this was headquarters for Maj. Gen. Arthur St. Clair, commander of the Pennsylvania Line who mutinied a year later near here. Legend has it that Wick's daughter Tempe, to hide her riding horse from mutineers, concealed it in a bedroom. Interior of the house is beautifully furnished with country antiques. Daily 1-5, from Feb. through Nov. Free.

Bettin Oak

A regimental clothier in the Pennsylvania Line told of some of the troops being "naked as Lazarus," in freezing weather. Housed in tents, the men in 1780 suffered through a winter worse than that of Valley Forge, with 28 snowfalls. Some of the ill-fed soldiers were buried like sheep under the snow. At times they went 6 days without bread, or without meat. When many enlistments ran out on Jan. 1, 1781, the Pennsylvania Line, long unpaid, mutinied. Capt. Adam Bettin who was killed by a mutineer is said to be buried under a great oak on Jockey Hollow Road. The tree fell in the 1960's.

Log Hospital and Officers' Hut (reconstructions)

On a snowy day it is easy to visualize the "log-house city" that the soldiers built here, to recall a winter when snow lay full 4 feet deep on a level, when the Delaware and Hudson rivers froze solid.

Jockey Hollow has many nature trails for the enjoyment of wildflowers and songbirds. Picnicking permitted, but no fires.

Take Tempe Wick Rd. W 3 mi. to Rte. 24 and . . .

MENDHAM

PRESBYTERIAN CHURCH 1860 Hilltop and Talmage Rds.

A beautiful old landmark with a spire visible for miles. The street leading to the church has many early houses.

BLACK HORSE INN   Rte. 24 at Hilltop Rd.,
Serving food and drink for over two centuries.

PHOENIX HOUSE   1820   Rte. 24 at Hilltop Rd.
BOROUGH OFFICES
Long an inn, the pillared Phoenix House was built and operated by a Mendham family of this name. The hostel's signboard, exhibited inside, depicts the legendary phoenix. Mon.-Fri., 12:30-4:30.

0.5 mi. W of Mendham Ctr. . . .
RALSTON GENERAL STORE   Rte. 24 at Roxiticus Rd.
John Ralston's general store, first opened in 1786, has been restocked to match some of the 200 items disclosed by early ledgers. Weekends and holidays, 2-5 P.M.

The 3-story white frame mansion (*private*) at the rear was built for the affluent Ralston who owned iron forges, a fulling mill, and gristmills nearby. At the adjacent corner is John Logan's Mill (*private*), sturdy stonework from about 1750.

The region south of Mendham has some of the most inviting lanes and villages in New Jersey, among them, Gladstone, Peapack, Far Hills, Liberty Corner, Oldwick, and Bernardsville. In the latter town, note especially John Bunin's Mill, converted to Borough Offices, on Mine Brook Rd.

VAN DORN STONE MILL   (*private*)   Rte. 202 at Childs
Rd., 2 mi. NE of Bernardsville
Fortress-like, this fieldstone mill took a year to build in 1842 and cost $5000 when a mason's wages were 50 cents a day. Stone foundations extend 20 feet below ground and walls are 7 to 9 feet thick, tapering toward the top, an amazing specimen of early masonry. Each of the 50 windows is fitted with a keystone. Ferdinand Van Dorn's mill was erected near the site of a red wooden mill, built in 1768 by Samuel Lewis, which ground grist for the American Army encamped amid snowdrifts at Jockey Hollow. The 14-foot waterwheel of the present stone mill contained 50 buckets of 17 gallons each. In

1934 William Childs, the restaurateur, had the mill put in operation, and flour was ground here as late as 1941. The Van Dorn homestead (*private*) is adjacent.

OLD MILL INN (*restaurant and hotel*) Opp. Van Dorn Mill, Rte. 202 (Morristown Rd.)

In 1930 an old barn, as sturdily built as the stone mill above, was moved from the Van Dorn property and converted by William Childs to a public inn. Original hand-pegged floors remain as do the partitions, even to 7 bents of the great haymow made into bedrooms. One of the latter has a rope-tied trundle bed for small fry. Displays of unusual early farm tools, original Currier and Ives prints.

Take adjacent Childs Rd. to Basking Ridge.

BASKING RIDGE

BASKING RIDGE OAK Center of village

Standing at the crossroads as some 300 years of history went by, this white oak tree is like a patriarch with arms outspread in benediction over the burial ground. Second in size only to the Salem Oak, this venerable tree stands 97 feet high, has a girth of 18 feet and a spread of 156 feet.

PRESBYTERIAN CHURCH

Mary (Polly) Kinnan of Basking Ridge in 1791 saw her husband and her daughter killed by Indians in Virginia as she herself was tomahawked and captured, then later sold to the Shawnee in Ohio. Joseph Lewis, her brother, visiting the Kinnans, had saved their sons. In journeys that took him as far as Canada he carried on a relentless pursuit and finally after three years and five months rescued his sister and brought her home. At the age of 84 Polly was buried here, in one of the oldest burial grounds in the State. Earliest headstone is dated 1736.

FINLEY'S CLASSICAL ACADEMY 1809
Oak St. W of Library

Now township offices, this academy founded by Dr. Robert Finley was rated one of the best in the nation. In 1827, students' board was $1.50 a week. The Rev. Finley was the prime organizer of the American Colonization Society which sought to establish a state in Africa for freed Negro slaves.

Over Rtes. 510 and 24 to . . .

CHESTER HOUSE 1812 (hotel) Main St., Chester

The town's first brick structure, built by Zephaniah Drake. Chester once had many mills powered by the rushing Black River.

From Chester take Rte. 24 W for 1.3 mi. At bridge turn left; 3 mi. to . . .

HACKLEBARNEY STATE PARK

Though only 193 acres, Hacklebarney is sometimes called the most beautiful park in New Jersey. A tumbling trout stream here flows between huge boulders. The Black River cuts a mile-long gorge through rugged terrain, bright in May with dogwood and laurel. A wildlife and nature sanctuary. Tables, fireplaces, and a refreshment stand.

Return to Rtes. 24 and 510. At triangle left of bridge, note group of early buildings. The large stucco mill was the Mountain Spring Distillery once famous for apple brandy.

FLANDERS VALLEY GOLF COURSE Rte. 206, 4 mi. N of Chester

An 18-hole course of championship quality on 315 acres maintained by Morris County Park Commission. Professional instruction available. Daily, in seasonable weather. Parking lot opens 6:30 A.M. The superintendent's house, built about 1812, has fine architectural details.

INVENTORS IN THE ORANGES

Millburn
Hartshorn Arboretum
Paper Mill Playhouse
South Mountain Reservation
Maplewood
Seth Boyden House
Historic Murals

Pierson's Mill
South Orange
New Jersey Fire
  Museum
West Orange
Edison Laboratory
Edison Home

MILLBURN—SHORT HILLS

CORA HARTSHORN ARBORETUM

Forest Dr. at Chatham Rd. From Five Corners on Rte. 24 follow Millburn Ave. 3 blocks, go left at Baltusrol Way to Short Hills R.R. station; left on Chatham.

Real bees in a hive, an ant farm and lighted fluorescent minerals are features of an instructive nature museum. Three miles of woodland paths in a 16-acre bird sanctuary. Frequent lectures on gardening and nature study. Free. 3-5 Tues. and Thurs., 10-12 Sat. Children only with adults. 201-376-3587.

From Old Short Hills Rd., first right after overpass to . . .

PAPER MILL PLAYHOUSE   Brookside Dr.

The "mill-on-the-burn" is an early local name attributed to Scotsman Samuel Campbell who bought this papermill soon after 1800. The Diamond Mill, which continued to turn out paper until shortly after World War I, is now a theater for Broadway shows and stock companies.

Continue on Brookside Dr. to South Mountain Reservation. Convenient for visitors without cars, the Erie-Lackawanna Railroad Station is just a brief walk from the forest preserve.

SOUTH MOUNTAIN RESERVATION   2048 acres

A minute away from traffic jams one can be in a mountain landscape of ravines and natural woodlands. Foot-trails and bridle paths wind over the hills, but at the low altitude the walking is easy, even for tenderfeet. From Millburn's railroad station a path leads to Washington Lookout, from the side of which trees seem to grow horizontally, an illusion that gave rise to the early name of the "Hanging Woods." Access from many points besides Millburn, for Route 510 bisects the tract, and Route 508 (Northfield Ave.) forms a northern boundary. Fishing in the Rahway River and Diamond Millpond. Inviting picnic spots, some with fireplaces and flowing springs.

Ice Skating Arena 560 Northfield Ave., W. Orange

From mid-September to mid-April hordes of hockey players, figure champs, and just plain skaters find room to glide in this indoor arena seating 2600. Skate rentals and instruction. Turtle Back Zoo near skating arena. Skiing and coasting slopes, S. Orange Ave., west of Brookside Dr. and Police Headquarters on South Orange Ave.

Information and large detailed maps, helpful in touring entire county, from Essex County Park Commission, Newark, N. J.

At Main St. go 0.5 mi. on Millburn Ave., turn left at Wyoming, continue to Rte. 510 (S. Orange Ave.) Sharp left up hill for 0.5 mi. Turn left at sign for Washington Rock. From sign to lookout crest, 1.7 mi. Two lookouts en route.

Washington Rock (alt. 544 ft.)
Deer Paddock

Less than five minutes' travel from busy Millburn and South Orange a herd of deer gambol among pines and rhododendron atop South Mountain, and seem utterly wild except that they approach the fence for popcorn. For the eye or the camera lens, some delightful scenes, especially after new-fallen snow.

Whether George Washington stood at the top of the escarpment named for him may never be known, but certainly some of his generals and scouts were here to spy on the British and the Hessians before the Battles of Springfield in June, 1780. A beacon here could have been seen for miles along the Continental lines to the west. Today a log summerhouse nestling in the treetops looks out on Millburn and Maplewood, and on clear days one can see the Manhattan skyline. Foot-trails lead to the base of the rock and to the 2000 acres of South Mountain Reservation.

Via Wyoming Ave. return to Millburn Ave., go E to Maplewood; en route . . .

VAUX HALL BRIDGE   Vaux Hall Rd., appr. 15 ft. from Millburn Ave.

On June 23, 1780, a bridge here was the site of an important skirmish when British troops detached from the main army proceeding to Springfield fought the Americans under "Light Horse" Harry Lee at this point. General Nathanael Greene later reported to General Washington that "the bridge was disputed with great obstinacy."

Return to Millburn Ave., continue E to Springfield Ave., Maplewood; turn right at Boyden Ave. to Seth Boyden School.

MAPLEWOOD

When this was Jefferson Village in 1796, a boy was born here who reached the age of 17 with little schooling. Apprenticed to an engraver in Newark, he drew classic Junos for banknote designs, and ultimately became one of his country's leading painters. The self-taught artist was Asher Brown Durand, founder of American landscape painting. He was also a founder of the National Academy of Design and its president for 16 years. His paintings sought after in his own lifetime, he lived his middle years in Greenwich Village, but then in 1869 returned to Maplewood, where he built a new house and studio on the site of his birthplace, now the southwest corner of Ridgewood and Durand Roads (the house no longer stands). Acquiring still more fame as a painter of Lake George scenes, the artist lived here to his ninetieth year. One of his paintings, "After the Storm," hangs in the Maplewood Library (51 Baker St.), two are in the Newark Museum, seven in the Metropolitan Museum, and many more are in nation-wide collections.

SETH BOYDEN HOUSE *(private)* 302 Boyden Ave., right of Boyden School

A legend in his lifetime, Seth Boyden, whose inventions flowed as from an eternal spring, at the age of 67 was given this retirement home by a group of Newark business men who had made millions from such inventions of his as patent leather, malleable cast iron and Russian sheet iron *(see Newark)*. Transplanted thus in 1855 to a rural spot known as Hilton, Boyden's inventiveness turned to horticulture, strawberries in particular. A Boyden berry weighing 1½ ounces was not unusual. What was unusual: Boyden freely passed on his berry lore to neighbors. Soon the area became famous for "Hilton berries," in heavy demand in the hotel market. Delmonico's paid a dollar a quart, when ordinary strawberries brought ten cents. Two years before his death Seth Boyden said that, given 20 more years, he could grow a delicious strawberry as big as a pineapple. Meantime Boyden was making no money from berries but was walking every day to work in a Newark hat factory, to the owner of which he had given his one and only patent. After Seth Boyden's death in 1870 Henry Jerolaman bought the property, found three rows of Boyden's best—No. 30—berries, added a mulch of salt hay, and, giving away no secrets, reaped bountiful crops and profits to become known as the "Strawberry King."

From Springfield Ave. take Tuscan Rd. to Valley St. Turn right to . . .

MAPLEWOOD MUNICIPAL BUILDING   574 Valley St.
Historical Murals of Maplewood
The distinguished style of this red brick modern Georgian edifice with portico and cupola set the trend in 1931 for a number of other suburban town halls. The council room was tastefully designed with arched niches for nine murals but the Great Depression struck before an artist could be commissioned. But 28 years later, these historic murals by Stephen Juharos were unveiled, on Flag Day, 1959, with an effect well worth waiting for. The luminous rich colors, remarkable depth of perspective, and the arched frame combine to give an illusion of windows opening on the past. Among the scenes are Seth Boyden and his locomotive *Orange* at the Maplewood Station, the Indian chief Tuscan, and Continental soldiers at the Timothy Ball House. Mon.-Fri., 9-4:30; Mon. eves. to 7 except June, July, Aug.

Go left on Valley St. (known in 1815 as Shitepoke Lane, its opposite end as Heathen St).

PIERSON'S MILL   1831   697 Valley St.
Never in its 142-year history has the mill been closed, not even after a fire in 1946. Though now grain is ground by electric- instead of water-power, the mill still has hand-pegged beams, the original stonework and structure. Five generations of Piersons, the first of them Lewis Pierson, have operated the gristmill. An earlier ancestor Samuel settled near here in 1766. Visitors welcome.

VAUX HALL   1843 *(private)*   693 Valley St.
With Grecian columns and classic pediment, the house of the affluent miller Lewis Pierson, which he named for London's famous public gardens, has been altered little since his wife wrote in her diary of Sept. 16, 1843, "We have taken tea in our new house this eve for the first time; not half our things are in." The diarist's descendants still live here.

Return on Valley St. to Municipal Bldg., take left turn at Oakview Ave. through Memorial Park (public);

*first right turn to Dunnell Rd.; then left on Jefferson
just past railroad; house on left, set back.*

OLD STONE HOUSE   c. 1776 *(private)*   22 Jefferson
   Ave., facing railroad

When *The Orange,* one of two wood-burning locomotives built in 1837 by Seth Boyden for the Morris &
Essex Railroad, chugged along these rails in front of
the Old Stone House, it was the flagstop for Jefferson
Village and so continued to 1859. About 1835 Asher
Durand's sister Betsy and her husband Daniel Beach
opened the Clinton Valley Store in the kitchen, which
later also served as the station waiting room. The delightful house of rosy brownstone blocks, which appears
to have more of its original construction left than any
other historic house in Maplewood, has been certified
in the federal survey as one of some 6000 historic structures "worthy of most careful preservation."

*Continue on Jefferson Ave. to Ridgewood, turn
right to . . .*

TIMOTHY BALL HOUSE *(private)*   425 Ridgewood Rd.

"T. & E. B. 1743" was the record cut into a chimney
stone of this house by the owners Timothy and Esther
Ball, the former a grandson of Edward Ball, who came
from Connecticut with Robert Treat in 1666 and
founded Newark. Timothy died in a smallpox epidemic
of 1758, but his widow lived on to see three of their
sons join the New Jersey Militia and to be hostess to
George Washington when he and his officers were scouting enemy maneuvers from Orange Mountain. The general in fact addressed members of the Ball family as
"Cousin"; his mother's name was Mary Ball. House
radically altered by addition of a portico in 1919.

Return to Valley St., continue NE to South Orange.

SOUTH ORANGE

Valley St. to S. Orange Ave. (Rte. 510); right to . . .

SETON HALL UNIVERSITY   S. Orange Ave.

Opening in Madison in 1856 with five students, Seton

Hall, Catholic university for men, now numbers over 2300 on this 31-acre campus. The first Catholic institution of higher learning in New Jersey, Seton Hall was founded by a convert bishop, James Roosevelt Bayley, whose maternal grandfather was James Roosevelt, great-grandfather of President Franklin D. Roosevelt. Bishop Bayley later became first Bishop of Newark, then Archbishop of Baltimore. First president of the college was the Rev. Bernard J. McQuaid, a frail young priest sent to Morris County, "where the air is pure." But though wholesome the campus was found to be too remote, and by 1860 it had been moved to its present site, where students and faculty started the day at 4 A.M. Now embarked on a broad expansion program, Seton Hall has several ultra-modern new buildings, among them a student center with a dodecagon auditorium for theater-in-the-round. At McLaughlin Hall, the library has changing exhibits of interest to visitors as well as to students. The college has pioneered in having a student radio station, WSOU-FM, with a 90-mile radius.

Father Vincent Monella Art Center. In 1973 a turreted, red-brick structure from the 1860's, once a carriage house and stable on the estate of Eugene V. Kelly, a New York millionaire financier, was opened with studios, lecture hall and an art gallery. Here the public is welcome for special events such as art exhibits, chamber music, films and lectures.

Continue on Valley St. to West Orange. At junction with Main St., continue for about 1 mi. to Lakeside Ave.

If not on tour, use Exit 147 of Garden State Pkwy., then go W on Park Ave. to Main St.

WEST ORANGE

THOMAS A. EDISON LABORATORY   *(U. S. National (Monument)*   Main St. Entrance at Lakeside Ave.

The world's most honored inventor in his lifetime, an Horatio Alger hero come to life, Edison, with a research team that he assembled, worked here for 44 years of his life, sometimes for 40 hours at a stretch. The many rooms and buildings are filled with originals and working models of some of the 1093 inventions he patented. Among 1700 silent films made by Edison's company was *The Great Train Robbery,* first movie with a plot. The archaic picture is projected for visitors in "The Black Maria," a reproduction of an early studio.

So attractively presented are the exhibits and so well informed the guides that visitors often spend half a day here. Mon.-Sat., 9:30-4:30. For large groups, 90-minute tours; advance reservations: 201 736-0550. Tickets to visit Edison's home, Glenmont, a half mile away in Llewellyn Park, must be obtained at the Laboratory.

GLENMONT   Glen Ave., Llewellyn Park
EDISON'S HOME

A private enclave, with guards at the gates which one cannot enter without proper certification such as a tour ticket for the Edison house, *Llewellyn Park* is fascinating in itself. A residential park with venerable trees, lavish plantings, and great rambling houses ranging from turreted Victorian to English manors, the section since 1857 has been restricted to a group of self-governing property-owners.

Edison's last home here, with original furnishings all in place and treasured possessions close at hand, gives the impression that the hosts may appear at any moment. In the two floors of the 23-room Victorian mansion that are open to public view, one of the most interesting items is what the inventor called his "thought bench," a massive table-desk with a view of Glenmont's sweeping lawns.

When Edison lay dying in this house, his son Charles informed anxious reporters, "The light still burns," a phrase of the inventor's when he was developing the first incandescent lamp. On October 18, 1931 the message was, "The light is out." But the electronics age, sparked by Edison's magical discoveries, was just beginning.

School groups and children under 16, free; adults, 50¢. 1-hour guided tours, Tues.-Sat., 10-4.

EARLY ART CENTERS

Vreeland House	Eagle Rock Reservation
Nutley Museum	Mills Reservation
The Enclosure	Grover Cleveland birth-
Montclair Art Museum	place

NUTLEY

Coming down the Minisink Trail on their annual trek to the sea, the Lenni Lenape found this green valley, where the Third River meets the Passaic, so beguiling that they paused for a harvest celebration or Yanticaw. Nutley residents are still digging up arrowheads in their gardens.

Robert Treat and his first settlers of Newark, who spread into what is now Nutley found the Indians quite friendly. The English and the Dutch found each other, rather than the Indians, the real obstacle. But 150 years later the rivalry had become mostly social, for in the 1840's the Stuyvesants and the Morrises lined the river with their country estates. A later group to find the valley beautiful were writers and painters, who established a colony here in the 1870's in a small park they called The Enclosure, which still exists. Mark Twain spent many weekends in Nutley as guest of Henry

BENNETS MILLS, BELLEVILLE, c. 1796
Watercolor by Archibald Robertson (1765-1835)

Cuyler Bunner, editor of *Puck*. The first writer to settle in Nutley, at 203 Walnut, was Frank Stockton who wrote his most famous story, "The Lady or the Tiger?" for entertainment at a local party. Bunner and his friends staged a hair-raising circus with a Nutley resident as star: Annie Oakley, who shot coins out of a man's hand while she turned cartwheels.

TOWN HALL   Chestnut St., nr. Franklin Ave.

Formerly a textile mill, the attractive brick building is a good starting point for a walking tour, some features of which are described below. Further information at Clerk's office; or write or call Nutley Women's Club, 201-667-1081.

VREELAND HOMESTEAD   1702

226 Chestnut St., opp. Town Hall

Long and low, the brownstone Dutch house was built for Abraham Van Giesen, a staunch Royalist. When the Declaration of Independence was read he left for New York and never came back. His property was claimed by a veteran of the Revolution, Captain Abram Speer. Now the home of the Women's Club.

Go E on Chestnut St. to Passaic Ave. (traffic light), then left to next street on left, which is . . .

THE ENCLOSURE

Frank Fowler built the first artist's studio in The Enclosure, at No. 16, most famous of all as it was occupied successively by Frederic Dana Marsh and his sons James and Reginald and by Guy Pène du Bois. James Marsh and his wife, Ann Steele Marsh, are co-founders of the Hunterdon County Art Center at Clinton. Next door to No. 16 was the Albert Sterner studio, later occupied by Charles W. Hawthorne, founder of the Provincetown art colony. No. 51 is the Abraham Vreeland House with the date 1838 in the doorstep.

OLD STONE PARSONAGE   213 Passaic Ave. at Park, within iron fence

Still used as a Methodist parsonage, this is another solidly comfortable Dutch house of the 1700's.

NUTLEY HISTORICAL SOCIETY MUSEUM 1875
65 Church St.

Mementoes of "Little Sure-shot, Lovely Lass of the Western Plains," as Annie Oakley was billed. Changing exhibits of New Jersey birds, mechanical banks, minerals, toys, antiques. A Colonial garden. Sun., 2-5, or by appointment: 201-667-7892. Free.

CAPTAIN SPEER HOUSE *(private)* 149 Church St.

Lower half of stone. Has original well. Captain Speer ran a tannery and a gristmill on Yanticaw River.

KINGSLAND MANOR 1796 *(private)* 3 Kingsland Rd., at Lakeside Dr.

Joseph and Richard Kingsland operated a mill near here where the first "safety paper"—to prevent currency forgery—was made, an idea of Thomas LaMonte of Virginia who later built his own mill on Kingsland Road.

GRACE CHURCH MURALS 200 Highfield La.

Clinton Balmer, an English painter, spent ten years creating murals for Grace Episcopal Church, only to see them destroyed by fire. A second series was completed in 1929. Lloyd Goodrich, Director of the Whitney Museum of American Art and a native son of Nutley, described the church as nearly unique for its size in the richness of its interior.

Take Franklin Ave. S to Hendricks Field golf course; then Belleville Ave. W to Bloomfield Ave. into . . .
MONTCLAIR

Late in the last century Montclair attracted many artists who wanted to get away from the grayness of big cities to the greenery of the Watchung foothills. One of America's greatest landscapists, George Inness, who spent much time in New Jersey, had a special fondness for Montclair, as did his son George, Jr., also a painter. The Montclair Art Museum owns two paintings by the father and one of his most brilliant works is titled *"Montclair."*

MONTCLAIR ART MUSEUM   Bloomfield and S. Mountain Aves.

One of the nation's notable small museums, the Montclair art gallery, opened in 1914, has become a creative arts center as well. American art predominates in paintings and prints. The Rand Collection of Indian art ranks among the first in the Nation. Important also is the Whitney Collection of British and French silver. From September to June, there are frequently changing exhibits of period costumes, oriental art, ancient glass, textiles, carvings, and traveling shows. Gallery talks and special programs for groups of 15 or more. From January to mid-March, 10 free concerts on Sunday afternoons. Daytime and evening classes in painting, ceramics, and weaving. Children's classes. Art library. Tues.-Sat., 10-5; Sun., 2-5:30. Free.

ISRAEL CRANE HOUSE   c. 1796 and 1840
   110 Orange Rd.

MONTCLAIR HISTORICAL SOCIETY *(museum)*

Constructed for "King" Crane, builder of an early toll road between Newark and Caldwell, this 3-story clapboard house now in the Federal style was saved from the bulldozer and moved here in 1965. Lined with stone, the house has attractive room settings, including a Federal dining room, Colonial parlor, and 19th century schoolroom. Frequent special exhibits and programs. Guided tours, $\frac{1}{2}$ hr., free. Sun. 2-5 or by appt. Closed June 15 through Labor Day.

EAGLE ROCK RESERVATION

The abrupt rise of this rocky outcrop to 664 feet makes a striking backdrop for Montclair. Long vistas from 400 wooded green acres.

From Valley Rd. in Montclair go N. at Watchung Ave. turn left uphill to Upper Mountain Ave.

UPPER MONTCLAIR

MOUNTAINSIDE PARK   500 Upper Mountain Ave.

Presby Iris Gardens display over 1,000 varieties about May 1. Clay tennis courts, playground, and skating.

Continue on Upper Mountain Ave., then go left up hill at Normal Ave. for two blocks.

MILLS RESERVATION

A hundred acres of unspoiled woodland, adjoining Mountainside Park, has nature trails and views of the cityscapes below. Obtain permits for picnicking.

Return to Bloomfield Ave., Montclair, and go west through Verona (Verona Lake on left) to Caldwell.

CLEVELAND BIRTHPLACE 1832 *(State historic site)*
207 Bloomfield Ave., Caldwell

The only President of the United States who was born on New Jersey soil first saw the light of day here March 18, 1837, and for the occasion a cradle, now on exhibit in this former Presbyterian parsonage, was borrowed from a neighbor. Beside the hooded cradle is a huge Victorian bed that President Cleveland slept in. Here too is a mammoth cane rocker he used in the White House and a large desk that was his as mayor of Buffalo, both items on a scale to fit the big frame of the man who was 22nd and 24th President. Largely self-taught, as a clerk in a Buffalo law office, Grover Cleveland's early years before being admitted to the bar were ones of severe self-denial. President Cleveland's five children have contributed numerous memorabilia of their father to the "Old Manse." His daughter Esther was the first child ever born in the White House.

About a mile W. on Bloomfield Ave., a lefthand road quickly leads to . . .

GROVER CLEVELAND PARK

These heavily wooded acres are a delightful spot for a travelers' picnic, but the park also offers attractions for those who tarry longer: tennis courts, a playground, shuffleboard, study of native plants, ice-skating in season.

Route 527 in Caldwell and through Essex Fells to Livingston is mostly a pleasant residential drive, leading to Hobart Ave. in the Short Hills–Summit area.

STAGECOACHES AND
CANAL BOATS

ALONG THE UNION STAGE LINE

From Rte. 22, S on Springfield Ave., at Cranford-Westfield Exit.

CRANFORD

RAHWAY RIVER PARK
A riverside green belt starting in the town of Rahway and extending to a broader section known as *Nomahegan Park* at the north end of Cranford, then joining *Echo Lake Park,* south of Route 22. Canoe rentals at Springfield Avenue and Orange Street.

CRANE HOUSE *(museum)* 124 Union Ave., next to Municipal Bldg.
CRANFORD HISTORICAL SOCIETY
Built by the Crane family, early settlers for whom Cranford is named, the Colonial house has exhibits of local history. Sat., 10-2; Sun., 3-5. **Free.**

WILLIAM MILLER SPERRY ASTRONOMY OBSERVA-TORY Union College Campus
A chance for the public to look at the stars through a high-powered, $12\frac{1}{2}$-inch reflector telescope. If skies are cloudy, slide lecture by the director. 7:30 Fri. eves., except third one of month.

From Cranford ctr. take 28W for 1.5 mi. into West-field. At E. Broad St. go right for about 1 mi.

WESTFIELD

SCUDDER HOUSE *(private)*   841 E. Broad St.

In a secluded setting, a low frame house with dormers and dropped wings, this was headquarters for one of Washington's leading generals, William Alexander, in 1777, when the British were bedeviling the Americans near Metuchen.

GALLOWS HILL

Nearly opposite the Scudder House is Gallows Hill Road. The hill above it is the one where James Morgan, an American soldier, was hanged for the fatal shooting of the Rev. James Caldwell, Presbyterian clergyman of Elizabeth, whose wife was earlier murdered by a Red-coat *(see Elizabeth and Springfield).*

PRESBYTERIAN CHURCH

Broad St. and Mountain Ave.

An earlier church here was the scene of James Morgan's trial and conviction of murdering the Rev. James Caldwell, chaplain in the Rebel army.

Return to Rte. 28; go W to Martine Ave.; turn right at bridge to Scotch Plains and continue 1.2 mi. to Front St. If on Rte. 22, go S at Scotch Plains to Park and Front Sts.

STAGE HOUSE VILLAGE   Park Ave. at Front St.

From its very beginning, in 1737, an important stage-coach stop on the Old York Road, a 2-day route between New York and Philadelphia, the Stage House Inn served travelers even down to modern times.

Today the restored inn is the focal point in a bricked courtyard with several shops, a number of them in original early buildings. The inn still has its original fire-places, hand-adzed beams, and a second floor "Long Room." At the bar is the cannon once used to announce the arrival of the Swift Sure Stage from New York.

Return to Rte. 28, W to . . .

PLAINFIELD

Plainfield's aspect in early 20th century is well described in *Scenes and Portraits,* Van Wyck Brooks' autobiography of his youth here and his school days at Cranford Seminary.

DRAKE HOUSE   1745 *(museum)*   602 W. Front St., W of Somerset Ave.

Victorianized in the 1860's, the Rev. Nathaniel Drake's house has been preserved because Washington made this headquarters before and after the Battle of Short Hills (near present Plainfield Country Club) on June 26, 1777. A fervent patriot, with four sons in the militia, the clergyman often opened his home to Washington for conferences with General William Winds and other officers of adjacent Blue Hills Military Post, in what is now Green Brook Park. The kitchen and dining room in the house have been restored with care and furnished with unusual, authentic pieces. Collections of Civil War mementoes, early china, guns and sabers. Also current art, crafts, and garden displays. Mon., Wed., Sat., 2-5 P.M. Donations welcomed.

GREEN BROOK PARK   W. Front St. and Plainfield Ave.

Site of the Revolutionary Blue Hills Military Post, a large earthworks fort, one of several that guarded access to the nearby Watchung hills and the American headquarters at Morristown.

Return via Front St. to Watchung Ave. Right to . . .

RELIGIOUS SOCIETY OF FRIENDS   1788 Watchung and North Aves.

Sandwiched between the U.S. Postoffice and a railroad embankment, this Quaker-gray shingled meetinghouse is a pleasing anachronism. Two stories high, green-shuttered, the house has plain time-worn benches. Services Sunday at 11 A.M. Visiting hours: 11:30-1:30, Mon. through Fri.

Continue on Watchung Ave. to Cedar Brook Rd. Go right one block.

MARTINE HOUSE 1717 *(private)* 950 Cedar Brook
   Rd. at Brook Lane
Oldest house in Plainfield and one of the loveliest in a city known for fine homes, this was built by William Webster. Once the home of Edmund Clarence Stedman (1833-1908), newspaper correspondent in the Civil War, critic and poet. Best known for his poem *Pan in Wall Street,* Stedman also wrote a poem about Revolutionary days: *Alice of Monmouth.*

CEDARBROOK PARK   Randolph Rd. W of Park Ave.
One of the largest iris gardens in the country displays prize varieties from May to mid-June. Opposite is a Shakespearean Garden containing flowers and trees found at Stratford-on-Avon or those named in the playwright's works. Chrysanthemum displays in autumn.

Return to junction of Front and Somerset Sts.; go N 0.7 mi. on Somerset; bear right on overpass to Watchung. From stop sign go left 1.2 mi., continuing around traffic circle to Watchung Municipal Hall. Turn right, up Mountain Blvd. for 1.5 mi. to sign for Washington Rock Park. Left turn up winding road to summit of hill.

WASHINGTON ROCK STATE PARK
From this natural rock outcrop with maplike, 30-mile vistas of the plain below, as far away as Newark Bay, Washington's scouts could spy on the Redcoats harassing a string of settlements in the West Fields, culmination of which was the Battle of Short Hills on May 26, 1777. Still with a splendid though more urban view, the 27-acre park is a favored lookout and picnic site. Coin-operated binoculars.

Take road S downhill (Washington Ave.) to Rte. 22. Turn right, go W to Bound Brook. (6 miles East of Washington Rock Rd. is entrance to 2000-acre Watchung Reservation; from Rte. 22, go N on New Providence Rd. to Coles Ave. See Summit for description.)
On Rte. 22 take Bound Brook Exit; at top of over-

pass turn left, toward hospital signs; then abrupt left up Middlebrook Ave., a wooded street; marker on right . . .

MIDDLE BROOK CAMPGROUND
Middle Brook Ave.

Now a tiny park, it was at this American encampment that the Stars and Stripes were first unfurled after their adoption by Congress on June 14, 1777. A replica of the first flag flies here day and night, one of the few places where, by order of Congress, the flag is never lowered at sunset.

Continue to Vosseller Ave., go left to Rte. 22, then right. At Chimney Rock Rd. go S, crossing Rte. 28 and take first left, a winding street which passes white frame house on knoll at left . . .

"CONVIVIAL HALL"   c. 1750   Bound Brook
AMERICAN CYANAMID CO. OFFICES

On April 12, 1777 Lord Cornwallis had breakfast here at Philip Van Horne's manor, and a few hours later host Van Horne was equally affable to his American dinner guest, Gen. Benjamin Lincoln. Next morning Cornwallis and 400 men surprised Lincoln's soldiers at *their* breakfast in Bound Brook and captured or killed 60 men as well as destroying supplies. Washington decided that Van Horne was carrying conviviality too far and ordered him picked up for questioning. After swearing allegiance to the Americans Van Horne was released, much to Washington's irritation, for he wrote: "I am sorry you did not keep old Van Horne under restraint."

Fine food and liquors in an elegant setting were only part of Convivial Hall's attraction. The real magnet was Van Horne's two pretty daughters, ages 16 and 23, who were equally charming to Tory and rebel. The very next year Mary, the elder charmer, married Washington's own aide-de-camp, Colonel Stephen Moylan. From then on the Van Horne Manor became Convivial Hall for American officers exclusively.

Restored in the 1930's, Convivial Hall is now handsomely furnished in period style; a painting of the manor graced American Cyanamid's Tercentenary calendar.

Return to Rte. 22 and continue to Somerville Circle.

SOMERVILLE

WALLACE HOUSE   1778 *(State historic site)*   38 Washington Pl., near Middagh St.

Fashion note of spring, 1779, was that George Washington appeared as host at a ball here in ruffles and a black velvet suit. No mention of what "Lady Washington" wore, though, at the celebration to honor the French ambassador, M. Girard, and the second anniversary of France's aid to the Americans. As the weather was mild and there was scant military action in New Jersey, that winter might be said to have been the social one of the war, with top brass such as Generals Knox, Alexander, and Nathanael Greene and their families housed in the Middle Brook Valley and giving rounds of parties. Resident at the Wallace House from autumn of 1778 to June, 1779, Washington stayed here longer than at any other place during the Revolution. For use of the house he paid the unprecedented sum of $10,000, but in depreciated Continental currency. Of special interest, among items of Americana, is his metal-covered campaign chest.

OLD DUTCH PARSONAGE   1751   *(State historic site)*   65 Washington Pl.

Bricks brought as ship's ballast from Holland form the walls of this sturdy house built for the Rev. John Frelinghuysen, who established the first Dutch Reformed Theological Seminary in America, which later became Queen's College and eventually Rutgers University. Formerly on the banks of the Raritan, the old Dutch house has been moved to a fitting site opposite Washington's Headquarters, as the general was a good friend of the vigorous patriot, Dominie Jacob Hardenbergh, who lived in the parsonage during the Revolution.

At Somerville Circle take Rte. 206 S to Dukes Pkwy. East; turn right at traffic light . . .

DUKE GARDENS

A sight to gladden all flower lovers are these 11 "gardens under glass," undoubtedly the most elaborate and beautiful floral displays in the State. On the estate of Miss Doris Duke, the conservatory gardens, designed with great artistry, vary from a serene Chinese garden to a tropical rain forest, from a formal French arrangement of rare beauty to an exotic East Indian garden. The late James B. Duke, who created Duke Farms in the 1890's, was an orchid fancier who developed some of the species now so lavishly displayed against jungle greenery.

Open daily except in July and August, the unique gardens are especially inspiring in winter when the outside world is bleak. Summer guided tours 1 to 5 P.M. last about an hour. Winter (Oct. 31-Apr. 1), 12-4 P.M. $1.75 per person. Reduced rates for groups larger than 10. By appointment only. 201-722-3700. No cameras or high heels. Special buses from New York Port Authority Terminal, 111 Eighth Ave., N.Y.C.: inquire there.

Rte. 206 S for 4.5 mi. to Millstone Rd., on left. (For Millstone and East Millstone, see following tour.) Follow Rte. 514 to . . .

WILLIAM L. HUTCHESON MEMORIAL FOREST

0.5 mi. E of East Millstone on Amwell Rd., Rte. 514

This 65-acre virgin forest of giant oaks and hickories has been growing undisturbed by man since at least 1701. From then until 1955 it was owned by one family, then through public gifts was given to the Botany Department of Rutgers, the State University, as a unique living laboratory and a forest sanctuary of great beauty. Early in May an interior forest of dogwood blooms beneath ancient oaks, some of them 90 feet high. Admittance only on free guided tours, arranged with Forest Director, Department of Botany, Rutgers, New Brunswick. Schedule supplied for certain Sunday afternoon tours.

VOORHEES HOMESTEAD   1793   Middlebush, Rte. 514
   (*private*)
The home of Garret Voorhees II was burned by Cornwallis while the owner was serving in Washington's army, and the present house was built after the war when the Government paid the Voorhees family £451 for their loss.

NEW BRUNSWICK

BUCCLEUCH PARK   N. end of College Ave.
A 73-acre city park on the Raritan River, just east of Landing Lane Bridge which marks one of the steamboat landings of the 1820's when New Brunswick was a major port for shipment of farm produce to Manhattan.

BUCCLEUCH MANSION   1739   In Park, near College
   Ave. and George St.
Hand-painted wallpaper murals of Paris and of tiger hunts are rare antiquities in this fine mansion built by Anthony White who married the daughter of Lewis Morris, New Jersey's Provincial Governor. In early days a duel was fought in an upstairs room and the victor escaped down a secret staircase to the banks of the Raritan. Collections of Colonial furnishings and costumes. Sat., Sun., 3-5, June to Nov. 1. 201-EL 6-1457.   ·

RUTGERS, THE STATE UNIVERSITY
Founded in 1766, the college has become a university with over 20,000 students enrolled in credit courses on three campuses, here in New Brunswick and at Newark and Camden. The eighth college to be organized in the Colonies, the institution was named Queen's College after Charlotte, Queen Consort. In 1767 classes were opened in New Brunswick in what had been a tavern, the Sign of the Red Lion. Organized by the Dutch Reformed Church in America, through the leadership of the Rev. Jacob R. Hardenbergh, the school had only a feeble thread of existence until about 1825 when generous endowments were made by Col. Henry Rutgers.

In New Brunswick the university has four campuses: a 50-acre plot around College Avenue; 950 acres at south New Brunswick, where Cook College and Douglass College are located, 1,100 acres on the north side of the Raritan River, site of a vast new Science Center, and Livingston College on the site of former Camp Kilmer. Since 1959 the State University has been engaged in a $50,000,000-expansion program, some results of which can be seen in the number of splendid new buildings in contemporary style.

Visitors are of course free to explore the campuses. Guides are provided only for large groups; advance arrangements with Public Relations Office.

Old Queens 1811 Hamilton, nr. College Ave.

The heart of Rutgers, Old Queens, the first structure on Rutgers campus, is a classical masterpiece of John McComb who also designed Manhattan's City Hall. Once heated only by 24 fireplaces, Old Queens still has a Dutch oven in one of the main floor offices.

College Field Plaque

This plaque in the gymnasium marks the site of the first American intercollegiate football game, played between Rutgers and Princeton on Nov. 6, 1869. Playing 25 men to a team, in a style more like rugby, Rutgers won, 6-4. A week later at Princeton, the Tigers won, 8-0.

Alexander Library College Ave. opp. Richardson St.

Incorporating modern features for efficient use, the library provides space for 1,500,000 volumes. Large collections of maps and manuscripts, also rare Jerseyana, including material on Walt Whitman. Special non-literary collections include old paper money, early American advertising art, antique prints, and some 40,000 Indian artifacts from the Charles A. Philhower Collection. Frequently changing displays of such items. Mon.-Sat., 9-5.

At right of the library is an unusual garden, its focus a brick map of New Jersey, surrounded by a rich variety of plants, all of them native to the State.

George H. Cook College (Formerly College of Agriculture)

In existence since 1864, the College, together with the New Jersey Experiment Station, has won a world-wide reputation for pioneering in agricultural research. A crowning achievement was the discovery of the antibiotic, streptomycin, by the late Dr. Selman A. Waksman, Rutgers alumnus and Nobel Prize winner, and his associates. Waksman Hall, home of the Institute of Microbiology, part of the Science Center on Busch campus, was built with streptomycin royalties.

Farm Museum

Hundreds of fascinating implements from early farms and homes. Groups only, by advance arrangement: Dean's office, Cook College. College Farm and gardens open daily.

Douglass College George St., 1 mi. from central campus

This is the women's college of the State University, with more than 3,000 students enrolled. It is a complete campus within itself, including not only dormitories, student center, and classrooms, but a theater, the Voorhees Chapel, and a library-study center.

JOYCE KILMER BIRTHPLACE *(State historic site)*
17 Joyce Kilmer Ave.

The New Jersey poet best known as the author of "Trees" was born here in 1886. Now state-owned, the building has been restored and houses the offices of the Arborists' Association of New Jersey and a museum of Kilmer memorabilia.

HENRY GUEST HOUSE 1760 60 Livingston Ave.
New Brunswick Art Center

Whaler, tanner, alderman and patriot, Henry Guest built this substantial house of ashlar stone. Guest's son Moses, a militia captain, helped capture the British raider, John Simcoe, near New Brunswick in 1779.

JOHNSON PARK River Rd. (Rte. 18), Highland Park, opp. Rutgers campus

In the 1820's Vanderbilt and Gibbons steamboats made connections here with stages bound for Philadelphia.

Present-day features on the bank of the Raritan range from a track for trotting horses to Sunday evening band concerts. Picnic grounds, fireplaces, tennis courts.

JOHNSTON HISTORICAL MUSEUM Rtes. 1 and 130. From N.J. Tpke., New Brunswick Exit.

National Headquarters, Boy Scouts of America. Scouting exhibits and displays such as a short-wave unit, a weather station, and a replica of the John Glenn space capsule. Also a 60-acre nature area. One-hour free tours. Daily, 9-5; Sun., 1-5.

THE DELAWARE–RARITAN CANAL

A tour for canoeists, hikers, and motorists. This can be an extension of previous motor tour, much of which parallels Route 22.

Now a canoeist's joy, the Delaware and Raritan Canal, the 140-year-old waterway built mainly to move Pennsylvania coal east was at its peak in 1866 one of the three most important canals in the Nation, with greater tonnage than the Erie Canal. A dam across the Delaware at Raven Rock diverted a continuous stream of water through a feeder ditch to Trenton, then through the canal itself which ran to New Brunswick, over 60 miles. At one time as many as 115 barges a day, hauled by mules plodding doggedly along the towpath, traversed the canal whose swing-bridges were opened by gate-tenders at the sound of a tin fish horn. In 1834 when the tracks of New Jersey's pioneering railroad, the Camden and Amboy, nearly paralleled the waterway it managed to survive the competition. In 1871, however, when the Pennsylvania Railroad leased both routes and later gave preference to railroad over canal, its decline began. By 1932 it ceased operation, and the railroad turned it over to the State of New Jersey.

Like the Morris Canal, a pick-and-shovel engineering feat, the Delaware and Raritan was scooped out, 75 feet wide and 8 feet deep, mostly by Irish immigrants, many of whom died in a cholera epidemic.

For 30 years canoeists have been exploring the Delaware and Raritan and camping along the towpath. A favored trip of several days, through quiet water, starts at Bound Brook, continues to Griggstown for 14 miles, then to Princeton and its Lake Carnegie, with a return trip via the Millstone River, an offbeat stream flowing north. Canal locks have been replaced by concrete spillways which keep the water level constant.

The most picturesque section of the 43-mile canal, now a State Historic Site, flows through the historic and still rural Millstone Valley, and is being developed as a State park.

A long ribbon of water, the Delaware and Raritan can be viewed at many places, but a convenient point for canoeists, hikers, and motorists alike is at South Bound Brook. From the junction of Routes 28 and 287, go south to the next exit: South Bound Brook. This brings the motorist to Canal Road. About a block east of here is the site of an old lock, but as it is less interesting than others west on the canal, motorists and hikers will want to return to the 287 Exit and follow along the waterway.

1.5 mi. W of exit at Rte. 287 is . . .
Bridge-Tender's House (private)

This tall and narrow white stuccoed house with the great sycamore at its door and the grassy plot around the spillway conjures up visions of mule-drawn barges and canalers. The property is posted against trespassers but can be viewed nearby.

About a half-mile farther on is a smaller, bridge-tender's house beside a footbridge.

Zarephath
PILLAR OF FIRE SOCIETY AND COLLEGE

Entrance to the Pillar of Fire community is at the bridge-tender's house, across the canal. The college is named for Alma White, wife of a Methodist minister, who founded the society in 1901. Coeducational students at the college earn their tuition and living in exchange for labor on the Society's farm. On State property, the self-contained community has its own fire department, postoffice, printshop, and store. It is the national and international center for 45 temples of the Pillar of Fire Society. Obtain written permission for campus tour.

Continue along canal until road swings left. At Elizabeth Ave. (Rte. 514) turn right to East Millstone. On Rte. 514, 0.5 mi. E of East Millstone is . . .

METTLER'S WOODS
HUTCHESON MEMORIAL FOREST

Unique in Eastern United States, the Forest has 65 acres of virgin woodland never cut over, burned, or otherwise disturbed by man. Open only for guided tours on application to Rutgers University. *See preceding tour.*

MILLSTONE   Rte. 533

On Oct. 27, 1779, Colonel John Simcoe and his Queen's Rangers made a lightning raid on Millstone, burned the courthouse to the ground, robbed an American supply base, pillaged the countryside, and returned to British headquarters in New Brunswick—55 miles of terror in about 24 hours.

WYCKOFF BLACKSMITH SHOP   1693

When Edward H. Wyckoff died in 1960, after being the smithy here for 72 years, the place had been a blacksmith shop for 267 years. Now the interesting Old Forge Museum. The rare Indian mortar was found on the Van Doren farm. Open 1-4 Sun. May-June and Oct. Mr. Robinson, the well-informed curator, will also respond to other Sunday calls left with owners of the adjacent River House antiques shop. The latter building was an early wheelwright shop. Near the studio gallery one can see remains of stone shoring for an early bridge across the canal. Canoes, for rent at the gallery, can be launched from a road near Elm and Market in East Millstone.

From Millstone, Route 533 to Griggstown follows closely beside the winding Millstone River. It was along the Millstone Valley that Washington led his army after the Battle of Princeton. Less than a mile south of Millstone, on the right, is the *John Van Doren House (see marker)* where Washington stopped on Jan. 3, 1777, and gave his victorious soldiers their first rest since their march from Trenton on New Year's Day.

GRIGGSTOWN

Visiting Griggstown in early morning or late day, or whenever travel is light, is to step back into another century. The mule-drivers' barracks, the bridge-tender's stone house, and the old swingbridge where willows dip into the placid canal combine to give the look of a 19th-century aquatint.

JOHN HONEYMAN HOUSE *(private)* Bunker Hill and Canal Rds.

Angry patriots tried to burn this house to the ground when they thought John Honeyman was hiding here, but Mrs. Honeyman produced a paper signed by George Washington, affording protection to the wife and children of "the notorious Tory." Honeyman actually was a spy for the Americans while serving the British army as a cattle dealer. Allowing himself to be captured, he brought word to Washington that the Hessians were prepared to relax and celebrate Christmas, and thus helped assure the surprise victory at Trenton on Dec. 26, 1777. After the Revolution Washington visited Honeyman at his Griggstown cottage and thus let the country know of the counter-spy's great service to the American cause.

Return on Canal Rd. to Griggstown and follow left bank of canal toward Princeton.

See Rocky Hill and Princeton for nearby tours.

ATLANTIC HIGHLANDS

CHEESEQUAKE, SANDY HOOK AND NAVESINK PARKS

Cheesequake State Park
Freneau Homestead
Matawan—Burrowes
  House
Belford Fishing Port
Leonardo State Marina

Atlantic Highlands
Navesink Lights State
  Park
Sandy Hook State Park
Rumson
Red Bank

From village of Cheesequake on Rte. 34 go S for 2 mi., turn left at marker and follow signs into park. Alternate route: Exit 120 on Garden State Pkwy.

CHEESEQUAKE STATE PARK

A wildlife sanctuary offering bountiful variety of plants and birds in its 975 acres of woodland, meadow, and salt marsh bordering Raritan Bay. Hooks Creek Lake has a sandy beach, bathhouses, lifeguard service. Many picnic groves. Freshwater fishing.

Return to Rte. 34, go S to town of Matawan (pop. 5097). At Rte. 79 turn right, go 1 mi. to homestead of Philip Freneau.

PHILIP FRENEAU HOMESTEAD *(house private; path open to poet's grave)*

"His paper has saved our Constitution, which was galloping fast into monarchy." So wrote Jefferson to Washington about Philip Freneau, called even in his lifetime "the poet of the Revolution." Today few know that here at Mt. Pleasant was the lifelong home and last resting-place of the man whose inflammatory poems against British tyranny inspired Americans to go on fighting when their cause seemed forlorn of all hope.

Even as a student at the College of New Jersey in Princeton, where Aaron Burr was a classmate and James Madison a close friend, Freneau was already pouring out patriotic, satiric verse. After six months' graduate study he had two volumes of poetry to his credit but no prospects of a career, so when chance offered he became a plantation manager in the West Indies, where some of his finest lyrics were written.

Returning to Mt. Pleasant in 1778 he enlisted in the militia. Later as a member of the gun crew of the *Aurora* Freneau came close to death, for the ship was seized by the English and he was thrown into the hold of the dread prison ship *Scorpion,* anchored in the Hudson. Held incommunicado, with men dying all around of fever, Freneau was released after six weeks, so ill he could scarcely walk and such a "perfect skeleton" that nearing home he took a path through the woods for fear of terrifying his neighbors.

When he recovered he blasted Tory cruelty with "The British Prison Ship." From that time almost until his death at 80, Freneau as fiery editor and lampooning poet sacrificed his lyric gifts and meager finances to battle oppression of all kinds. As editor of the *National Gazette* in Philadelphia he was bitterly attacked by Alexander Hamilton, John Fenno, and their coterie whom the Jeffersonians regarded as kingmakers.

Here at Mt. Pleasant in 1794 the poet began writing and printing *The Monmouth Almanac,* and the next year, *The Jersey Chronicle,* unsuccessful ventures that led him back to his alternate career of sea captain. In 1818 his house, printshop, and many manuscripts burned, but a dwelling being built next door for his daughter gave shelter to all the family. Locust Grove, his father's 1000-acre estate in 1752, was sold off bit by bit to pay debts. When he was in his seventies the poet worked on Monmouth County roads to pay his taxes. At his request Freneau was buried on a knoll which still has a view of green Navesink hills which he loved so much. His contemporaries composed the words cut in the marble shaft:

His upright and honorable character is in the memory of many and will be remembered when this inscription is no longer legible.

MT. PLEASANT TAVERN   1784   Rte. 79, ½ mi. toward Rte. 34

Now called "The Poet's Inn," this tavern was undoubtedly host to Philip Freneau and his celebrated Whig friends. In the lobby is a modern portrait of the poet, of special interest because Freneau, though "his countenance was intellectual," always refused to sit for his portrait, even for Rembrandt Peale.

For 1.3 mi. continue N on Rte. 79, crossing Rte. 34 to Main St. in Matawan. On left . . .

BURROWES MANSION   1723 *(private)*   94 Main St., Matawan

Few patriots in the Revolution suffered more from the pointed vengeance of the British than did Major John Burrowes, Jr., who organized the First New Jersey Company of militia and whose father was a Matawan grain merchant called the Corn King. On June 3, 1778 about 200 of Skinner's Greens led by local Tories burned the Burrowes gristmills and vessels, then set out to capture the owners. Today a splatter of blackened bullet holes at the top of the stairwell attests to the fracas in this house. The Corn King was seized and later thrown into a Manhattan Sugar House prison. Missing capture by minutes, Major Burrowes escaped by a rear window, to Matawan Creek, and hid for two days without food. His wife Margaret took to her room and would not be questioned. When an officer mounted the stairs she appeared on the landing but refused to talk. The officer demanded her silk shawl to bind up the wounds of one of his soldiers. She retorted that no shawl of hers would staunch Tory blood. Thereupon the officer struck her in the breast with the hilt of his sword, with such force that she fell unconscious.

Margaret Burrowes did not die on the spot, and later she and her husband were re-united. But the wound eventually caused her death, it was said. Neighbors in nearby Rabbit Lane must have wondered if they dared stand up and be counted as Americans in 1778, for the hapless Burrowes family had friends in high places: Margaret was a Forman of the prominent Monmouth clan, and a sister-in-law of Philip Freneau.

Burrowes Mansion, notable for its fine woodwork and handsome fireplaces, was built by John Bowne, Jr., son of one of the early Monmouth settlers.

Continue NE for 1.3 mi. via Rte. 516 to Rte. 35; turn right. Rte. 516 rejoins 35 twice more; take last 516 going East, then Rte. 36 into town of Atlantic Highlands (pop. 4119). En route here, interesting sorties are Belford, a small workaday fishing port favored by salon photographers and painters; and Leonardo, its State marina crowded with pleasure craft.

SCENIC DRIVE, ATLANTIC HIGHLANDS

Rising abruptly from the wharf area in the town of Atlantic Highlands, Ocean Boulevard affords a panorama not only of Sandy Hook just below but of Manhattan and Long Island. Mt. Mitchell *(alt. 250 ft.)* is the highest point on the eastern shore of the United States and the first landfall seen from ocean vessels coming into Hudson River Harbor.

Philip Freneau was inspired to write a now-forgotten poem on these "Hills of Neversink." But all America became aware of the Atlantic Highlands when James Fenimore Cooper's bestseller, *The Water Witch,* appeared in 1831, for the setting was an actual villa here, where lived a mythical Huguenot maiden and her Dutch uncle. The hero was a mysterious sea rover, "Skimmer of the Seas," who in his vessel *The Water Witch* hid out among the coves of Sandy Hook.

Follow ocean drive down to Rte. 36 to Highlands (pop. 3536). Just before bridge leading to Sandy Hook, make abrupt right up Beacon Hill (alt. 200).

NAVESINK TWIN LIGHTS STATE PARK

(*museum*)

As early as 1746 this headland became a beacon when the English lighted cauldrons of whale oil to alert the citizenry against marauding French ships. In the Revolution these heights again flared with fire to warn against privateers. By 1828 the present castellated brownstone towers were built.

At the Chicago World's Fair of 1893 the French exhibited the world's most powerful lighthouse lens, designed by Antoine Fresnel. Later the United States bought this 9-million-candlepower lens and installed it at Navesink, a light visible 22 miles at sea. In World War II Navesink was the scene of early tests of radar, a British invention that finally blacked out Fresnel's light forever. It now rests in a Boston museum.

Open to visitors, the north tower offers vistas of Staten Island, the Verrazano Bridge, even the spires of Manhattan. Center of the building houses an interesting marine museum.

What seems to be a pair of pioneer space ships are life-saving vessels used by the U.S. Coast Guard in the 1870's. Small rockets with a line attached were fired at or from a ship and made fast. Then one of these man-sized metal capsules was slid down the line, a passenger scrambled inside, pulled the lid down after him and was hauled ashore. The rescue boats are housed in the first Federal lifesaving station, set up at Sandy Hook in 1848.

NAVESINK TWIN LIGHTS

Now a State marine museum, the historic lighthouse overlooks Sandy Hook State Park and the Atlantic Ocean. Painted by Granville Perkins in 1879.

Lighthouse and museum open between Memorial and Labor Days, 1 to 4:30, except Mondays. Free.

For Sandy Hook Park, cross bridge, turn left at seawall.

SANDY HOOK STATE PARK

Henry Hudson may have slept here—out in the open. For Robert Juet of the *Half Moon*'s crew recorded in 1609 that a shipmate, John Colman, slain by Indians "with an Arrow shot into his throat," was buried at a place his companions named Colman's Point, generally agreed on today as being Sandy Hook.

From this storied neck of land rises the oldest lighthouse still in use in the western hemisphere. Octagonal, nine stories high, Sandy Hook Beacon was first lighted, with "48 Oil Blazes," on June 11, 1764, and was maintained by a group of New York merchants levying tonnage dues on ships.

As the British controlled Sandy Hook during the Revolution, it was here that Sir Henry Clinton and his army found refuge in 1778 after the Battle of Monmouth.

Of such military value was this 1600-acre sandbar that no sooner had the Colonies united than the new Federal government took over Sandy Hook Light. By 1807 the U.S. Army had designed fortifications and ever since has held a firm grip on the Hook. The off-limits sign was moved north in 1962 when the Federal government leased a third of the Hook to New Jersey for an unspoiled seaside park, now 730 acres.

Here in 1893 Hudson Maxim tested his smokeless powder, a weapon believed so hideous that he hoped it would end war. Modern Fort Hancock had its inception at Sandy Hook in 1892, was a troop-training center in World War I, an antiaircraft base in World War II, and in 1951 became a major radar and missile base. As early as 1848 the U.S. Coast Guard set up its first lifesaving unit here and now maintains a major station.

Where today striped bass are the prized catch of surf

fishermen at Sandy Hook, in Colonial times it was whales, and Spermaceti Cove on the bay side was a favored site for rendering blubber. Now a wildfowl preserve where egrets and herons stalk the shallows, Spermaceti Cove offers a spectacle during the spring and fall migrations of ducks and Canada geese. Near here is a wild holly forest of 79 acres, one of the finest stands in the Nation.

In the late 17th century buccaneers were so common off the Atlantic coast that New York's Governor, the Earl of Bellomont, sent out Captain Kidd to prey on pirates. On Kidd's last voyage, before he was hanged in London in 1701 (for killing a mutinous seaman, not for piracy), he put ashore at the Highlands. A spot on Sandy Hook is still known as Kidd's Meadow and "pieces of eight" have been found on the Highlands.

But today the real bonanza is the smooth sweep of sandy beach, half reserved for surf fishermen, half for swimmers. Bathhouses, lifeguards. Nature guides for groups. See Supplement for Ft. Hancock.

Heading next for Rumson, the motorist at Highlands has two choices: (1) following Ocean Blvd. S to Sea Bright, then Rte. 520 into Rumson; or (2) traveling W on Rte. 36 for 1.5 miles to the Rumson road S across the Navesink River for 3 miles via Rte. 8A. As the ocean view is blocked by concrete bulkheads into Sea Bright, the second tour is more scenic, past country lanes and well-kept houses.

RUMSON

On the Shrewsbury River and just south of the Navesink, Rumson is one of the liveliest boating centers of the Northeast and the setting for sailing, motorboat, and iceboat regattas. A prosperous residential town, Rumson has many attractive streets and surrounding drives.

To reach Red Bank from Rumson continue SW on Rte. 520 or take River Road on the southeast bank of the Navesink.

RED BANK

At the head of the Navesink River, Red Bank, like Rumson, has long been a center for the exciting sport of iceboating and headquarters for yachtsmen.

THE OLD UNION HOUSE   1791 (*restaurant*) 11 Wharf
   Ave. at Marine Park

A stagecoach inn during post-Revolutionary times, the Union House must have been a beehive of activity in the 1830's when James P. Allaire, inheritor of Robert Fulton's mantle, kept a flotilla of steamboats plying between his marine-engine works in Manhattan and Red Bank. The inn was a transfer point for goods brought by wagon from Allaire's Howell Works, an iron-making village, much of it still standing today near Farmingdale *(see Allaire Village)*.

MARINE PARK   Wharf Ave.

This small park on the Navesink River is a vantage point for watching boat races and is the setting for summertime concerts. At the marina, a sort of community center, barn dances are open to the public.

Just W of Red Bank via Rte. 520 is Entrance No. 109 of the Garden State Pkwy.

MIDDLETOWN: OVER THREE CENTURIES OF HISTORY

Marlpit Hall	Stout House
Hartshorne House	Shrewsbury
Christ Church	Allen Homestead
Baptist Church	Friends Meeting House
Hendrickson House	Christ Church
Holmdel Park	Monmouth College
	Long Branch

From Garden State Pkwy., Exit 114 to Middletown.

MIDDLETOWN

Middletown is one of the oldest continuous settlements in New Jersey. About 50 families, mostly Dutch, were already living here in 1650. The first Indian purchase, from Chief Popomora, was made in 1664 by Richard Stout, Captain John Bowne, and four other Baptists who had been persecuted out of Long Island. The next year these men and six others received from the Duke of York the celebrated "Monmouth Patent" which gave the founders not only a great tract of land here but guaranteed "free liberty of conscience without any molestation or disturbance whatsoever in the way of worship."

Penelope van Princis, a young woman who would not die, also was a founder of Middletown in the early 17th century. Just as she approached the New World the ship carrying her and other Hollanders was wrecked off Sandy Hook. Indians attacked the survivors, and Penelope was so badly tomahawked that she was left for dead. Later, two more compassionate Indians found her, took her to their village, and restored her to health. After a time her New Amsterdam friends, hearing that she was alive, persuaded Penelope to leave the Indians and brought her to Manhattan. There she met and was wooed by the Englishman Richard Stout. As man and wife they returned to Middletown. By the end of their lives their descendants numbered in the scores.

Middletown's King's Highway, 100 feet wide, was planned that way in 1719 as being ideal for horse racing. The first cup won in these pioneer contests bears the date 1699. From that distant time Monmouth County has never let die its reputation as one of the first great racing centers in America.

MARLPIT HALL   1684, 1720 *(museum)* 137 King's Highway

Owned by the Monmouth County Historical Association, this long, low, shingled house shows the Dutch influence, though for many years it was the home of Englishmen from Kent, George and Edward Taylor, who operated a tannery in Middletown. Described by the U.S. Department of the Interior as "worthy of most careful preservation" for its exceptional historic and architectural interest, Marlpit Hall is said to have most of its original paneling, hardware, and doors, one of the latter with rare bull's-eye panes. The classic drawing room is depicted in the book by Helen Comstock, *One Hundred Most Beautiful Rooms in America*. The entire house is furnished with choice antiques, among them, an early Dutch *kas* or cupboard decorated *en grisaille*, of which only about a half-dozen are known in the nation. Furnishings and portraits of the Taylor family. 11-5, Tues., Thurs., Sat.; 2-5, Sun. Closed Jan. Make advance reservations for groups: 201-462-1466.

CHRIST CHURCH 1836, restored 1972
LEEDS MONUMENT (King's Highway)

In 1700 Lewis Morris, who had sown considerable wild oats in his youth, as Colonial Governor wrote the Bishop of London that at Middletown were perhaps "the most ignorant and wicked people in the world." In response to this plea for salvation the Church of England sent to New Jersey one of its most renowned missionaries, George Keith. His hymn, "How Firm a Foundation," is known wherever Christians gather. But his crowning achievement may well have been the conversion of William Leeds, right-hand man of Captain Kidd. In the yard of Middletown's Episcopal Church, founded by the Rev. Keith, is a marble shaft to Leeds, in "appreciation of his benefactions." His bones lie buried at the doorway of the sister church in Shrewsbury. Since 1739 both churches have derived income from the "glebe" of 438 acres of William Leeds, who lived for some time on the high seas but died in his bed at Leedsville, now Lincroft.

BAPTIST CHURCH 1832   King's Highway

Organized in 1688, this was the first Baptist congregation in New Jersey, among the founders, such early settlers of Middletown as Richard Stout, Jonathan Holmes, Obadiah Holmes, and Captain John Bowne, who is buried in the Presbyterian cemetery on the opposite side of King's Highway. Near the Baptist Church was an often-used whipping post.

HARTSHORNE HOUSE   c. 1670 *(private)*   King's Highway at New Monmouth Rd.

A Quaker upholsterer in London, Richard Hartshorne found great riches in New Jersey for he received a grant from the Crown of 2000 acres, an enclave that embraced all of Sandy Hook and Portland Point, the peninsula which juts into the Navesink River. By 1675 Hartshorne was sending glowing letters to London friends about the "fertile soile" that grew:

Gooseberries, Cherries, and peaches in abundance, having all sorts of green trash in the Summertime. . . . We can buy a fat Buck of the Indians . . . for a pound and a half of Powder or Lead . . . and a peck of Strawberries the Indians will gather, and bring home to us for the value of 6 pence. . . . In short, this is a rare place for any poor man, or other . . .

Two of the most famous Quakers, William Penn and George Fox, visited the Hartshornes here. In his Journal Fox tells that in 1672 Hartshorne carried the preacher and his party and horses by boat "over a great water," a day's journey to Long Island. The burying ground adjoining the house was a gift of Richard Hartshorne, whose grave is now unknown.

Tucked in among the lanes around Middletown are many more privately owned houses dating from early Dutch times, which are sometimes opened for tours.
Take Holland Rd. W of King's Highway for 3.5 mi. to Crawfords Cor. Rd., then Longstreet Rd.

HENDRICKSON HOUSE   c. 1715 *(museum)*   Longstreet Rd., approx. 1 mi. E of Rte. 4

A uniquely preserved example of an early Dutch house, this one, formerly on the site of the Holmdel

Bell Telephone Laboratories, was given by the firm to the Monmouth County Historical Association, Freehold, whose members have furnished the 14 rooms in 18th-century antiques. Prior to restoration the house had never had plumbing, electricity, or a heating system and hence is of prime interest to antiquarians. Interior original woodwork is virtually intact. Tues., Thurs., Sun., 1-5. May to Oct.

0.2 mi. SW of Hendrickson House is . . .

HOLMDEL PARK   Longstreet Rd.

Opened as part of New Jersey's Tercentenary celebration, this 170-acre Monmouth County park, nearly half of it in wooded land with winding brooks, sets aside welcome green acres in an area rapidly converting to light industry. Picnic groves and a natural pond for fishing. Nature trails, guided tours. Ball fields. Free.

Near Hendrickson House, take Roberts Rd. on left for 0.5 mi. to . . .

BELL TELEPHONE LABORATORIES

Crawfords Corner-Everett Rd.

Looking as if made from blocks of jet this striking 6-story building is among the last creations of the late Eero Saarinen, world-renowned architect. Inside, creation of a different sort takes place, for this is a "think factory" of the space age. This Holmdel headquarters of Bell Laboratories and the Crawford Hill center a few miles north have pioneered in many fields but particularly in communications satellites. When Echo I, the 10-story balloon, was set aloft from Cape Kennedy on August 12, 1960, the sensitive horn antenna at Crawford Hill picked up the message, marking the start of communication by orbiting satellites. Both laboratories paved the way for the great break-through of July 10, 1962, when television pictures were transmitted from Europe to America via the satellite Telstar. Laboratories *not* open for tours.

STOUT HOUSE *(private)* Crawfords Corner Rd., opp.
Bell Laboratories

This early Dutch house is said to be that of David Stout, son of Penelope Stout, who after having been left for dead by Indians lived to bear 10 children, become a founder of Middletown, and reach the age of over a century.

Go S on Crawfords Corner Rd. to Rte. 520 E; at Rte. 35 go S to Shrewsbury.

SHREWSBURY

Broad Street at Sycamore is one of the most historic crossroads on the Jersey shore. Even before the white man arrived, the red man had cut a wide trail here, for Sycamore Avenue was once the end of the great Minisink Path which began at the village of that name on the upper Delaware River and led all the way to the sea. Once a year the Minisink Trail was crowded with whole villages of Indians headed for the ocean, to gorge on seafood, to bathe in salt water.

ALLEN HOMESTEAD 1667 NW cor. Broad and Sycamore Ave.

MONMOUTH COUNTY HISTORICAL ASSOCIATION

In the civil war between Loyalists and Patriots in Old Monmouth this house, one of the oldest in the county, saw much violence. A British spy was slain here by Continentals and his blood stained the stairway for over a century. At another time some Tories hiding behind tombstones in Christ Church cemetery surprised a dozen unarmed Virginians in the Allen tavern, killed three, and carried the rest off to the Sugar House prison in New York City. Restored in 1973, the house will be furnished as a Colonial tavern.

FRIENDS MEETING HOUSE 1816 NE cor. Broad and Sycamore Ave.

The eloquent George Fox, just after he had led the Shrewsbury Quakers in "a precious meeting" on this spot in 1672 was credited by the congregation with performing a miracle. John Jay, a Quaker planter from Barbados, was thrown from his horse and was picked up as dead, apparently of a broken neck. George Fox put his hands upon the man's head, and suddenly he came alive again. But the Quaker preacher took no credit for miracles, telling in his journal that the man's neck was dislocated, not broken.

CHRIST EPISCOPAL CHURCH 1779 SE cor. Broad and Sycamore Ave.

In the Revolution, patriots tried to shoot down the British crown that tops the spire but only riddled it with holes. Christ Church has one of only 8 known "Vinegar" Bibles, published at Oxford in 1717, in which the "Parable of the Vineyard" has the latter word misprinted as "Vinegar." The canopied pew for the Colonial governor is believed to be the only such in the United States. The silver communion service was given by Queen Anne. Just outside the vestibule is the grave of William Leeds *(see Middletown, above),* wealthy convert to the church in 1735 and a former chief cohort of Captain Kidd who, though often called a pirate, actually held a commission from New York's governor to "exterminate pirates."

From Broad St. continue S on Rte. 35 to Rte. 36. Go E. then S on Monmouth Rd. to West Long Branch.

MONMOUTH COLLEGE West Long Branch

The campus of Monmouth College is a composite of several estates. Shadow Lawn, one of these properties, was the official summer White House in 1916 when President Woodrow Wilson lived here. Destroyed by fire in 1927, Shadow Lawn was replaced by a chateau and grounds that cost a retired president of the F. W. Woolworth Company some ten million dollars. Patterned after the Palace of Versailles, the 140-room mansion is now the central unit of Monmouth College. Classes are held in rooms with sculptured stone fireplaces and carved paneling. Mosaics in some of the rooms are of special interest. Opposite the main campus the former Guggenheim residence is now the library of this coeducational college.

Roads east to Ocean Ave. and the beaches of Long Branch.

LONG BRANCH

Because it had a seaside boarding house as early as 1792, Long Branch vies with Cape May City for title of "oldest ocean resort in the nation." But while Cape May retains the nostalgia of a Victorian postcard album, Long Branch shows little trace of the noted and notorious who have summered here for 181 years.

CHURCH OF THE PRESIDENTS   Ocean Ave. nr. Takanassees Bridge

Besides Ulysses S. Grant and James A. Garfield, four other American presidents worshipped here during summer sojourns: Rutherford B. Hayes, Benjamin Harrison, William McKinley, and Woodrow Wilson. An odd bit of seaside architecture, the former church is now headquarters of the Long Branch Historical Society.

In the nineties glittering gambling casinos flourished at Long Branch, and Diamond Jim Brady used to drive Lillian Russell in an electric coupé brightly lighted inside so that all could see the beauty and her jewels. In the Naughty Nineties it was considered improper for a woman to bathe in the sea without a male escort. If an escort was not available or a belle preferred variety, paid companions offered their services—the first gigolos in America.

OLD MONMOUTH

LEE'S RETREAT AND
MOLLY PITCHER'S CHARGE

Freehold

Clinton's Headquarters

Monmouth County His-
torical Association

St. Peter's Church

Tennent Church

Englishtown Inn

Monmouth Battlefield

Molly Pitcher Spring

Colt's Neck Inn

The Phalanx

Tinton Falls

Asbury Park

Ocean Grove

Rte. 9 to Freehold traffic circle

FREEHOLD

One of the five major Revolutionary battles fought in New Jersey takes its title from Freehold's early name: Monmouth Court House. In humid heat close to 100 degrees on the Sunday of June 28, 1778, officers whose names now rank among the "greats" of the time were lined up in opposition for a final struggle over New Jersey. In control of Freehold were Sir Henry Clinton, Lord Cornwallis, and the redoubtable Hessian, Baron von Knyphausen. Resolute for victory were not only Washington and Lafayette but Nathanael Greene, Alexander Hamilton, William Alexander, Anthony Wayne, and von Steuben. And Charles Lee. But for the latter's inexplicable retreat leaving his men leaderless, the Americans might have completely routed the British. As it was, with casualties six times those of the rebels, the enemy stole away at midnight to Middletown, without waking the exhausted Americans. London was right in referring to the Battle of Monmouth as "Clinton's escape."

Freehold, its many elm-shaded streets bordered with green-shuttered, white houses, is an enjoyable place for sightseeing.

CLINTON'S HEADQUARTERS   ca. 1750   150 W. Main
MONMOUTH COUNTY HISTORICAL ASSOCIATION

At the Battle of Monmouth this house, now oldest in Freehold, was headquarters for Sir Henry Clinton and his officers. After the war William Forman, sea captain and brother-in-law of the Revolutionary poet Philip Freneau, lived here with his brothers and sisters. During the War of 1812 they welcomed Capt. James Lawrence here by strewing roses in the naval hero's path. Freneau's poem "The Seafaring Bachelor" was dedicated to Forman, who died a bachelor.

Open by appointment: 201-462-1466.

MONMOUTH COUNTY HISTORICAL ASSOCIATION
(Museum) 70 Court St., N of Main St.

Deemed one of the finest small historical museums in the nation, this modern Georgian building houses many rarities in New Jersey furniture, ceramics, glass, and paintings, arranged in tasteful and authentic room-settings. Among many choice pieces are the desk of James Wilson, a Signer of the Declaration of Independence, a painting by Benjamin West, and one by Leutze of the Battle of Monmouth. A British flag captured in the battle, a copy of the Monmouth Patent, and court-martial papers of General Charles Lee are among scores of unusual items. Rotating exhibits of special collections such as guns, porcelains, primitive paintings, toys, New Jersey pottery, horse-racing mementoes, and New Jersey documents. Thousands of school children visit the outstanding Junior Museum. The library, open 2nd and 4th Saturdays only, has an excellent collection of maps and manuscripts, also a complete file of Monmouth County newspapers. Daily, except Mon., 11-5; Sun., 2-5. Closed latter half of Dec. and July. Free. Appointment needed for group tours.

MONUMENT STATE PARK Court St. opp. museum

A 94-foot shaft is surrounded by 5 bronze bas-reliefs depicting scenes of the Battle of Monmouth, one of which shows Molly Pitcher manning a cannon. A border of splendid copper beeches edges the tiny triangular park. It was near this spot that a spirited skirmish preceding the major battle took place between General Dickinson's New Jersey militia and enemy troops.

ST. PETER'S CHURCH 33 Throckmorton St.

A Quaker meetinghouse in 1683 at Topanemus, 4 miles north of Freehold, the structure was moved here by the congregation who were converted by the Episcopalian, George Keith. The church is believed to have housed wounded during the Monmouth fighting. Sunday services; weekdays, inquire at rectory next door.

AMERICAN HOTEL 1842 18 E. Main St.

The restaurant is now completely modernized but has attractive displays of antique racing prints.

Take Throckmorton St. W (Rte. 522 W) for 4.5 mi. to Rte. 3, turn right to . . .

TENNENT CHURCH 1751 Off Throckmorton Rd. on Rte. 3

From the belfry of this cedar-shingled church on a hill a scout would have had a sweeping view of Monmouth battlefield stretching three miles south and east toward Freehold. Many Continental soldiers are buried in the churchyard. Some years after the war, citizens of Freehold demanded that the Revolutionary martyr Joshua Huddy be buried here. Once called Old Scots, the Presbyterian Church is named for the Rev. William Tennent, pastor here for 43 years, who lies buried beneath the center aisle. Sunday services.

Continue on Rte. 522 NW to Englishtown.
ENGLISHTOWN

THE VILLAGE INN   1732

Believed to be the oldest tavern in continuous operation in New Jersey, this was where Washington and his officers gathered and dined on June 27, 1778, the eve of the Battle of Monmouth, while the British held Freehold. After the battle in which the Americans were confounded by the retreat of General Charles Lee, Washington and one of his most loyal generals, William Alexander, Lord Stirling, met at this inn to draw up plans for the court-martial of the officer whose behavior quite probably cost the Americans a clear-cut victory. Prints of George Washington and Revolutionary relics are on display in the tavern.

Return via Rte. 522 to Freehold. En route . . .
MONMOUTH BATTLEFIELD *(State park)*
E of Rte. 3 and N of Rte. 522   1450 acres

Although the British burned houses as far away as Smithburg, the Battle of Monmouth was fought mainly on the land southeast of Tennent Church toward Freehold. In 1963 the New Jersey Department of Conservation and Economic Development bought 1000 acres here in the heart of the battlefield and plans to create a museum. Of all the Revolutionary battlefields, the Monmouth site is reputedly closest to its original historic appearance. Apple orchards, grain fields, and terrain are almost identical to the situation of 1778 when Washington, riding along the Englishtown Road, was startled to find Lee's soldiers in what von Steuben called "senseless retreat." Famous for his self-control, Washington galloping up to Lee was livid with rage, according to eyewitnesses Knox and Lafayette. The latter afterwards said, "Never had I beheld so superb a man," as Washington rallied the confused troops and marshalled his generals.

Longest battle of the Revolution, with the cream of both armies engaged, the fight went on, amid searing heat and thunderstorms, until darkness stopped it. Exhausted, even the generals slept on the field. At dawn the Americans discovered that the enemy had decamped in a retreat to Sandy Hook, with a baggage train of loot from Philadelphia homes.

Writing insulting letters to Washington, Lee later demanded a court-martial to clear his name. He got what he wanted, but also a surprise: the court found him guilty of "misbehaviour before the enemy." The penalty was light—suspension for a year without pay—but Lee never returned to the army and died disgraced.

MOLLY PITCHER SPRING   SE cor. Wemrock Rd. and
     Rte. 522

The actual spring from which soldiers on Monmouth field sought to assuage heat and thirst is on the left side of Wemrock Road, just beyond the overpass, and was never a "well." A real person who carried pitchers from the spring to men collapsing of heatstroke, Molly, a young woman from nearby Allentown was the wife of one of the Monmouth cannoneers, John Hays. When he fell exhausted she continued to help in firing the gun, bravery for which she was commended by Washington himself. Amid cannonading and musket-fire, men and horses fell dead without a wound. It was death by dehydration. Officers especially, in full regalia of woolen uniforms, were the victims. No wonder the cry went out, "Molly! Pitcher, Molly!" Many of the Hessians declined to fight, and lived to fight another day. (*See also Allentown, birthplace of Molly Ludwig Hays.*)

Rte. 522 to Freehold, then Rte. 537 E to . . .

COLT'S NECK INN   1717   Rte. 535 at Rte. 34

At one time the tavernkeeper here, Captain Joshua Huddy, on a night in 1780, was surrounded in his adjacent house by 70 "Pine Robbers." Led by Colonel Tye, a mulatto Tory, the band set fire to his home, and captured him. Miraculously Huddy escaped but on March 20, 1782 while defending the blockhouse at Toms River he was again seized. A month later, without charges or trial he was hanged at Atlantic Highlands. Public indig-

MOLLY PITCHER AT THE BATTLE OF MONMOUTH
Newly discovered oil painting depicts the New Jersey heroine, Molly Pitcher, in the thick of the Revolutionary battle west of Freehold. Painting attributed to Alonzo Chappell (1828-1878).

Courtesy of the Tillou Gallery, Buffalo, New York

nation was enormous and Monmouth citizens petitioned for reprisal. Obtaining no satisfaction from the English, Washington ordered that a captured officer be executed, and the lot fell to a youth of 19, Captain Charles Asgill. Through the intervention of the French foreign minister, the boy's life was finally spared, and the British did not atone for Huddy's lynching.

From Colt's Neck intersection go N on Rte. 34 for 0.9 mi., then right and continue to site of the Phalanx, on left.

NORTH AMERICAN PHALANX *(site*)*

The block of a building glimpsed through trees was a *phalanstery,* common house of the *North American Phalanx,* most successful of many utopian societies which failed in America. Following the tenets of the French philosopher Charles Fourier, the Phalanx, established in 1843, had such backers as Horace Greeley, editor of the *New York Tribune,* and Albert Brisbane. Strong president of the Phalanx and responsible for much of its 12-year financial success was John S. Bucklin, grandfather of Alexander Woollcott, playwright and critic in the 1920's who was born and grew up here.

Some ideas promulgated by the Phalanx have since become widely accepted: equal rights for women, a 30-hour week, profit-sharing, day nurseries for children of working mothers. A disastrous fire in the factory buildings marked the end of the Phalanx but non-resident stockholders received 100 per cent of their investment.

* Destroyed by fire in 1972.

Continue on to Lincroft, go right on Swimming River Rd. into New Shrewsbury (Tinton Falls).

NEW SHREWSBURY

The first successful ironworks in New Jersey was operated here by Henry Leonard as early as 1674, then sold two years later to a Barbados merchant, Colonel Lewis Morris. His wealth and 3500-acre estate "Tintern" were inherited by his nephew and namesake who became the first provincial governor of New Jersey (1739-1746) and chief justice of the provincial court. All trace of the mines is gone but an old mill (early 18th century) is still here near Tinton Falls and now used as an art center.

Rte. 537 E to Eatontown, then Rte. 35 S to Asbury Park.

ASBURY PARK 1870

Founded by a militant reformer, James A. Bradley, as a reaction to the high life of Long Branch during the escapades of Jim Fiske, Lilly Langtry, and Diamond Jim Brady, Asbury Park is now a major convention center, with big hotels, a mile of boardwalk, a convention pier, and, of course, a beach. The Sea Queen beauty contest is held here in August.

OCEAN GROVE 1869

Another resort that Senator Bradley founded for summer camp meetings still draws faithful Methodists and others seeking a quiet temperance village. From Saturday midnight to Sunday midnight no motor traffic moves on Ocean Grove streets. Many religious conferences and musical programs are held in the Auditorium which, like Solomon's temple, is built without nails.

Shore roads lead north to boating centers on the Navesink and Shrewsbury rivers and to historic Sandy Hook.

NEPTUNE

SHARK RIVER COUNTY PARK   School House Rd., off Rte. 33
Picnic area, playground, fishing, ice-skating.

SHARK RIVER HILLS MARINA   Riverside Dr.
Deepsea fishing boats.

ALLAIRE'S IRON-MAKING VILLAGE

From Garden State Pkwy. use Exit 96 South or 97A North, then Rte. 524 to Allaire Village.

Allaire Village is a convenient extension of the Freehold Tour. From Freehold take Rte. 33 to village of Farmingdale; then Rte. 547 and E on Rte. 524.

ALLAIRE VILLAGE AND STATE PARK

When Robert Fulton died prematurely in 1815 before he had enjoyed the fruits of his arduous labor on The Steamboat, who carried on his work? The man was James Peter Allaire, who in 1822 began building this iron-smelting village in the New Jersey pines so as to have raw material for his steamboat engine works in Manhattan. By 1840 Allaire's village had become the largest iron furnace in the young nation. Having built the engines or the cylinders for a number of the Fulton boats, including the great *Chancellor Livingston,* James Allaire went on to become the foremost marine engine builder of his day and the inventor of such improvements as the multi-cylinder steam engine for marine use. One of his proudest achievements was making the cylinder for the *S. S. Savannah,* first steam vessel to cross the Atlantic, on May 22, 1819.

At the peak of his fortunes, Allaire's little realm of 11,000 acres held probably 3000 people and some 70 buildings. Ten of the latter are still standing, including the rarest prize—the beehive furnace stack. Dependent on bog iron and charcoal, Allaire's village began to decline about 1846 when hardrock iron ore and anthracite were discovered side by side in Pennsylvania.

When it was considered radical to advocate free education Allaire actually established a free school here, supporting it for 16 years, until his own fortunes declined. Still in the village is the Episcopal Church which he built and financed, where no one, contrary to then prevailing custom, had to pay pew rent. In the custom of his time Allaire employed some indentured workers, yet he strove to create a good life in a garden community for his people. Still at Allaire Village are two of the sturdy brick row-houses built for workmen.

James P. Allaire was once known as the man who gave the U.S. Mint a run for its money. He issued his own currency, coppers and bills, which changed hands fast in his 4-story department store.

Ovens still intact, the community bakery now houses a museum displaying the ironworks money, utensils made in the village, Allaire documents, and letters carried by the ironmaster's flotilla of steamboats. Allaire was first to establish a line of coastwise steamers from New York to Charleston, S.C.

Today Allaire's department store is open and stocked with old-fashioned goods, much of it for sale, and country antiques. Here too are an old-time postoffice and the original elevator, one of the earliest known. At Allaire's wheelwright shop a craftsman demonstrates carpenters' tools of a bygone era. The foreman's cottage is open to view, and a farmhouse of the mid-18th century has been charmingly furnished with antiques. The blacksmith shop has been rebuilt and is in frequent operation.

Besides unique historical sightseeing, wooded Allaire Park offers recreation for a day's outing. During the summer many special events are scheduled such as photography, philatelic, and art exhibits. The mill brook, overhung with willows, is stocked with trout. The general store has a snack bar, and there are outdoor fireplaces and picnic tables. Apr.-Nov. 1, 10-5. Parking, $1.00; 25¢ per passenger.

PINE CREEK RAILROAD   Allaire Park

Rail fans of all ages come here to ride behind antique steam locomotives, in cars which run on narrow-gauge tracks. The circle ride is part of the New Jersey Museum of Transportation, a non-profit project organized by adult hobbyists. Trains run weekends and holidays, 12-6, May through November.

SHORE RESORTS

From Belmar to Brielle is a string of seaside resorts each with its own personality. *Manasquan,* now with summer cottages jammed together and few trees, in 1888 was host to Robert Louis Stevenson on his way to the South Seas where he died. At the Union House, since burned, he wrote part of *The Master of Ballantrae.* *Spring Lake* is a shady residential place but not very receptive to beach-hungry strangers. *Belmar* does have a good public beach. *Brielle* has the busy look of a fishing and boating center. It is at the mouth of the Manasquan River, down which James P. Allaire used to float barges filled with iron to be loaded into vessels bound for New York.

Original furnace stack now in Deserted Village of Allaire where Jersey bog iron was smelted in the 1830's.

Photo by Adeline Pepper

Robert Fulton's successor as marine-engine builder, James P. Allaire also built this village as a source of iron for his Manhattan shops. See p. 107.

See p. 107.

Photo by Adeline Pepper

"MIDDLE OF THE SHORE"

LAKEWOOD'S PINES AND ISLAND BEACH

Lake Carasaljo
Georgian Court College
Ocean County Park
State Quail Farm
Lakehurst, U.S. Naval
  Station
Toms River
Pine Beach

Forked River State
  Game Farm
Forked River State
  Marina
Island Beach State Park
Upper Barnegat Bay
  Resorts
Point Pleasant Beach

Coast Guard Station

Garden State Pkwy., Exit 91, then Rte. 9 to . . .

LAKEWOOD

A century or so ago when pine-laden air was regarded as more salubrious than just *plein air,* the locale of what is now Lakewood, with fine stands of evergreens in a dry pleasant climate, suddenly became the ultimate in winter resorts. By the Gay Nineties New York's "400"—Astors, Vanderbilts, Goulds, Rhinelanders, and Rockefellers—vied with one another in building ever more lavish houses on their country estates around Lake Carasaljo, a "Gold Coast" 10 miles inland from chill sea breezes.

Even though the rambling mansions surrounded by garden statuary have become obsolete status symbols, Lakewood continues to attract visitors, over 150,000 annually, to 75 or more hotels and condominiums. Besides its agreeable all-season climate Lakewood offers wide recreational latitude: golf, riding, tennis, ice- and roller-skating, swimming in all-weather pools, sports tournaments, parachute jumping, night clubs, and concerts.

During the War of 1812 when a need arose for cannon-balls, a bog-iron smelter was erected here, Washington Furnace, later called the Bergen Iron Works. In 1833 the settlement became Bricksburg in honor of the iron-master Joseph W. Brick. "Tokens" he issued as currency in 1840 still circulate among coin collectors.

LAKE CARASALJO

Named for Brick's daughters, Carrie, Sally, and Josephine, the lake still has groves of pine and cedar in spite of reckless cutting to fuel the bog-iron smelter. Boating, fishing, and swimming are summer recreations here, and bridle paths skirt the shore, as on nearby Lake Manetta.

GEORGIAN COURT COLLEGE

At the north end of Lake Carasaljo, the 200-acre campus of this Catholic college for girls is one of the most beautiful in New Jersey. And no wonder, for New York financier George J. Gould lavished some of his multimillion-dollar fortune in glorifying this, his country estate, with Japanese gardens, fountains, sunken gardens, sculpture, and formal Italian gardens.

OCEAN COUNTY PARK   Rte. 88, about 1 mi. E. of Lakewood

The man who built this park was at the same time building one of the half-dozen greatest fortunes in America. He was John D. Rockefeller, Sr., and in his time this 575-acre estate was sacrosanct, hidden by soldierly groves of pine. But now the arboretum with over 150 species of trees and shrubs is public property. John D.'s mansion, a pile of rooms that includes 14 guest suites still stands, but a far greater attraction now is the herd of a hundred tame deer· that roam about. Vying in appeal are the horse-drawn carriages, now a tradition at Lakewood. Ponds and picnic grounds.

Rte. 528 W of Lakewood to . . .

STATE QUAIL FARM

BUTTERFLY POND   Hunting and Fishing Grounds

COLLIERS MILLS   Hunting and Fishing Grounds

This land west of Lakewood is a sportsmen's happy hunting and fishing ground, the route well marked. Even those who are not hunters or fishermen may enjoy the State bob-white farm.

Rte. 527 SE then 547 to . . .

LAKEHURST   Rtes. 547 and 37

U.S. NAVAL AIR STATION

From this 7400-acre Federal Reservation in 1923 the first American rigid airship, the *Shenandoah,* took off in successful flight. In 1937 the *Hindenburg,* most luxurious dirigible ever built, flown here from Germany, was within 200 feet of landing at Lakehurst when it was consumed by flames, taking the lives of 35 persons.

Among 8 unique Naval Air Commands at the base is a school of aerology and one for parachute riggers, who work with space equipment. Two helicopter squadrons rescued over 1000 persons in 1962 storms and many survivors in marine disasters such as the collision of the *Andrea Doria* and the *Stockholm* in 1956.

Public tours are welcomed on Sundays and holidays, with guided trips by bus from 1 to 4:30 P.M. Informative 2-hour tours for groups of adults and children over 12 years; write Service Information Officer.

At the southeast corner of the base is the Gothic style *Cathedral-of-the-Air,* nondenominational memorial to the heroes of flight.

Rte. 37, 9 mi. to . . .

TOMS RIVER

A fishing and boating center, Toms River seems to have forgotten two of its most colorful figures. One of them, Captain Joshua Huddy, became a *cause célèbre* when a vengeful Tory, Richard Lippincott, and his companions on April 12, 1782 lynched the patriot Huddy who had been captured while defending the Toms River blockhouse. Public revulsion was explosive, and even Sir Henry Clinton expressed remorse over the "barbarous outrage." Although Lippincott went unpunished, the crime put an end to unauthorized raids by Loyalists, which in New Jersey had been marked by unparalleled atrocities.

In the 1890's Simon Lake, Jr., developed a submarine that could rest on three legs at the bottom of Toms River. After a successful test of his *Argonaut, Jr.*, at Highlands in 1895, Lake charted secret experimental mines that the U.S. Navy had planted at Hampton Roads, then presented his charts to Navy officials. Result: no sale. But in short order, Lake sold 7 submarines to the Russians who offered him a fortune to come over and build more. He did visit Russia but was too shocked by upperclass morals to stay. The Germans, finding he had not registered his American patents in Germany, proceeded to bilk Lake out of royalties and to build up their deadly U-boat armada of World War I. Lake is credited with the first successful periscope and with pioneering in polar submarines for Sir George Hubert Wilkins in his explorations at the North Pole, as well as building the *Explorer* for William Beebe's oceanographic research. Capital steadily dwindling, the brilliant Simon Lake in old age lost his mortgaged house because of mounting debts.

SIDE TRIP TO FORKED RIVER

Rte. 9 S for 1 mi. to Beachwood, then left to Pine Beach and Ocean Gate Beach; public swimming areas.

ADMIRAL FARRAGUT ACADEMY   Pine Beach

A waterfront campus on the south bank of Toms River is the pleasing setting for the first naval "prep" school in America, which now attracts students even from abroad.

Rte. 9 S to Forked River, 8 mi.

In mid-18th century Forked River was the scene of a salt works where ocean brine was evaporated in sun pans to produce the commodity so essential to the colonists' survival.

FORKED RIVER STATE GAME FARM

E of Rte. 9, 0.5 mi. N of Forked River traffic light

On this 550-acre farm hundreds of that exotic northern fowl, the ring-necked pheasant, can be seen. Some 35,000 are reared each year and released to State hunting grounds. Visitors may walk and drive around the farm to see the colorful birds in their pens. Guided tours of incubating rooms for school groups only; phone ahead.

Holmes House

The superintendent's residence at the game farm is a capacious house built for Joseph Holmes, a sea captain, in the early 19th century. In the house a graceful mahogany and white balustrade, imported from England, so attracted the fancy of the financier George J. Gould that he offered $700 for the elegantly-turned railing. The State declined the offer.

FORKED RIVER HOUSE *(restaurant)*

Captain Joshua Huddy whose callous hanging, without formal charges or trial, by the Refugees so incensed the Americans, used to stop at the original stage-house on journeys to inspect the Colonial militia. The two early dwellings which form the present structure are said to have been built for sea captain Ed Loman in the 1820's.

FORKED RIVER STATE MARINA   Just S of Forked River House

This harbor for pleasure craft is interesting even for vacationers without boats. Deepsea and surf fishing. Visitors allowed on the State buoy boat.

_____

Return to Toms River via Rte. 9 N; take Rte. 37 to its end, which is Seaside Heights, an amusement resort on the ocean. Go S for about 1 mi. to Island Beach.

ISLAND BEACH STATE PARK

Known during the Revolution as Lord Stirling's Island, for its owner, the American general William Alexander of Basking Ridge, Island Beach was then in physical possession of "Pine Robbers": pirates who preyed on Whig and Tory alike, ashore or afloat. Later, through decades of disuse, the island became a treasure trove of botanicals.

One of the few remaining unspoiled barrier beaches along the eastern edge of North America, Island Beach came close to being subdivided in 1926 by Henry Phipps, Andrew Carnegie's multimillionaire partner-in-steel, but realtors' dreams of glory for these beautiful dunes were shattered by the 1929 stock-market crash.

Visitors today are not allowed to walk on the dunes except in guided nature tours at the northern section, but along some parts of the 10-mile white strand, even beach buggies are permitted. The southern tip is a wildlife refuge, with surf-casters allowed to use the shore. The mid-section has a well-kept bathhouse and snack bar. Alert lifeguards are on hand, as the roaring rollers that pound this beach are not exactly for timid swimmers.

April and May are good seasons to see the golden pine-barrens heather, beach plum, sandwort, turkeybeard, and other unusual plants. Warblers en route north stop here, and ospreys often nest nearby. Write or phone for group nature tours.

Return to Rte. 35 N to Point Pleasant, through the oceanside resorts of Ortley Beach, Lavallette, Normandy Beach, Mantoloking, and Bay Head.

UPPER BARNEGAT BAY RESORTS

Sports fishermen and yachtsmen favor this narrow stretch of barrier beach sliced by Route 35; Barnegat Bay (part of the Intracoastal Waterway) on the west provides sheltered saltwater sailing while the Atlantic on the east appeals to cruisers. At *Lavallette's* excellent sand beach the surf-casting season culminates with prize contests in July. Each day at *Mantoloking* commercial fishermen chug out to sea about 3 A.M. and return with their catch in time for breakfasting tourists to enjoy the sight. *Bay Head* is a center for weekend sail and speedboat races and also snug harbor for yachts that rove as far as the Caribbean.

POINT PLEASANT
POINT PLEASANT BEACH

U.S. COAST GUARD STATION

How rescues at sea are carried out with electronic equipment is explained in guided tours. The complex devices seem light-years away from the covered metal lifeboat invented by Joseph Francis of Toms River, which was maneuvered on a line launched by a mortarball, the invention of William A. Newell of Manahawkin. But even these primitive contrivances proved their worth in an 1850 blizzard when the bark *Ayreshire* ran aground a few miles north of Point Pleasant, at Squan Beach. Of 201 passengers aboard only one was lost. Thanks to Joseph Francis and Dr. Newell, who later became Governor of the State, the U.S. Life-Saving Service—now the U.S. Coast Guard—first began in New Jersey. Advance reservations needed for tours.

STATE MARINA

One of four State marinas, this one is especially popular with boatmen as it is close to good beaches and to the Garden State Parkway and Routes 9 and 70.

ABSECON LIGHT TO BARNEGAT'S BEACON

Atlantic City
Absecon
Brigantine Wildlife
    Refuge
Smithville
Port Republic
Chestnut Neck

Bass River State Forest
Tuckerton Shell Mounds
Manahawkin Hunting
    and Fishing Grounds
Long Beach Island
Barnegat Light
Barnegat

ATLANTIC CITY

In spring, summer, and autumn the "Queen of Resorts" has a population increase totaling over 21 million visitors. Tourists spend close to a billion dollars here a year, probably more than at any other resort city in the world. It's scarcely a surprise that the first ramshackle beach houses have disappeared from such valuable property, but almost forgotten is "the Father of Atlantic City," Dr. Jonathan Pitney.

In 1819 a physician fresh from Columbia College, Dr. Pitney, then 22, arrived in Absecon after having traveled on horseback all the way from his native Mendham. His restless presence was to create a social revolution, for almost from the day he set foot on Absecon Island he envisioned it as a health resort and "bathing village." The magic touch would be a railroad to bring tired souls from the cities. Pitney's idea of a line from Camden to barren Absecon Island was laughed off as a "railroad with only one end." But with the financial backing of industrialists such as Samuel Richards the first railroad to the Jersey shore—the Camden and Atlantic—became a reality. On July 1, 1854, the first locomotive, named *Atsion,* and a train overflowing with distinguished citizens, pulled into the village which the railroad's designer, Richard B. Osborne, named Atlantic City.

* Atlantic City hotels and 'bus companies often arrange sightseeing tours to such points as Smithville and Batsto Historic Village. Even a taxi trip to Brigantine Bird Refuge or Smithville is not excessively costly for a group.

ABSECON LIGHT   1857   Rhode Island and Pacific
Aves.

At the stroke of midnight opening New Jersey's Tercentenary in 1964 Absecon Light, dark since 1933, once
again beamed out to sea. The light served to focus also
on the dark past when so many lives and ships were lost
off this shore, for lack of a beacon. For twenty years Dr.
Jonathan Pitney battled for this very lighthouse. While
he tended the sick, wrote vainly to Congress, and gathered petitions, dozens of vessels were wrecked off this
coast. The whole nation was shocked when on April 16,
1854, the *Powhatan* foundered at Little Egg Harbor, with
the loss of all aboard: 311 immigrants and the crew. Had
it been built then, Absecon Light could have guided the
mariners. At last Congress was convinced of the need for
a beacon, and within three years the 167-foot tower was
completed. Daily, except Mon., Memorial Day to Labor
Day. 25¢.

STATE MARINA

One of the most modern marinas along the Northeast
coast this one is popular even with land-lubbers because
of the waterfront dining room.

ABSECON

*Rte. 30 N to Rte. 9 (N. Shore Rd.). Large white
house on left . . .*

DR. JONATHAN PITNEY HOUSE *(private)*   57 N. Shore

Dr. Pitney liked the Absecon climate so well that he
stayed here for the last 49 years of his life, during which
he never ceased working for the public good. The lower
part of this house was built about 1795, the upper part
and the captain's walk in the 1860's.

DOUGHTY HOUSE *(private)*   Mill Rd.

A general in the War of 1812, Enoch Doughty had
charge of the triumphal tour of Lafayette through New
Jersey in 1824. General Doughty and Dr. Pitney were
leaders in securing a State charter for the Camden and
Atlantic Railroad.

METHODIST CHURCH 1829, 1856 Church St. and Pitney Rd.

A pleasing example of Greek revival architecture this brick church, with white cupola and Corinthian pillars, has been marked for preservation in the Historic American Buildings Survey.

Historic houses in Absecon are sometimes open for Maytime tours. In Absecon Highlands, *Gross' Winery* offers free tours.

BRIGANTINE NATIONAL WILDLIFE REFUGE
Headquarters: 1 mi. E of Oceanville on Rte. 9 (a bus route); 11 mi. from Atlantic City

Primarily for protection and management of waterfowl in the Atlantic Flyway, these 13,100 acres of brushy upland, marsh, and tidewater have a winter population of over 150,000 birds such as brant, Canada geese, ducks, gulls, and terns. A mecca for birdwatchers, the refuge is also used by sport fishermen, and in three posted areas hunting is permitted subject to State and Federal laws. Ferry service for hunters, $5.00 per person. Write Box 72, Oceanville. Picnicking allowed but no special facilities. Free. The Refuge is bisected by the Intracoastal Waterway.

From Oceanville go 1 mi. N to Smithville, a privately-owned historic village, open to the public. Rte. 9.

SMITHVILLE INN AND VILLAGE
A major stagecoach stop on the run from Leed's Point to Berlin (which the Indians called Long-a-Coming), Smithville Inn, long renowned for good food and hospitality, was falling to ruin when, in 1949, it was restored by its present owners who have since brought in a dozen early New Jersey buildings once marked for destruction. Here, around the millpond are the fine old gristmill from Sharptown, Hosea Joslin's tiny chapel from May's Landing, the Brower House from now-vanished Hewittown, and the minuscule cobbler's shop from Seaville. The

general store from New Gretna has many country antiques and part of the Smithville collection of 1200 decoy ducks. Early American antiques are used lavishly in the décor of the inn; of special note: redware ceramics such as were made in New Jersey's first potteries. Seeking to recreate the atmosphere of early "down Jersey," the owners feature rides in a stagecoach that once lumbered over the old roads, skating and sleighing parties, and regional dishes. On the north side of the lake, the stately old Mathis farm is open with antiques and furnishings authentically South Jersey. Surrounding land will be farmed, and cattle, sheep, and ponies will be on hand for the edification of city folks.

The village is free, the only charge being for meals, drinks, and articles bought in the shops. Open daily.

Rte. 9 N, first left turn to Port Republic, on Rte. 575, 2 mi. to . . .

PORT REPUBLIC

FRANKLIN INN   c. 1750 *(private)*   W side of Mill Rd., millpond dam

Among the first Americans to be granted government letters-of-marque-and-reprisal—equivalent to a privateer's license—sea captain Micajah Smith, who with malice aforethought named his ship the *Sly,* was a leader in the "nest of rebel pirates" (so dubbed by the British), who raided English vessels from the nearby port of Chestnut Neck. After the Revolution Captain Smith became part owner of this substantial coaching inn on Nacote Creek. In 1835-1837 the inn was owned by the Colwells, ironmasters at famous Weymouth Furnace (interesting ruins visible northeast of Routes 322 and 559).

METHODIST CHURCH   1870   Main St.

Dazzling white with incisive lines that stand out against blue sky, this is often called "the Christmas Card Church."

Return to Rte. 575, go N 2 mi. to Chestnut Neck Minute-Man Monument, facing bay.

CHESTNUT NECK "MINUTE MAN"   Rte. 9 E of Garden State Pkwy.

The havoc wrought here on Oct. 6, 1778 by 400 armed men aboard a British flotilla must have pleased Sir Henry Clinton who had ordered them to "pillage, burn and destroy," yet the vengeful raid did not accomplish its real goal: to expunge the "nest of rebel pirates" at The Forks, American privateering base 30 miles up the Mullica; nor the more desirable end of destroying the munitions furnace at Batsto. But Captain "Pat" Ferguson's men did level Chestnut Neck Fort—for it had no cannon—and then scuttled 10 prize vessels. Rushing overland from Trenton, Count Casimir Pulaski's men arrived at Tuckerton too late to be more than a threat. Then the enemy committed another of their night atrocities: the bayonetting of 44 men in a picket post as they slept. With the countryside now aroused and Colonel Proctor's artillery arriving from Batsto, Ferguson ordered an abrupt departure. In the haste, the splendid new flagship *Zebra* ran aground and so the British set her afire. One by one her guns exploded as she burned and sank into Little Egg Harbor Inlet. Never again did the British trouble this part of Jersey.

N on Rte. 9 to New Gretna; then follow signs to Bass River State Forest. Entry also from Tuckerton.

BASS RIVER STATE FOREST

Loblolly and white pines which fringe Lake Absegami are the product of forest management carried out here since 1905 by the State Department of Conservation and Economic Development. Now 8418 acres, New Jersey's oldest public forest offers one of the most economical family vacations. Rustic cabins and campsites for tenting can be had at a modest rental and are clustered around Lake Absegami which has an excellent sand beach and a good bathhouse. Weather-tight camp shelters are also available. Deer are often seen close to the narrow winding stagecoach roads, and hunting is permitted in season. A pleasant base for exploring nearby historic sites such as Batsto.

Take Rte. 9 N to Tuckerton.

TUCKERTON

Settled as early as 1699, Tuckerton was a great port of entry for goods from England and the West Indies when sailing ships were queens of transport. Known in Colonial times as Clamtown, the village was such an abundant source of the bivalves that contracts for indentured servants used to specify that they would not have to eat clams more than three times a week.

Diagonal rd. E of Rte. 9 and S of bridge. About 1 mi. on right . . .

INDIAN SHELL MOUNDS

This grass-covered hummock, about ten yards from the road, rising above marshland is one of the largest shell mounds left by Indians along the Atlantic coast.

LAKE POHATCONG

Swimming and picnicking.

Rte. 9 N to Manahawkin (boyhood home of Governor William Newell). At Rte. 72 go E to Ship Bottom. On N side of Rte. 72: Manahawkin Hunting and Fishing Grounds.

LONG BEACH ISLAND   End of Rte. 72 E

An 18-mile sandbar paralleling the mainland, Long Beach Island in midsummer swarms with *aficionados* of sun, sand, and breakers. Causeway to the island crosses the Intracoastal Waterway, on which cruises, including moonlit ones, can be arranged at Beach Haven. Informal vacationing, in contrast to sophisticated hotel life at Atlantic City. Bay, surf, ocean and deepsea fishing.

BARNEGAT LIGHT 1858 *(State park)* N. tip of Long Beach Island

In the early 19th century when the coast was uncharted and lighthouses were rare, Barnegat shoals became a graveyard for ships. In 1837 the *Newark Daily Advertiser* told of the arrest and conviction of William Platt, his son, and others for robbing two vessels wrecked off Barnegat. Embroidered by James Gordon Bennett's *Herald* and other New York newspapers, reports soon read that false lights on the Absecon-Barnegat shore lured ships to their doom, that survivors, the dead, and the cargo were robbed and that even corpses were held for ransom. Since that day many a writer has carelessly tossed off unverified tales about "Barnegat Pirates" and the "Jersey Wreckers." How different were the actual facts is described in an intriguing bit of literary detective work by Prof. Oral S. Coad in *Proceedings of the New Jersey Historical Society,* July, 1963, who shows that the fact-finding commission of 1846 found no evidence of plundering ghouls and decoy lights.

"Old Barney" was designed by George Gordon Meade, later a Civil War general and a hero at Gettysburg. F. Hopkinson Smith, author, playwright, and engineer, also aided in building the tower. Although it is 207 steps to the lantern, the 20-mile view from here on a clear day is worth the climb. Beach picnics and swimming permitted, but no fires.

BARNEGAT Rte. 9 N of Manahawkin

Not the same as Barnegat Light, the town has been a shipbuilding port since early days and now also has charter and U-Drive boats for hire. Sportmen's headquarters, for duck, quail, pheasant, and fish. A center also for blueberry and cranberry industries.

FRIENDS' MEETING HOUSE 1767 E. Bay Ave.

One of the oldest churches in the county is still open for meetings in summer.

On Rte. 9, bet. Barnegat and Lanoka Harbor . . .

THOMAS POTTER CHURCH   1766, 1841

A farmer, Thomas Potter, built the original church here, and when a shipwrecked young man appeared one day, Potter persuaded him to stay on as minister. The latter, John Murray, became founder of the Universalist faith in America.

BATSTO, ATSION, AND WHARTON STATE FOREST

Historic Batsto, reception center for the 96,000-acre Wharton State Forest, can be reached via the Garden State Parkway, New Gretna Exit to Rte. 542 W. From Philadelphia, take Rte. 30 E, then go 6 miles E on Rte. 542, near Hammonton.

MULLICA RIVER

Placid except for summertime motor boats, this tidal river takes its name from a Swedish navigator, Erik Mullica, who in the mid-17th century sailed up the stream, then settled near Batsto (or *badstu,* a Swedish word meaning "steam bath") at The Forks. The latter, head of navigation, was crowded during the Revolution with American privateering vessels and others seized from the English. It was to wipe out these South Jersey raiders that the British sent one of their cruelest, ablest officers, "Pat" Ferguson, with a flotilla and 400 men who sacked the Chestnut Neck Fort, perpetrated a night massacre at Tuckerton, but failed to reach The Forks or destroy munitions-making Batsto.

From Wading River Bridge on Rte. 542 go W 2.6 mi., then S 1.5 mi. to Mullica River and Lower Bank . . .

LEEK BOATYARDS   Lower Bank

An English surveyor and shipbuilder, Captain John Leek, came to the Mullica about 1715, began building boats from the plentiful, durable swamp cedar, and established Leek's landing, a busy port on the nearby Wading River. The captain's direct descendants form the present-day firm of C. P. Leek & Sons, Inc., which since 1914 has been building speedy craft, from revenue cutters to yachts, and is now one of the largest makers of fine cruisers. Much waterfront activity here. For group tours (high school age or over), phone, or write Box 337, Egg Harbor.

GREEN BANK   Rtes. 542 and 563

GREEN BANK STATE FOREST
Mostly a white cedar swamp of 1833 acres, the forest is inaccessible for recreation, but hunters and fishermen are admitted. Just east of the bridge on Route 563 is a small picnic ground and open-air shelter with a good view of the Mullica from a high bank.

SOOY CHURCHYARD   Picnic grove to end of road
Preceding even Erik Mullica, a Dutchman, Joos Sooy, settled in these parts in the early 17th century and left progeny so numerous that today Sooy reunions are still held in Green Bank. Many headstones around the little country church have names of early Sooys.

In August the marshes south of Green Bank Bridge are filled with pink mallows. Peak of the laurel season in the Wharton area is often the first week in June.

CROWLEYTOWN LANDING   Rte. 542, in Wharton State Forest
Marked now as a picnic grove on the Mullica, this is the site of a glass-bottle factory built by Samuel Crowley in 1851. The first successful Mason jar, patented by John L. Mason of Vineland in 1858, was blown here, creating a revolution in food processing as significant as that of freezing in modern times.

Upstream a few yards is a convenient dock for launching boats. This is near the site of the ore docks for early Batsto Furnace.

WHARTON STATE FOREST *96,000 acres*
Main entrance, Rte. 542, at Batsto

Travelers who see New Jersey only at such heavily industrialized cities as Hoboken and Camden are astonished that this wilderness of 150 square miles exists so close to main highways. Five times the size of Manhattan, Wharton State Forest offers 60 miles of canoe routes along shores banked with pine, cedar, and laurel. Long known as "the deer woods," this uninhabited region is open for gunning and bow-and-arrow hunting in season. Some 50 million years ago a sea floor, this unique botanical tract, where the Great Glacier brought down Arctic natives like bearberry to mingle with flora of the Everglades, has fascinated nature lovers since 1749 when the Swedish traveler, Peter Kalm, reported on its wonders.

BATSTO

In 1766 thousands of piney acres became fuel for the bog-iron smelter built by Charles Read. In the Revolution when Batsto Furnace produced quantities of cannon balls and camp kettles for the Americans, the ironmaster was Colonel John Cox, assistant quartermaster-general. After the war William Richards set up a family dynasty of ironmasters. When bog-iron smelters came upon hard times, the Richards in 1846 turned to making window glass, but that too failed and Batsto became a ghost town. Archeologists have discovered ruins of both the iron furnace and the glass furnace.

In 1876 Joseph Wharton, pioneering industrialist and philanthropist, bought the Batsto property with the idea of using its rivers to supply water to Philadelphia but his hopes were dashed when the New Jersey Legislature forbade export of water. Wharton spent thousands of dollars rebuilding Batsto after a fire in 1874, and installed the 80-foot tower for an hydraulic water system.

Many of some 30 rooms in the ironmaster's mansion, open for guided tours, have been handsomely furnished with period-style settings. Among many other attractions in Batsto Village: the post office and archaeology exhibit;

the blacksmith shop; the gristmill and its hand-made turbine; the street where tenant workers lived, which has two houses open for inspection; a display of early carriages, including a stagecoach that ran in the region; displays of farm tools. Grounds are open free, but visitors to buildings must be accompanied by guides. Groups by appointment only: Batsto Visitors Center, R.D. 1, Hammonton, N.J. Phone: 609-561-3262. Permits for camping in Wharton Forest should be obtained at Batsto Visitors Center. Memorial Day to Labor Day, Mon.-Fri., 10-6. Balance of year, 11-5 daily.

ATSION   Rte. 206 N of Hammonton

Samuel Richards, son of William, was the ironmaster here who in 1826 built the Greek Revival house which until recently had 13 iron pillars cast at Weymouth Furnace. Since demolished, Atsion Furnace made ammunition for the War of 1812 and many stoves such as that at Crosswicks Meeting House. Now being restored, Atsion Mansion is not open, nor is the store-and-postoffice beside it. Pretty little Atsion Lake attracts swimmers, and there is a picnic grove near the highway. This spot is also favored for launching canoes.

PLEASANT MILLS CHURCH   1809   W of Batsto, Rte. 542 and Pleasant Mills Rd.

Francis Asbury, first Methodist bishop in America, after dedicating this small church on April 21, 1809, wrote in his Journal: "At the Forks on Friday, I preached in our elegant chapel, on John XII . . ." As early as 1762 there was a log meetinghouse here, donated by Colonel Elijah Clark, a member of the Provincial Congress, where circuit-riding preachers such as Philip Vickers Fithian of Greenwich and David Brainerd, missionary to the Lenni Lenape, held services. Among the unusual tombstones are slabs cast of bog iron. Jesse Richards, Batsto ironmaster, is buried near the church. Sunday services.

Take narrow road back of church to parking lot for . . .

BATSTO NATURE AREA

Much of the flora and fauna of the 1¼ million acres of the now lush Pine Barrens are telescoped into this 150-acre nature preserve. The golden pine-barrens heather, a traveler from northern tundras, mingles with orchids, of which New Jersey has 55 known species. Canadian trailing arbutus blooms here in early spring, and in midsummer, the prickly pear cactus. The impression is one of limitless wilderness where amber colored streams wind among white sand hills and pines grow close to water-lily pools. The 130 plant species are all native here. Visitors can explore the nature area free by following marked trails but because of the uncommon plants a guided tour is advisable. Inquire at Batsto reception center. Appointments needed for large groups. Picnicking, fires, and hunting forbidden.

0.2 mi. E of Rte. 542 and Pleasant Mills Church . . .

PLEASANT MILLS PLAYHOUSE   *(private)*   Pleasant Mills Rd.

Now a multi-roomed studio on several levels with gardens in the manner of an Italian villa, the playhouse was in active use in the 1950s. The whole is an imaginative creation from early cotton and paper mills, the first of which opened in 1822.

KATE AYLESFORD HOUSE   1762 *(private)*   Opp. Playhouse

Although built by Elijah Clark, Revolutionary militia officer and privateer, this charming old house, once owned by Batsto ironmasters, is best known as "the Kate Aylesford Mansion." Kate was the heroine of a melodramatic novel of the same name, published in 1855 by Charles J. Peterson, reputed to have once been an iron molder at Batsto. Steeped in local color, the book tells how the dangerous Pine Robber Joe Mulliner, an actual bandit of Revolutionary times, swooped down and kidnaped for ransom "the maid of Sweetwater," now thought to have been modeled after lovely Margaret Wescoat, whose father Richard owned this house from 1779 to

1782. There is no record, though, that the real-life heroine was shipwrecked at Little Egg Harbor, spirited away, tracked by a bloodhound, and miraculously saved by her sweetheart, as Peterson described.

Continue on Pleasant Mills-Weekstown Rd. 1.8 mi. to grave marker on right . . .

"JOE MULLINER—HUNG 1781"

No figment of novelist Peterson's imagination, Joe Mulliner was one of the wiliest of Pine Robbers who terrorized this part of South Jersey. Along with pillaging and burning, he and his band had a way of dropping in at dances and taking over the parties and the girls. Once too often he did this, at nearby Indian Cabin Tavern, where he was captured by an old Indian fighter, Captain Baylin. Convicted in Burlington Court of high treason, Mulliner was hanged on Gallows Hill, August 8, 1781. And here lies the man of whom *New Jersey Gazette* then recorded, "the whole country, both whigs and tories, were his enemies."

HIGH BANK

At this bend in the Mullica the bluffs afford a view of the general area of the historic Forks. Boat rentals at nearby Sweetwater Casino, riverside restaurant.

OCEAN DRIVE TO OLD CAPE MAY

Somers House and
    Museum
Ocean City
Corson's Inlet Beach
Stone Harbor Bird
    Sanctuary
The Wildwoods

Cape May City and
    Point
Cold Spring
Cape May Court House
Dennisville
Belleplain State Forest
Seaville Meeting House

Tercentenary Holly

SOMERS POINT
On Rte. 52, at circle . . .

SOMERS HOUSE   c. 1720   *(State historic site)* Mays
    Landing and Shore Rd.

Richard Somers, American Naval hero who perished
in a suicide mission during the Tripolitan War in 1804
was the great-grandson of the first Richard Somers who
built this house, now restored.

In a desperate plan to blow up ships in the harbor of
Tripoli, whose ruler was extorting tribute from several
nations and had seized the Jerseyman Capt. William
Bainbridge and his warship, the *Philadelphia,* young
Somers had made his ketch, the *Intrepid,* a floating mine.
With 12 other volunteers Commandant Somers planned
to sail into Tripoli harbor by night, light a fuse in his
explosive ship and row quickly away. The *Intrepid* did
blow up with a mighty roar but Somers and his men
never returned to the vessel awaiting them at sea. Six
U.S. Navy ships have since borne the name *Somers.*

Two Chippendale chairs and a highboy formerly owned by the Somers family are part of the large museum of the Atlantic County Historical Society.

Take Rte. 52 across bridge over Great Egg Harbor Bay, to Central Ave., Ocean City, and turn right (south).

OCEAN DRIVE

"The Flight of the Gulls" is the roadside marker to follow if one would travel the easternmost route from Ocean City to Cape May City. Sometimes called a "land cruise," the route crosses four islands, connected by five county toll bridges (5 tickets for $1.). With the Atlantic to the east and the Intracoastal Waterway to the west, the road passes through flat tidelands and the resort towns of Strathmere, Sea Isle City, Townsend's Inlet, Avalon, Stone Harbor, and The Wildwoods. Some of the Northeast's finest beaches for swimming and fishing lie along this coast but can best be enjoyed only if motorists take time to park and really get down to the sea, for "Ocean Drive" is often routed through business districts.

OCEAN CITY

This resort was founded about 1880 by Simon Lake and his two brothers, all Methodist ministers, as a temperance retreat for family living and church conferences. Simon Lake, Jr., a brilliant but little-known inventor, is perhaps most deserving of the title, "father of the American submarine," although he sold 7 undersea vessels to the Russians before the U.S. Navy was willing to invest in his ideas.

Through its Music Pier, Ocean City has become known for excellent summertime concerts. Stone Harbor, famous for its heronry, is built on 7 man-made lagoons. Avalon is noted for its good beach, sand dunes, and nesting ospreys. In July and August several of the resorts have fishing tourneys with generous cash prizes.

See Supplement: Ocean City Museum and Art Center.

S of 59th St., Ocean City, follow Central Ave. to its end at 59th St., which adjoins beach.

CORSON'S INLET *(State beach, undeveloped)*

A calm curve of beach stretching about 1½ miles south. No bathhouse or other facilities as yet, but the public may swim and fish at the excellent beach. Free.

Return to 55th St. and follow "Ocean Drive" signs W and S. Road crosses . . .

OCEAN CREST ISLAND *(State fishing grounds)*

This extension of Corson's Inlet Beach consists of about 300 acres of islanded salt-meadow. Motorists may park along the road just above the toll bridge and fish the banks. Boat livery on property.

In Stone Harbor go S to 111th Street. Parking for heronry here.

STONE HARBOR BIRD SANCTUARY

Great flights of exotic birds, many of them regular migrants from the tropics, furnish a thrilling spectacle here from late March to November. Finding ideal nesting grounds, long-legged wading birds—green herons, little blue herons, glossy ibises, cattle egrets, American egrets—now form a summer colony numbering over 5000. The birds can be viewed without even getting one's feet wet. Best season for watching nesting waterfowl is April through July, but the spectacular flights of birds leaving the refuge for the feeding grounds just after daybreak and returning to their nests during the two hours before sunset can be seen from late March through October. Two coin-operated binoculars. On first and fourth Mondays of July and second and fourth Mondays in August the Witmer Stone Club offers public lectures on nature subjects in Stone Harbor.

At 110th Street is a fine white beach.

CAPE MAY CITY

Hark back to 1847 at Old Cape May. In that Victorian era a tall and eloquent Congressman from Kentucky's glamorous frontier, Henry Clay, was being chased along the Cape May strand by a bevy of females brandishing scissors. Squealing with delight, they were after snippets of Henry's hair.

In 1849, "A. Lincoln and wife" registered at the same hotel, the Mansion House, but their presence went unnoted. In Cape May's long colorful history as a resort 5 American Presidents have stayed here: Franklin Pierce, James Buchanan, U. S. Grant, Chester A. Arthur, and Benjamin Harrison.

In 1905 young Henry Ford brought one of his then unknown automobiles down to compete in a race on Cape May sands. He lost the race (as did "the Ace French driver, Chevrolet") and in order to get railroad fare back to Detroit, sold his racer to Daniel Focer. Later, Focer's became the first Ford agency in America.

As early as 1760 a poem by John Drinker of Philadelphia told about "the fam'd Amusements of Cape May," and by 1766 an advertisement in the Pennsylvania *Gazette* described the Cape as a spot "where a number resort for Health and Bathing in the Water." In 1801 Postmaster Ellis Hughes built the first hotel, a bleak sort of dormitory, but when Capt. Wilmon Whilldin, friend of Capt. Cornelius Vanderbilt, established regular steamboat service to Philadelphia, "America's first resort" mushroomed with elaborate hotels. When the fabulous Mount Vernon opened in 1853, with 2000 rooms and as many private baths, plantation society moved in to stay—until the War Between the States.

A postwar boom brought more of the vast hotels with lacelike façades, horse-racing, railroad excursions, and yachting, the latter culminating in the Cape May Challenge Cup Race, from Sandy Hook to the Point. Then in 1869 and again in 1878 fires swept away many wooden structures but Cape May, while some shore resorts were becoming citified, clung to its romantic antebellum look.

Today Cape May City, according to the National Trust for Historic Preservation, has the largest and most interesting concentration of Victorian edifices east of the Mississippi. Cape May citizens are embarked on an unusual urban renewal plan: to protect and restore the many tasteful examples of Victorian architecture. Freshly painted houses and inns trimmed with "carpenter's lace" are set off by trees and lawns, with touches of wisteria and azalea in spring. The aura of the past is most vivid on summer evenings when gas lights cast flickering shadows.

A ferry operates between Lewes, Delaware, and Cape May. From Memorial Day through Labor Day: 12 daily scheduled crossings; 4 extras on weekends and holidays. Fare is $5.00 per car and $1.50 per person. The 16-mile run takes about 80 minutes and leads to Ocean Hiway, down the Delmarva Peninsula, then across Chesapeake Bay via the 17.6-mile bridge-tunnel. 609-886-2718.

In 1970, the entire area of Cape May City was named to the National Register of Historic Places. Antique trolley rides and walking tours are conducted by the Mid-Atlantic Center for the Arts. The rides start at 2 P.M., Mondays through Thursdays. The Cape May County Art League conducts tours of county historic sites on the second Saturday in July.

CAPE ISLAND MARINA

Turn left just after crossing bridge into Cape May.

A kaleidoscope of harbor life swirls around this colorful marina. Attractive waterfront dining rooms, fish markets, much small-boat traffic.

FISHERMAN'S WHARF   (Schellenger's Landing)

Opp. marina on bay side of road

Largest privately owned fishing dock on the New Jersey coast. Cape May County ranks second among the State's counties in pounds and dollar-value of the fish catch. During the mackerel season in April, even the fishing fleet of Gloucester, Mass., comes down here. Boats leave near dawn and return with catches of 50,000 to 90,000 pounds of marine life.

THE VICTORIAN MANSION 1856 *(inn)* 635 Columbia Ave. (Beach Ave. to Stockton Pl.)

A famous gambling casino before the Civil War, this beautifully proportioned house of 22 rooms was built by R. R. Lear, a noted black-face ministrel. From cupola crowning the roof to a wooden bathtub inside, the house epitomizes Victoriana at its most charming.

THE CHALFONTE 1876 Sewell Ave. and Howard St.

Some of the Victoriana of Cape May was created by Henry W. Sawyer, a carpenter who lived obscurely in Cape May from 1848 until he enlisted in the Union army 13 years later, and then was catapulted into the headlines. The harrowing events began June 9, 1863 when Capt. Sawyer was wounded, captured, and thrown into the dread Libby prison. A month later when his name was drawn in a "lottery of death"; he was sentenced to die on the gallows, with a Capt. John Flinn, in retaliation for the unrelated death of two Confederate captains. Bravely, Henry Sawyer wrote his wife: ". . . only let me see you once more and I will die becoming a man and an officer . . ." Instead, his wife and Capt. Wilmon Whilldin raced by stagecoach for an audience with President Lincoln. In Washington it was discovered that the son of Gen. Robert E. Lee had been captured by Unionists on the same battlefield where Sawyer fell. A day before the scheduled execution the warning went to the Confederates that Gen. William Lee and another Southern officer would die unless Sawyer and Flinn were spared. The South relented. But months dragged on before the exchange of prisoners took place, while Sawyer and Flinn, unaware of efforts to save them, lived in daily fear of the gallows. Released at last in March, 1864, Capt. Sawyer soon was back in action with the New Jersey cavalry and before his unit was discharged in 1865 he was twice wounded. He came home to Cape

May as a lieutenant-colonel. In 1876 he built the Chalfonte and managed the hotel for several years. Before his death in 1893 he served in many civic posts, among them, superintendent of the U.S. Lifesaving Service for the New Jersey coast.

CONGRESS HALL   1879   Beach Ave. at Congress

This vast porticoed brick hotel, now modernized, was just one of a half-dozen similar, some even larger, in the 1870's, most of them wooden and eventually destroyed by fire. The first Congress Hall was built in 1816.

WINDSOR HOTEL   Beach Ave. at Windsor

An old wooden chain sets off the rolling lawns. Now white with maroon shutters, the big L-shaped hotel was built by Thomas H. Whitney, who put up tents for the overflow of guests.

DOHERTY HOUSES   1848 *(private)*   24 Congress St.

These twin houses were built for the daughters of Southern summer visitors and once were connected by a second-story front porch. Cooking was done in small separate buildings at the rear.

THE BLUE PIG   1845 *(private)*   North and Windsor Sts.

One of Cape May's three famous gambling establishments in antebellum times. Henry Cleveland, the North's most notorious gambler, built the Blue Pig, then named for its pale blue tint (now white), on the lawn of Congress Hall. Only the rich gambled here: chips for less than $5 were not accepted.

THE PINK HOUSE   *(private)*   33 Perry St.

Pink clapboard with white detailing of its ornately bracketed pillars creates the charm of an old-fashioned Valentine.

EMLEN PHYSICK ESTATE   1878   1050 Washington St.
Mid-Atlantic Center for the Arts
Cape May County Art League
Victorian Village Museum

An ornate, 19-room mansion, perhaps most notable for its 8 tiled mantels and carved woodwork, this house was designed by Philadelphia architect Frank Furness. In process of restoration, the building is now a busy art center offering frequent exhibits and special events. Daily, 9-5, July 1 to Labor Day; other seasons, weekends. Donation, 75¢. Carriage-house shows, free.

VICTORIAN HOUSE   1863 *(inn)*   720 Washington, at
Jefferson St.

In a setting of tree-shaded grounds occupying a full block, this great square house, with cupola and 14-foot green-shuttered windows, suggests the Deep South. Inside, wall-length mirrors and sculptured ceilings hint of the earlier luxury of this private house.

CAPE MAY COUNTRY STORE   1877   Jefferson and
Page Sts.

Visitors can watch candle-dipping here, and craftsmen are often at work refinishing furniture. *Carriage House,* next door, also dates from 1877.

JACOB LEAMING HOUSE   1879 *(private)*   712 Columbia Ave.

Hoping to encourage construction of impressive homes, the Pennsylvania Railroad offered a free annual pass to Philadelphia to anyone building a house that cost $2000 or more. Wanting a pass for his son, a law student in the Quaker City, Jacob Leaming built this house, but when the cost was reckoned it came to only $1800. Hurriedly, some extras were added to the building, and young J. Spicer Leaming got the pass.

BREWSTER HOUSE   *(private)*   655 Hughes St.

Pristine white with black shutters, and its high peaked dormers edged with "lace," this house is high-style Victorian. Note also the Dambach House, 651 Hughes Street.

HISTORICAL AND COMMUNITY CENTER   1853
417 Lafayette St.
Classic antebellum architecture, this was once a church, but now, deconsecrated, is open for civic activities.

For Cape May Point, follow shore road: Broadway to Sunset Ave., then left to Bird Sanctuary; latter often has southern species not normally seen in New Jersey.

CAPE MAY POINT

A Cape May visitor as early as 1796, Com. Stephen Decatur kept data on erosion at the Point from 1804 until 1824 and estimated that 3 miles of land had been lost within historic time. Near here an entire whaling settlement, Town Bank, long ago fell into the sea, as did two early lighthouses.

Amateur prospectors comb the beach for Cape May "diamonds," though these clear quartz stones are becoming hard to find. Largest known of these semi-precious stones weighed 14 ounces.

CAPE MAY POINT BEACH *(State Park)*

At this southernmost tip of New Jersey, a half mile of oceanfront beach adjoining the lighthouse is excellent for sunning, shelling, fishing, bird watching. No special facilities for swimming.

CAPE MAY LIGHTHOUSE   1859

First lighted by kerosene wick, the present tower, successor to two others (one known as the "Flash Light"), is among the largest on the Atlantic coast.

LAKE LILY   Lighthouse Road

Known to ancient mariners as a source of sparkling fresh water, this 10-acre pond is now a bird sanctuary supervised by the Audubon Society. In the War of 1812 when there was a naval engagement off Cape May as well as a British blockade, local patriots retaliated by digging a ditch from the tidal marshes into Lily pond to salt it so that enemy sailors dared not fill their water casks here.

Around 1700, reports of pirates were frequent. A letter from Col. Robert Quary to the British Lords of Trade tells of 60 pirates arrived here from "Malligasco": "They are part of Kidd's gang. About 16 of them quitted the ship and are landed in ye government of West Jersey at Cape May."

Return to Rte. 9, go N and W 3 mi. to Cold Spring.

COLD SPRING PRESBYTERIAN CHURCH   1823
Seashore Rd.

With a hardy congregation, the "Old Brick" was heated and lighted only by sunshine. The call to services was the blowing of a conch shell. Pews were auctioned off to the highest bidders; still in the balcony are stalls where slaves stood during the long sermons.

Return to Rte. 9, go N to . . .

CAPE MAY COURT HOUSE

HISTORICAL MUSEUM   Basement of Courthouse

Although crowded, this museum has worthwhile displays of whaling implements, ship models, early tools, "mined" cedar shingles, Cape May County documents, early glass and china, and a Colonial period room. Saturdays, July and August. Free.

Next door is the court house built in 1848 by Daniel Hand, who studied the works of Sir Christopher Wren before beginning construction.

JONATHAN HAND HOUSE   c. 1803 *(private)*   12 N. Main St.

Sarah Moore Wilson, before she became the bride of Jonathan Hand, won fame as one of the 13 girls who at Trenton strewed flowers in the path of George Washington on his triumphal way to New York to assume the Presidency in 1789.

Rte. 585 to South Dennis and Dennisville.

DENNISVILLE

Just a block off the highway is a little eddy remaining from the 1820's, where prosperous shipbuilders have left

SAWING CEDAR-LOGS, AND MAKING SHINGLES

CEDAR "MINING", CAPE MAY COUNTY, 1856
Prehistoric cedar trees buried deep in swamps near Dennis Creek made the most enduring shingles, it was discovered in the early 1800's. Independence Hall was re-roofed with the prized shingles.

Courtesy of the New Jersey Department of
Environmental Protection

their substantial homes. On nearby Dennis Creek there was a shipyard where vessels of 200 to 1000 tons were launched. The following houses marked with plaques are among those usually opened for tours on the second Saturday of July.

NATHANIEL HOLMES HOUSE 1822 No. 36

A spacious dwelling built by a ship chandler, and a founder of a glassworks here. Furnished with many South Jersey antiques, the house has unusual mantels by a noted builder, William Armstrong.

LODGE HOUSE 1852

Attractive Victorian Gothic.

DIVERTY HOUSE 1825 No. 80

Interior woodwork by William Armstrong.

CRANDALL HOUSE 1807

Some original cedar paneling inside.

WILLIAM J. TOWNSEND HOUSE c. 1833

0.1 mi. N of Dennisville marker on Rte. 47

Built by a merchant who shipped goods to Philadelphia, the house with picket fence lies close to the highway, has slave quarters at the rear.

CEDAR MINING

The whine of a power saw and a nondescript Dennisville shed where nonagenarian Capt. Ogden Gandy cut cedar logs as late as the 1930's are sole reminders of a lost industry: cedar "mining," grappling for giant logs in a sunken prehistoric forest deep in the ooze of Great Cedar Swamp. In the 1800's settlers discovered that these trees, despite their having been buried for centuries, when cut into planks or shingles not only had the aroma of fresh-hewn cedar but were phenomenally resistant to water and wear. One customer of the Dennisville sawmill complained that water tanks of "mined" cedar lasted a lifetime, too long to make their sale profitable. When Independence Hall needed a new roof at the turn of this century, 25,000 shingles of Cape May cedar did the job. In 1868 a Cape May cedar was dredged up that had

1000 annular rings. Although much "treasure" still lies in the 12-mile-square swamp east of Dennisville, mining is not profitable in these affluent times.

Rte. 47 NW to Rte. 557. N to park entrance near Woodbine . . .

BELLEPLAIN STATE FOREST

Cool even on a hot day, the road bisecting the park is canopied with leaves, and entrance to Lake Nummy is through a grove of tall white pines. Small but clear, with a well-kept sandy beach, Lake Nummy deserves to be better known as a summer recreation spot. Beachside picnic grove. Dressing rooms. Lifeguard. Large groves for tenters, and near the lake a few log lean-tos. Riding horses and pony rides. Much of the 6492 acres still a forest preserve. Hunting permitted in season.

Return to Woodbine; Rte. 550 E through Great Cedar Swamp; then first road or Rte. 9 N to Seaville.

SEAVILLE QUAKER MEETING HOUSE   Shore Rd.

Moved to this shady plot in 1730, but probably built about 1716 at Beesley's Point, the Friends' Meeting House is still open for Sunday services in summer.

Garden State Pkwy. between mileposts 22 and 23; entrance at No. 17 or 25 . . .

THE TERCENTENARY HOLLY TREE

"Engineer, spare that tree!" was the word that went out when the Garden State Parkway was being constructed. And so this tree which the Holly Society of America calls the oldest holly in New Jersey has been saved. Sixty feet high and its trunk 30 inches in diameter, the holly pre-dates the founding of New Jersey as an English colony. The tree is usually trimmed with colored lights for the Christmas holidays.

Batsto ironmaster's mansion in Colonial Village, founded 1766, where shot and shell were made for Washington's army at Valley Forge. See Wharton State Forest, p. 127.

UP THE DELAWARE—
DOWN THE APPALACHIANS

HILLS OF HUNTERDON

Lambertville	Clinton Art Center
Stockton	and Old Mills
Raven Rock	Spruce Run
Sergeantsville	Voorhees State Park
Flemington	New Hampton

For centuries the bread-basket of New Jersey, Hunterdon County has few major historic shrines, yet its peaceful villages and undulating landscape are restful and appealing to city-dwellers hemmed in by stone and steel.

LAMBERTVILLE

Known from 1732 to 1812 as Coryell's Ferry, Lambertville was the point where Washington's army crossed the Delaware, July 28, 1777. Today, pontoon boats at New Hope provide short scenic tours up the Delaware and return.

Downstream about half a mile is Wells Falls. Within memory of persons now living, raftsmen used to pole their way down the Delaware from as far north as Port Jervis, with goods for Philadelphia, but at Wells rapids they risked losing their whole cargo. Just south of Lambertville, Goat Hill is a landmark also known as Washington's Rock. Lambertville's interesting old houses and side streets can best be explored on foot.

LAMBERTVILLE HOUSE *(restaurant)* Bridge St.
Opened as a hotel in 1812 when John Lambert built a bridge, set up a post office and changed the name of the town, which the Coryells called "Lambert's villainy." George Coryell, who was one of Washington's pallbearers, lies in the Presbyterian churchyard.

MARSHALL HOUSE *(state historic site)* 60 Bridge St.
Back in 1832 Philip Marshall whose house this was caught his son James shining his shoes on Sunday. A quarrel arose. Young James, then 22, threatened to leave home—and did, for the Far West. By 1848 he was a prospering partner in a lumber business in the Sacramento Valley. And there he had riches in his hands, for while building a mill he had discovered gold in the stream bed. When the news seeped out, he was driven off his land by gangs mad for gold. James Marshall was the man who touched off the frenetic race to California. He himself became a prospector, and died poor.

JOHN HOLCOMBE HOUSE c. 1730 *(private)*
Homestead Farms   N. end of Main St.
George Washington's bill for board and lodging testifies to his stay with Quaker John Holcombe in this handsome stone house in July, 1777, and June, 1778.
Rte. 29 to Stockton.

STOCKTON-ON-THE-DELAWARE

The road to Stockton runs near the feeder of the Delaware and Raritan Canal, a great waterway completed in 1834. *(See Delaware-Raritan Tour)*. A quaint and quiet little river settlement, Stockton and nearby roads have many interesting old houses, restored mostly by gentlemen farmers. The winding road to Flemington abounds with wild roses in June. With many picturesque sections, the stream and its towpath along which mules once hauled barges is a favorite with canoeists and hikers.

STOCKTON INN   1832 *(restaurant)*

Opened when the Delaware and Raritan Canal was being scooped out by hand labor, this rambling inn built by Asher Johnson is largely in its original state, and its hospitable old-time air suggests that a stagecoach may come rolling up to the door.

Rte. 29 N to . . .

RAVEN ROCK   Bull's Island State Park

A dam built across the river here gave the Delaware and Raritan Canal its endless flow of water. See Supplement.

Go S to Rte. 519, then N (left) to Rosemont.

SERGEANTSVILLE COVERED BRIDGE

Sole survivor of New Jersey's many early covered bridges spans Wichecheoke Creek, midway between Rosemont and Sergeantsville.

Take Rte. 523 N to Flemington.

FLEMINGTON

In 1898 Flemingtonians could greet 54 trains a day on three different railroads. Now a tourists' railroad, the BR&W, which works valiantly as freight transport in winter, carries nostalgia-seekers to Ringoes and back, a huge attraction.

The popularity of the railroad has created a proliferation of other related ventures here, among them the village of Turntable Junction in the heart of Flemington, Liberty Village with its several historical museums, and various craft shops on adjacent streets. Maps are available at Turntable Junction. See Supplement.

Tourists might well want to spend several days exploring Flemington and using it as a base to visit Lambertville on the Delaware and Somerville's Wallace House and Duke Gardens and its Oriental museum.

FLEMING CASTLE 1756 5 Bonnell St.

A small white stucco house, this was the home and inn built by Samuel Fleming for whom the town is named. Open by appointment with the Daughters of the American Revolution.

CHIEF TUCCAMIRGAN'S GRAVE

A friend of John Kase, Flemington's first settler, the Delaware Indian chief asked to be buried beside the man he considered his white brother. In 1925 a marble marker to Chief Tuccamirgan was placed among crumbling stones of the Kase family in this private cemetery west of Fleming Castle.

FULPER-STANGL POTTERIES Railroad Ave.

Beginning as Fulper Bros. in 1805, this pottery was owned by one family until 1929 and is now the oldest in New Jersey. Although the ceramics are now made in Trenton, the showroom here has part of the old kiln, and some early buildings remain.

RURAL HUNTERDON

Not truly rural perhaps, because many of the farms are likely to be inhabited by exurbanites who have restored capacious old houses. The following is a lovely road typical of many to be found in New Jersey by venturesome motorists:

From Flemington go N on Rte. 69 to Woodschurch Rd. on right. At next main crossroads, also marked Woodschurch, go left and follow this winding route to next main road. Continue on Rte. 523 through White House Station to Rte. 22 W.

The following three villages on Rte. 579 are accessible either via Rte. 12 W of Flemington, the more scenic way, or Rte. 22 W of Clinton.

QUAKERTOWN—PITTSTON—BLOOMSBURY

These three charming villages offer a pleasing glimpse

backward of historic rural America. At Quakertown the old Stone Meeting House dates from 1720 and is still open for Sunday services. Note, too, the stone house and well on the main street. At Pittstown the 3-story Century Inn is a stone hotel built by Moore Furman who was deputy quartermaster for the Continentals and sheriff of Hunterdon County. Furman's mill is now a local lumberyard. Among many interesting structures at quaint Bloomsbury is a great frame mill beside the Musconetcong River. On the nearby hill is a stucco house that once was an important stagecoach inn. Close by are several fine early houses of brick and stone.

CLINTON

HUNTERDON COUNTY ART CENTER
In the heart of town at the Raritan dam three buildings from early times, an inn and two handsome mills, form a cluster from which a stimulating and photogenic art center has sprung. The stone mill offers an excellent setting for shows of paintings and antiques. "Live" theater is staged at the Hunterdon Hills Playhouse, and frequent concerts are held. Behind the red mill, which contains a museum, are old lime-kilns, remnants of Colonial industry. Good fishing in the Raritan.

CLINTON HOUSE   1743, 1836
Though by-passed by express Route 22, the old inn, once a prominent stage-stop on the Easton Road, is now sought out by tourists.

From Rte. 22 go N on Rte. 69 to Rte. 513 N through High Bridge to . . .

VOORHEES STATE PARK

Threaded with trails and drives, much of this 429-acre park was the gift of Foster M. Voorhees, New Jersey's Governor from 1899 to 1902. Many of the woodlands are interesting examples of reforestation by the State Department of Conservation and Economic Development. Picnic sites, fireplaces, and playfield at Hoppock Pond.

SPRUCE RUN RECREATION AREA (State reservoir) Rte. 31 about 3 mi. N of Rte. 22 and Clinton

A 1,300-acre man-made lake, Spruce Run, in 1973 became the focus of a $5,400,000 recreation complex covering 2,000 acres. A pavilion of 7 buildings surrounded by tiled walkways overlooks a sand beach accommodating 3,000 bathers, with a pool for toddlers. Unprecedented for a public beach is a 4-ton metal sculpture symbolizing the Hudson Palisades and surrounded by fountains. The sculptor is Sahl Swarz.

The lake is open for small boats and fishing, with a pier designed especially for the elderly, as are various walks and ramps. Parking, $1, 25¢ per person. Children under 12 and Jerseyans over 65, free, latter with identification. 201-638-6990.

ROUND VALLEY STATE PARK Access via Rte. 31 S of Rte. 22 nr. Clinton

The 2,350-acre, man-made lake in the crater of Cushetunk mountain is second in size only to Lake Hopatcong. Fishing, small boats, and hunting in season. Campsites under construction in the 4,000-acre park.

NEW HAMPTON

NEW HAMPTON GENERAL STORE

Formerly the Union Hotel, the store is a period-piece, complete with cracker barrel and pot-bellied stove. 9-6, weekdays; 12-6, Sun. Free.

DUSENBERRY MANSION c. 1812 *(private)*

A substantial stone house by a master builder.

AMERICAN HOTEL c. 1865 *(residence)*
DANIEL MORGAN FOUNDATION

General Daniel Morgan was celebrated for his bold courage in the battles of Saratoga and Cowpens.

By continuing N on Rte. 69 to Oxford Furnace, motorists can connect with the Delaware Water Gap Tour.

LAKE HOPATCONG AND THE
MORRIS CANAL

Hopatcong State Park
Morris Canal
Stanhope
Netcong
Musconetcong State
Park

Waterloo Village
Stephens State Park
Saxton Falls
Hackettstown
Rockport State Fish
Hatchery

LAKE HOPATCONG STATE PARK

*West shore of Lake Hopatcong; access via Rte. 206
at Netcong or Rte. 46 at village of Landing. From Lakeside Blvd. follow signs to park, about 0.8 mi.*

Hopatcong is New Jersey's largest lake, with 45 miles
of shoreline, most of it privately owned. Only 107 acres,
the State park nevertheless has a sweeping vista of the
lake, a good beach, modern bathhouses, and lifeguards.
A tree-topped rocky hill along the shore makes a delightful picnic grove and along the beach are charcoal grills.
Speedboat tours can be arranged at the State dock in
Landing. Ice-boat races bring crowds in winter to this
lovely lake.

THE MORRIS CANAL   1831

A barge waterway of 106 miles that joined the Delaware River at Phillipsburg to the Hudson, the Morris
Canal, dug by hand with pick and shovel, was America's
greatest engineering feat in its day. Designed by Prof.
James Renwick of Columbia College, this was the first
American canal to climb hills, which it did by means of
23 separate inclined planes. Set in giant cradles, boats
were hauled up rail tracks by chains to water levels as
high as 100 feet. And sometimes the chains gave way, as
at Port Colden where a crashing boat killed a woman
and two children. At Boonton a boat loaded with pig
iron, zoomed down the plane, skidded over a 20-foot

MORRIS CANAL, SUMMIT OF AN INCLINED PLANE
Canal boats put in cradles on tracks could climb mountains when pulled up inclined planes like this one, formerly at Drakesville, today Ledgewood. Portions of the 106-mile

embankment and landed upside down in the trees. The captain's wife and two children emerged unscathed from the boat's cabin. Here in Hopatcong Park, to the left of the beach, is a huge iron waterwheel, from Plane No. 3, which operated chains, later wire cables, pulling up the boats.

At the gate control house, near this old turbine, one can see the locks under water, at the edge of the lake. Just west of the pumping station and the turbine, the broad declivity was the basin of the old canal which continued on toward Lake Musconetcong. Still in the park is the gatekeeper's and paymaster's house, built about 1826 and now occupied by the Lake Hopatcong Historical Society. Among the exhibits are a model of the Canal and a plaque giving its history.

Most prosperous year of the Morris Canal was 1866 when it carried 889,229 tons of freight. The canal's history has been called a riches-to-rags story: chartered in 1824, two years after George P. Macculloch dreamed up the idea while fishing in Hopatcong, built and enlarged at a cost of five million dollars, and abandoned a century later. The canal atrophied when railroads proved they could move coal as cheaply and faster. To go from Phillipsburg to Jersey City, 106 miles by mule-drawn barge, took an average of 5 days.

From Hopatcong Park return toward Landing, but at fork in road marked Port Morris turn right, go about ¼ mi. to N. Main St. to . . .

PORT MORRIS
SITE OF INCLINED PLANE

A few yards from the main road, right of North Main Street, is stone masonry of one of the inclined planes of the Morris Canal. The latter followed along the present shoreline of Lake Musconetcong and the highway, toward Route 206. When the water level is lowered, the canal towpath becomes clearly visible along the entire length of the lake bed.

MUSCONETCONG STATE PARK   Rte. 206 at Stanhope

All of Lake Musconetcong is included in the park's 343 acres. The lake and nearby streams, such as Lubber's Run, are well stocked with trout. Near the highway is a small bathing beach, with boats for rent close by. All around the locality are landmarks of the Morris Canal to be explored, such as the old locks at Netcong.

At Rte. 206 and the lake turn left to Stanhope.

STANHOPE

Plane Street is named for the inclined ramp of the Morris Canal, which began here, to meet the high rise of Lake Hopatcong. At the end of Plane Street to its left is the bed of the waterway which went on to the canalport of Waterloo *(see below)*. Stanhope has the stamp of an early canal town, including some canalers' boarding houses, with "chicken feather" shingles. The quaint village was known as Sussex Iron Works in the Revolution and in 1841 had the first American iron furnace fired by anthracite.

Continue N on Rte. 206 for 2 mi. from canal marker at Lake Musconetcong. Turn left at road marked to Waterloo and continue for 2.5 mi. to . . .

WATERLOO   *(State historic site)*

As you turn a sharp corner into this little village of about a dozen buildings it is like seeing an old print come to life: on the hill at the left a white-spired church like a sentinel; opposite, the bright waters of the Morris Canal; and down the winding road, a yellow stone mill and white clapboard and stucco houses. This was the busy canalport of Waterloo, a few years ago so overgrown with a jungle of vines that 2-story houses were not visible. The charming restoration of existing buildings is the work of two interior designers who use Waterloo as headquarters. The entire village was part of

Andover iron forge built on the Musconetcong in 1763 by William Allen and Joseph Turner, Tories whose property was confiscated to make cannonballs for the Americans. The splendid coaching inn dates from the early 19th century but the Smiths' store, which did an annual business of $75,000, was not opened until after the canal was completed.

Costumed guides and craftsmen at the store, the smithy and other of the dozen buildings. Admission and guided tour, $2.50; children, $1.00. A series of first-rate concerts on frequent summer weekends. Mid-April to Christmas, 11-6 daily.

Return to highway and go left 2 mi. on Hacketts-town Rd.

STEPHENS STATE PARK AND SAXTON FALLS

Although only 246 acres this is one of the most popular State parks, especially among photographers and fishermen, because of the rushing waters of the Musconetcong River, its rocky winding course stocked with trout. Anglers can practically whip their catch into the pan, as charcoal grills are set up in a wooded grove along the river. Beside beautiful Saxton Falls is the guard-lock once used to adjust water levels of the Morris Canal, and now one end of the lock provides a fine "swimmin' hole."

Return to highway and go S to Hackettstown and Rte. 46. This tour connects directly with Delaware Water Gap Tour.

DELAWARE WATER GAP TO JENNY JUMP

Hackettstown   Pahaquarra Mine
State Fish Hatchery   Old Mine Road
State Game Farm   Blairstown
Oxford Furnace   Hope, Moravian Village
Worthington Tract   Jenny Jump State Forest

HACKETTSTOWN

In the Musconetcong River Valley ringed by high hills, Hackettstown since pioneer times afforded a natural route for adventurers seeking the way West, through Delaware Water Gap. A town with a New England flavor, it is today a gateway to some of the loveliest and most interesting country in New Jersey. Hackettstown is a place where sportsmen converge for fishing in the Musconetcong, in the Pequest which winds along Route 46, and in the Delaware.

2 mi. S of Rte. 46 is . . .

CHARLES O. HAYFORD STATE FISH HATCHERY
Grand Ave.

Largest freshwater hatchery in the world, with over 300 ponds and 3 hatchery buildings, this fish assembly-line—10 miles of water—produces millions of rainbow, brook, and brown trout. State streams were almost trout-less in 1912 when the hatchery was created, but now about half a million trout are released annually when the season opens in April. A new true breed, the golden rainbow trout, has been hatched here. Free guided tours, 1 to 1½ hours; 8-5 daily.

4 mi. S of Rte. 46 on Grand Ave. is the . . .

ROCKPORT STATE GAME FARM

Over 20,000 pheasants bred here are released each year before the fall hunting season. A pioneer in pheasant breeding the farm owes much of its advancement to a Scottish family of game keepers, headed by the late Duncan Dunn and his son-in-law, Robert S. Buntain. The black-necked pheasant from the estate of the Duke of Argyll was introduced here by Robert Buntain.

Return to Rte. 46 W; go S on Rte. 69 to . . .

OXFORD FURNACE *(State historic site)* Nr. Methodist
Church.

A rare relic of early American industry is this charcoal-blast iron smelter, so old that it produced cannonballs for the French and Indian Wars. An Irishman,

Jonathan Robeson, who built the furnace in 1742, was succeeded as ironmaster by Philadelphians Dr. William Shippen, Sr., and his son Joseph. This furnace stack is in marked contrast to the one standing at Allaire Village, not only in design but in that Oxford used hardrock ore, not bog iron. Operations continued at Oxford until 1884.

The Methodist Church is built from a gristmill which was part of the ironworks. Across the street is *Shippen Manor* (1750), where Benedict Arnold is said to have visited; he was married to Peggy Shippen, a cousin of Joseph.

Return to Rte. 46 and continue NW toward Delaware Water Gap.

BELVIDERE Rte. 519

Perhaps the most peaceful county seat in the State, this delightful town seems light-years away from harried cities. Downstream a few miles is the spot known for centuries as Foul Rift because of dangerous rapids in the river. Since largely blasted away, the rocks deterred navigation and forced the Dutch to build the *Old Mine Road* in order to remove copper from the Kittatinny Mountains to the Hudson. In June the annual Down River canoe races start from Foul Rift.

COLUMBIA

Two decades ago this little village was connected to its twin, Portland, on the Pennsylvania side by a long, covered bridge which became a casualty of spring floods. Now an uncovered bridge reserved for pedestrians provides a good view of the Delaware, for those who don't get dizzy.

DELAWARE WATER GAP

Changed by blasting for railroads and highways, Delaware Water Gap has lost the wild beauty revealed in early paintings, but the notch carved in the Kittatinnys by the river is still an impressive sight. Travelers will quite likely want to view the Gap from several angles by crossing the bridge to Stroudsburg.

For this tour just before Delaware Bridge, turn right off Rte. 46 and follow the river's east bank to Worthington Forest, 3 mi. N of the bridge. With trees meeting overhead and the stream far below, this road hints of pioneer days, especially when deer come bounding out of the woods. The river can be seen to best advantage when trees are budding.

WORTHINGTON STATE FOREST

A rich man's deer preserve has become a wonderful public park. The industrialist, C. C. Worthington, had herds of deer here which, since released, have created a bountiful harvest for hunters in recent years. A wilderness of 6200 acres with 4 miles of Delaware shore, the Worthington tract also has 6 miles of the hiker's hallowed ground, the Appalachian Trail, which runs on northeast into Stokes State Forest, High Point State Park, and Wawayanda State Park. Reward for climbing the steep slopes east of the road is Sunfish Pond, described in 1870 as "a sheet of pure transparent water . . . strangely and unaccountably situated on the very Summit of the mountain." Rhododendrons and tall ferns abound, even close to the road where campsites have been set up along the Delaware. Although riverside picnic tables are convenient for family groups, the forest, undeveloped, is recommended for experienced campers and hikers, not young children.

The island opposite the ranger's house is Buckwood and the second one above it is Tock's, a name that now inspires anxiety among nearly all residents along the Old Mine Road, fear that the proposed billion-dollar Tock's Island dam project will cause the Delaware waters to drown history, wildlife, and rare scenic beauty.

E side of Delaware River Rd., about 12 mi. from Columbia and 8 mi. from the Gap is . . .

PAHAQUARRA COPPER MINE *(Federal Property)*

End of the mysterious Old Mine Road, which the industrious Dutch hacked out of the wilderness from the Hudson River to the Delaware, appears to have been near this copper mine, one of about 18 openings known to exist in the vicinity. Unlike most abandoned mines, usually found in areas made barren by man, this one is in a rhododendron glen. Even the mine entrance is picturesque: the mossy stratified rocks athwart one another form a ceiling, so that it is possible to walk into the mine horizontally. All except about 75 feet of the narrow tunnel is blocked off. Old as is the white man's history here, the early red man, who had copper beads, undoubtedly worked these mines before him.

OLD COPPER MINE INN   N of Worthington Tract, W side of highway

Turn-of-the-century on the outside, the stone interior of this inn is a 1710 house built by one of the Shoemakers, among the very first settlers in frontier Indian country here. Close to the river bank an early road is plainly visible.

From Pahaquarra Mine north, the highway follows much of the Old Mine Road, a 100-mile route wide enough for ox-carts to haul copper all the way to Kingston, N.Y. Some authorities believe that the road was completed by 1659, an astonishing feat for its time and the wilderness conditions.

DELAWARE WATER GAP

This gap in the Appalachians opened the way to early exploration of the American West. Scene above is near the Old Mine Road, 100-mile wilderness route to the Hudson River, built by the Dutch in the mid-1600's. Painted by Granville Perkins in 1872.

MILLBROOK

Here the left road to Flatbrookville is a continuation of the old Dutch road, a scenic drive which can be approached from the north (*see High Point Park Tour*). For this tour, take *right* road over the hill to Blairstown. A backward glance from the crest of the ridge gives a rewarding view of the Delaware. Many old stone fences from frontier times can be seen along the Blairstown Road.

At the fork a 3 mi. side trip on the Marksboro road is highly picturesque. At a bridge beside the rocky stream is a stone gristmill that has been operating since 1750, but now with electric power. The first residence on the right, overlooking the mill is . . .

MARK THOMSON HOUSE *(private)*

In a region of many Tory sympathizers, Colonel Mark Thomson was a leading patriot, wounded in the Battle of Princeton, a friend of Alexander Hamilton. After the Revolution, among his many public honors, he was one of five New Jersey Congressmen serving during Washington's Presidency in 1795. Now carefully restored, the large white house has exquisitely sculptured woodwork and paneling as befitted a mansion of one of the largest landholders in the State.

Return to Blairstown Rd.

BLAIRSTOWN

What other American town can boast of an old mill on its main street, with the raceway flowing under the highway? This is Blairstown, and for more quaint charm there are balconies over some of the store fronts, western style. The early mill is now part of the campus of Blair Academy, a "coed" preparatory school, founded in 1848 by John I. Blair, Lackawanna Railroad millionaire. The school has purchased the old Blair homestead, the square flat-topped mansion which surveys the town from the hill above the mill. The small house beside the Blair mansion was the company store, as well as the post office. Another flat-roofed mansion up the hill was owned by Dr. William Vail, a manager for some of Blair's many projects.

Rte. 521 S to . . .
HOPE

Moravians, a German Protestant sect from Bethlehem, Pa., who first settled Hope in 1769 must have expected it to endure for a thousand years, judging from the care they put into its buildings. The talk of the Colonies, their 4½-story stone mill was grinding grist until recent years. With the crudest of tools then available, the Moravians cut the raceway 22 feet deep into slate rock. Some 14 Moravian structures still stand, among them their *Gemein haus* or church, now a local bank, with drive-in window. Wearing a "Pennsylvania Dutch" type of uniform, holding their lands and buildings in common, the Moravians, a singing people, had a trombone choir. A booklet on the local Moravian experiment is obtainable from the Hope Historical Society which has an interesting museum (not Moravian) at the bridge house. Open Sunday afternoons.

Rte. 519 NE to . . .
JENNY JUMP STATE FOREST

Its true origin unknown, the name "Jenny Jump" Mountain was mentioned as early as 1747 in the diary of a Swedish missionary Sven Roseen. Beloved of hikers and campers, this forest of 967 acres has elevations up to 1108 feet with panoramas of the Delaware Water Gap, 12 miles to the northwest. Maintained for water conservation and timber protection, Jenny Jump Forest has one public area open. Hunting in selected areas. Well marked trails and forest roads with broad vistas.

JOHNSONBURG

This tranquil little hamlet was known as the Log Gaol when from 1753 to 1761 Sussex County courts convened here. The log jail was abandoned when prisoners found it too easy to break out. The site is the small frame-and-stone structure beside the Robert Blair place, an attractive white house. Close by are the Episcopal old stone meetinghouse and the 3-story structure that was an eighteenth-century inn owned by Dr. Jonathan Pettit.

On the road to Allamuchy is a milestone 270 years old, telling travelers it is "2 TO LG"—two miles to Log Gaol. The milestone came to rest in 1964 after kidnapings by rival historians, and is now watched over by all of Warren County.

HIGH POINT, STOKES FOREST, AND THE OLD MINE ROAD

NEWTON

SUSSEX COUNTY HISTORICAL SOCIETY *(museum)*
82 Main St.

The exciting but hard-to-track-down history of Sussex County and its scenic beauty can be viewed at first hand by exploring part of the 100-mile Old Mine Road, dating from the 17th century, along the Delaware, and such quaint historic hamlets as Hope.

The names one still hears in Sussex County are of Tom Quick, the Indian slayer, who killed redmen in revenge for his father's death, the White Pilgrim, a traveling preacher who rode a pale horse, and Dark Moon Tavern near Johnsonburg—real people, real places, long ago.

Valuable and well-displayed Indian relics, many from such richly historic sites as Minisink, the former Lenni Lenape village on the upper Delaware, form the nucleus of this Sussex County collection. Displays of Revolutionary weapons, documents, maps, and a large library. Mon.-Fri., 1:30-3:30. Free.

THOMAS ANDERSON HOUSE 1750 *(private)* Main St., beside Episcopal Church

The early owner supplied horses and fodder for George Washington and his staff when they stopped in Newton on July 26, 1782 en route to Newburgh, N. Y.

EPISCOPAL MANSE 1750 *(private)* Top of Dunn St., back of 122 Main St.

A choice example of a substantial early stone house, of which Sussex County is said to have more than any other in the State. Many houses were laboriously built of stone rather than of more plentiful timber because frame houses were too easily fired by the Indians.

LEVI MORRIS HOUSE 1840 *(private)* 132 Main St.

A Greek Revival mansion of the prosperous era sparked by the opening of the Morris Turnpike, which ran from Elizabethtown via Morristown to Newton.

From Newton ctr. take High St. (Rte. 94SW) out of town for 3 mi. Turn right at Paulinskill Lake Rd. (Rte. to Stillwater). Turn right at road paralleling railroad tracks (Swartswood Station Rd.) . . .

BOUNDARY BETWEEN EAST AND WEST JERSEY

Follow this narrow road for a few yards through woods. At the sharp left jog in the route, extending ahead is a straight stretch of the Swartswood Road, which may be the only visible trace remaining of the famed boundary of 1664, created when the Duke of York divided his province of Nova Caesarea into halves. Land to the left of this road was in West Jersey which the Duke gave to his friend John, Lord Berkeley, while the two present-day red houses on the lane to the right would have been in East Jersey, awarded to Sir George Carteret. The boundary was not firmly established until after a survey known as Lawrence's Line of 1743.

HANKINSON HOUSE *(boarding kennels)* Second red house up lane to right of Swartswood Rd.

Early deeds of this house show the above-mentioned boundary as the dividing line between the provinces of East and West Jersey. Records of the clapboard house trace back to 1755.

Return to Stillwater Rd., bear right to Paulinskill Lake (private) and dam. Below dam and left (SE) of brook, cross narrow bridge next to overpass and follow road along the stream (3 mi.) to Stillwater.

THE PAULINS KILL

One of the loveliest in New Jersey, this meandering stream is lively with trout, especially from Paulinskill Lake to Stillwater.

At Stillwater the kill becomes a favorite starting point for canoe trips, especially during high water in spring. Flowing into the Delaware just north of Columbia the Paulins Kill glides through a richly varied scene with ever-changing views of the Kittatinny Mountains to the north, past historic places like Blairstown, between sheer cliffs at Hainesburg. Portages around some half-dozen mill dams are not difficult but conditions along the route should be checked in advance. No canoe rentals here. Route 94 runs close to the Paulins Kill.

STILLWATER

Drowsing as if under a spell cast in the 18th century, this tiny village, once a gristmill crossroads, was the earliest settlement in the Paulinskill Valley. Stillwater had a miller as early as the 1740's when Caspar Schaeffer came here as a pioneer from Philadelphia. A venerable stone mill, two stories and sturdily made, is still here, to the left of it the miller's white house as well as other early buildings. Stillwater is but one of several charming, isolated hamlets in Sussex County, which give a better idea of what life was like in early days than do visits to a half-dozen museums.

From Stillwater, take Rte. 521 N to Middleville, another quiet, peaceful little village. From Middleville follow Rte. 521 around Swartswood Lake. At Swartswood, turn right to entrance to . . .

SWARTSWOOD LAKE STATE PARK

Most of the park's 704 acres are covered by lovely Swartswood Lake which has a sand beach and affords excellent fishing. Small boats can be rented but motorboats are not allowed. Bathhouse but no locker service. Lifeguard. A favorite picnic grounds is Emmons Grove with its stand of stately hemlocks. Fireplaces.

Return to Rte. 521, go NE to Rte. 15 N. Stokes Forest entrance about 1 mi. N on right.

STOKES STATE FOREST   N of Branchville

Atop the wooded Kittatinny Ridge which runs the length of Sussex County, these 12,495 acres offer some of New Jersey's finest mountain country, of outstanding beauty in May and June, when dogwood, laurel, and rhododendron are in bloom, and in its autumn coloring. The forest, which includes part of the Appalachian Trail, has a great attraction for wilderness campers and hunters but at the same time offers smooth paths and motor roads for the less vigorous. Lake Ocquittunk is a center for water sports, and Big Flat Brook nearby offers some of the finest trout fishing in the State. At Tillman Ravine a mountain stream cascades down a rocky course, the slopes covered with hemlocks. Sunrise Mountain at an elevation of 1653 feet provides a beautiful vista. The New Jersey School of Conservation is at Lake Wapalanne.

From Branchville, take Rte. 519 to . . .

HIGH POINT STATE PARK

A gift of 12,857 acres from Colonel and Mrs. Anthony R. Kuser, this lovely mountain park in Sussex County has the highest point of land in New Jersey, 1803 feet above sea level. The mountain is topped by a 220-foot granite shaft, a memorial to New Jersey's war heroes. From the summit there is a 360-degree vista that includes the Poconos, the Catskills, and the Kittatinny range. High Point Lodge, former home of the Kusers, has rooms for overnight stays, and a modern motel. Nearby High Point Inn offers diningroom service. A number of attractive rustic cabins are also available.

Lake Marcia, 1600 feet above sea level and spring fed, invites swimming, and Sawmill Lake is a delightful place for family camping. Good fishing. Open for winter sports. Vivid autumn foliage along scenic drives.

Follow Rte. 23 N to outskirts of Port Jervis. Here at N.Y.–N.J. border take Rte. 521 S (Old Mine Road). *Check speedometer reading at border in order to locate some pioneer houses.*

THE OLD MINE ROAD   17th century   Part of Rte. 521

Almost half a century before the first English settlers of New Jersey put up four log huts in Elizabethtown, the Dutch had constructed at least one stone house along the 100-mile Old Mine Road. Solid as a rock is one such dwelling from 1620, near the Kingston-on-Hudson end of the ox-cart path that Hollanders built all the way to their copper mines at Pahaquarra, about 10 miles north of Delaware Water Gap. As early as 1641 the *Journal of the Netherlands* told of mineral riches and a crystal mountain in this land. Silver and gold were probably the real lure that produced the wilderness road. Traces of silver, as well as amethyst and quartz, have been found in the Kittatinnys, but the glitter was probably fool's gold: pyrites.

Minisink Island, just south of Montague, was a Lenni Lenape capital to which, like spokes in a wheel, led Indian trails from afar. The earliest Dutch, who had built their own Minisink Village opposite the island, were on such cordial terms with the Indians that most spoke only the Delaware language: when some Philadelphians explored the upper river in 1730 they had to find an Indian interpreter in order to talk to the white men!

As a rule, the route nearest the river is the original Dutch and Indian path. The distance from the State line to Pahaquarra Copper Holes is about 33 miles. *(See Delaware Water Gap Tour.)* Houses described below *(private)* are a few of the remaining homes, which often were forts as well, built by hardy pioneers.

ABRAHAM SHIMER HOUSE   1750   *5.9 mi. from State line. W side, N of ravine*

White frame structure with a stone house inside. Captain Shimer, a commander of British troops, and his slaves fended off an Indian attack here.

ARMSTRONG HOUSE   *6.7 mi., W side*

Once a hotel where river raftsmen used to stop off. From this height one can see the bend in the Delaware where rafts were moored.

Continue S on Old Mine Rd., crossing Rte. 206 through village of Montague.

EVERITT HOUSE   1725   *9.5 mi., N of brook, W side*

One of only three dwellings remaining from the now almost legendary village of Minisink.

BELL or WESTBROOK HOUSE   1701   *(posted against trespassers)*   *1.7 mi. S of Everitt House, W side*

Until recently, 10 generations of Westbrooks lived in this house with the steeply pitched roof and a look of growing out of the soil. Another survivor from Minisink Village.

Do not take road across Dingman's Bridge, but follow the nearby river route south.

ISAAC VAN CAMPEN INN 1750 *19 mi., E. side*

This 3-story building of cut limestone was a fort as well as a famous inn. In November, 1763, 150 men, women, and children took refuge from the Indians here. Count Pulaski was sent to Van Campen's with 600 men to protect the frontier. In 1776 General Gates and 7 regiments on their way to aid Washington at Trenton had to camp here because of a heavy snowfall. John Adams, riding horseback all the way from his home in Massachusetts, rested at Van Campen's en route to joining Congress in Philadelphia.

FORT SHAPPANACK WALL 1755 *(private)*
About 250 ft. N of Van Campen Inn

With the outbreak of barbarous Indian warfare, Shappanack was one of half a dozen stone forts built on the upper Delaware in 1755 at a cost of £10,000. Present owners permit visitors to see this rare relic of the early American frontier.

FLATBROOKVILLE

At this tiny settlement the road *south* crosses Big Flat Brook, one of the best trout habitats in all of New Jersey. The road *west* of Flat Brook is a lovely one, where deer sometimes graze in herds, but takes the motorist back in a circle to the Delaware.

The right fork at Millbrook is a continuation of the Old Mine Road, while the scenic highway over the hill goes to Blairstown *(see Delaware Water Gap Tour)*.

Note: As the Federal Government is buying private property along the Old Mine Road, some landmarks are disappearing.

Esplanade beside State Museum at New Jersey's Arts and Science Center, Trenton.
Photo by Adeline Pepper

TURNAROUND IN THE REVOLUTION

WASHINGTON'S CROSSING AND TRENTON

Washington Crossing
State Park
McKonkey Ferry
Museum
Trenton State Capitol
Old Barracks

Trenton Battle
Monument
State Museum
Trent House
Old Masonic Lodge
Douglass House

Watson House

Start tour at Rtes. 29 and 546 on the Delaware River. Many tourists may want to begin the trip where Washington and his men in 1776 embarked on the crossing, now a state park on the Pennsylvania shore opposite.

WASHINGTON CROSSING STATE PARK

Even if this 369-acre park were not the shore to which George Washington transported 2400 troops in a Christmas night crossing of the ice-choked Delaware, the arboretum here would still be memorable. In spring the masses of pink and white dogwood and redbud against the green of hemlocks are a beautiful sight, a living memorial to men who marched with bare feet bound up in rags. One of their number, Sergeant Thomas McCarty, a Virginian, summed up the epochal event in terse words: "Came there about daybreak and beat the damn Hessians and took 700 and odd prisoners. And the worst day of sleet rain that could be."

The site of Bear Tavern where the two American columns separated for the dawn march to Trenton is at the west end of the park. General Sullivan's forces followed Bear Tavern Road while Washington went by way of Pennington, for a pincers attack. Boulders mark the routes.

McKONKEY FERRY MUSEUM

The bar-and-grill and the common room of this quaint inn dating back at least to 1748 are furnished with great attention to authentic detail. Upstairs is the simple room where the innkeeper persuaded Washington to rest briefly before the advance on Trenton. Old-fashioned garden. Picnic groves. Excellent fishing in the Delaware, especially shad and herring in May.

Take River Rd. to Trenton.

TRENTON

Trentonians in 1784 spruced up their French Arms Tavern, for the Federal Congress was about to convene here on November 1, in search of a National capital. The impression left by Trenton was so favorable that Congress authorized a fund of $100,000 for a "federal house" on the banks of the Delaware. Great was the jubilation in Trenton, but pressures from southern states, and from Washington himself, were so strong that the money was never appropriated.

But Trenton got its capital after all. In 1790 it became officially the seat of State government. Over the years industry in this strategic location proliferated so rapidly as to overshadow governmental aspects of the city, but now in a vast riverfront renewal plan handsome modern buildings, some opened in the Tercentenary year, will provide more efficient quarters for government services.

THE STATE HOUSE   121 W. State St.

The legislative chambers house one of the oldest parliamentary bodies in the nation, its 196-year history being longer than that of the Federal Congress. Land

THE BATTLE GROUND AT TRENTON

New Jersey's capitol now rises close to this spot, depicted in a 19th century view. Washington's successful surprise attack on the Hessians here in 1776 marked the turning point in the Revolution.

Courtesy of Rutgers University

for the original capitol, a building which measured only 60 by 100 feet, was the gift of Joseph and Susannah Brittain. Among many famous visitors, the Marquis de Lafayette was welcomed and spoke in the Assembly in 1824. Another distinguished visitor was Abraham Lincoln who, en route to his Inauguration in 1861, addressed the Legislature. Lining the corridors are portraits of State Governors and other noted Jerseymen.

The New Jersey State Police provide guide service for group tours which include the Assembly and Senate chambers and the Governor's reception room. Call State Police, Capitol Bldg.

STATE LIBRARY John Fitch Way

Repository not only of the New Jersey Archives, the State Library, now in its long-needed modern quarters, is also noted for the large collections on genealogy and history. Many of the 300,000 volumes may be borrowed by New Jersey residents through local library loans.

THE STATE MUSEUM W. State St., near the Capitol

At the close of the Tercentenary Year the State Museum moved into a complex of three handsome modern buildings: the museum proper with a Hall of Natural History, a Hall of Cultural History, and an entire floor devoted to the fine arts; a 400-seat auditorium; and a 165-seat planetarium.

Drawn from the museum's large and varied collections, displays are frequently changed. Dinosaurs and other prehistoric fossils and habitat groups of New Jersey fauna are outstanding features of the Hall of Natural History, as are exhibits from the geological collection, one of the most important in the State. In the Hall of Cultural History the development of man in New Jersey, from prehistoric Indians and Colonial settlers down to modern times, is dramatized with dioramas and rotating exhibits, such as Lenni Lenape artifacts, New Jersey pottery, glass, silver, and furniture, and electronic inventions.

Having celebrated its Diamond Jubilee in 1965, the State Museum has long been an invaluable aid to teachers and an inspiration to school children who visit here in great numbers.

Guide service for organized groups; arrange in advance. Numerous films available for showing to visiting groups and for loan. Weekdays, 9 to 4:30; Sun. and holidays, 2-5. Free.

TRENTON BATTLE MONUMENT   1893 *(State historic site)*   N. Broad St. and Pennington Ave.

An heroic-size statue of George Washington topping this 155-foot granite shaft, designed by John Duncan, marks the spot near which American artillery on December 26, 1776 opened fire on the unsuspecting Hessians. A Sergeant Joseph White later wrote how he, Captain William Washington, and Lieutenant James Monroe (who became fifth President) captured a major fieldpiece from the enemy here. While the Revolution was still going on Lord Germain told the English Parliament, "All our hopes were blasted by that unhappy affair at Trenton."

OLD STONE BARRACKS   1758 *(State historic site)*
    S. Willow St., Capitol grounds

When the French and Indian Wars broke out England, in 1756, sent shiploads of soldiers for frontier defense. At first, His Majesty's troops were billeted in taverns. Some 250 soldiers moved in on Trenton, a town of only 100 homes and three or four taverns. Almost immediately officers usurped the best featherbeds of the citizenry. In Trenton 10 or 15 soldiers sometimes moved in on one little cottage. And not usually peaceably. By 1758 protesting petitions from all over West Jersey poured into the capital at Burlington. Joseph Yard and his associates came up with a plan: build barracks. The British acceded and ordered 5 to be erected at a cost of £2600 each at Burlington, New Brunswick, Elizabeth Town, and Perth Amboy, as well as Trenton. Troops were housed in these barracks every winter until the Treaty of Paris was signed in 1763, stripping France of Canada.

The "shot heard 'round the world" re-opened the Old

Barracks doors with a bang. But two weeks before Christmas in 1776, it was not Americans but 1500 Tories and Hessians who were garrisoned here. As their commander Col. Johann Rall had laughed off advice that the rebels might cross the Delaware, the Germans were celebrating Christmas night. The American pincers attack came at eight next morning, a total surprise. Some of the Hessians made a futile stand, others fled, and 909 were taken prisoner, 106 were killed or wounded.

The only one of the 5 barracks remaining, the handsome structure houses a varied museum, including mementoes of Washington's triumphal procession through Trenton on April 21, 1789, en route to his New York Inauguration. A mural of this scene, by N. C. Wyeth, is in the First Trenton National Bank. Museum: weekdays, 10-4.

Free map of Trenton from Chamber of Commerce, opp. Old Barracks.

TRENT HOUSE   1719 *(City historic site)*
    539 S. Warren St.

Trent Town was named for a Scot, William Trent. The elegant house he built on about 800 acres has proved such an enduring and satisfying Colonial monument that scores of societies and individuals have contributed to the lovely 18th century furnishings. New Jersey's first Chief Justice, William Trent, was but one of several political leaders who resided here. The first Royal Governor of New Jersey, Lewis Morris, lived here his last four years. When Colonel John Cox moved here after selling Batsto Furnace at a handsome profit in 1778 he called the house Bloomsbury Court and gave gay parties presided over by his wife and 6 charming daughters, with such distinguished guests as the Washingtons, Lafayette, and Rochambeau. A learned judge, Philemon Dickerson who became Governor in 1836, made Trent House his home from 1835 to 1838. After a career in the U.S. Navy, Rodman Price lived in Trent House as Governor from 1854 to 1857.

Antiques in the mansion have been selected to match as nearly as possible the "True & Perfect Inventory" of the Chief Justice's goods. Weekdays, 10-4; Sun., 1-4.

MASONIC LODGE HOUSE   1793   NE cor. S. Willow and Lafayette Sts.

Believed to be the oldest Masonic temple in the Nation, this one is unique in having the meeting room furnished as it was in Colonial times, even to the Rising Sun emblem and All-Seeing Eye which was in the original ceiling. Trenton was the center for much Masonic activity in Colonial America, and as early as 1730 a prominent Trentonian, Col. Daniel Coxe, was named the first Grand Master in the New World. The museum here contains such unusual items as the gavel used by Washington when he was a member of the Williamsburg Lodge, and a Bible produced by Isaac Collins, Burlington printer, who published the State's first newspaper, the *New Jersey Gazette*. Mon. to Fri., 10-4 (closed at noon); Sat., 10-12. Free.

WAR MEMORIAL BUILDING   opp. Masonic Lodge

A memorial to soldiers and sailors of World War I, the limestone building is also a community center for important civic events and cultural programs. It is here that the inauguration of New Jersey's governors takes place.

DOUGLASS HOUSE   Stacy Park, opp. War Memorial

Late on the night of Jan. 2, 1777, after the bloody fight of Assunpink Bridge, sometimes called the Second Battle of Trenton, Washington held a council of war in this house just before he ordered his weary soldiers to march secretly and circuitously to Princeton. Campfires were kept burning all night at the bridge, and the surprise of Cornwallis when he found the Americans had vanished was total. Original location of the Douglass House was 193 South Broad Street.

FIRST PRESBYTERIAN CHURCH 1841 114 E. State

Many patriots in the Revolution are buried here and also Abraham Hunt, a rich Trenton merchant who gave unwitting aid to the Americans as host, on Christmas night of 1776, to the Hessian commander Rall, when a spy came to warn the rebels were crossing the Delaware. Absorbed in a card game and holiday cheer, Colonel Rall, without reading the note, stuffed it into his pocket and was not aware of the American advance on Trenton until a short time before he fell mortally wounded next morning.

FRIENDS MEETING HOUSE 1739 NW cor. E. Hanover and Montgomery Sts.

Governor Richard Howell who as a young man was a ringleader in burning British tea at Greenwich in 1774 is buried here (grave unmarked), as are George Clymer, a Signer of the Declaration of Independence, and General Philemon Dickinson. Here, too, lies Dr. Thomas Cadwalader, first Chief Burgess of Trenton and founder of the first public library in New Jersey and one of the early advocates of inoculation against smallpox.

ST. MICHAEL'S EPISCOPAL CHURCH 1819 140 N. Warren St.

Of unique design, the crenellated roof derives from Norman architecture. Buried here is Pauline Joseph Ann Holton, the child born to Joseph Bonaparte, who in exile had a great estate at Bordentown, and his beautiful Quaker mistress, Annette Savage. David Brearley, also buried here, was a noted, early Chief Justice of New Jersey.

ST. MARY'S CATHEDRAL 1871 157 N. Warren St.

Much of the fighting in the Battle of Trenton took place at this spot and the Hessian leader Rall died in a house that formerly stood here.

From the Old Barracks, go E on Lafayette 2 blocks to Broad St.; turn right and continue on Park St.; turn right and follow to end. Parking here; walk to house.

WATSON HOUSE 1708   Broad Street Park

For many years Isaac Watson's home on the bluffs of Watson's Creek was the handsomest in Nottingham Township, named for his English birthplace. Owned by the Mercer County Park Commission, the fieldstone house and its 7½ acres have been leased as headquarters for the New Jersey Society of the Daughters of the American Revolution, with the proviso that the D.A.R. undertake authentic restoration.

Beautifully restored, the house is an impressive setting for parlor, dining room, kitchen and three bedrooms furnished in rare 18th century antiques. Free, but by appt. only: 609-888-2062.

Take Calhoun St. or Princeton Ave. to their inter-section. Then take nearby Prichart St. to Fairfacts St.

EDWARD MARSHALL BOEHM STUDIOS

25 Fairfacts St.

At the age of 38 Edward Boehm was a Maryland cattle-breeder and scientific farmer. Two years later, in 1952, he found himself leading a totally new life, as a success-ful sculptor-ceramist. In less than a decade "Boehm's Birds" had become world-famous. Setting up his studio in Trenton, known since 1880 as the Staffordshire of America, because of the excellence of its clays and the skill of its potters, he created animals and birds in true-to-life colors and milieus. Described as America's first true porcelain of a quality matching that of the Orient, Britain, and Europe, limited editions of Boehm's sculp-tures are in the Metropolitan, the White House, the Smithsonian, the Vatican, among other collections. In 1958 President Dwight D. Eisenhower commissioned Boehm to create "The Polo Player," which was presented to Queen Elizabeth and Prince Philip. After Mr. Boehm's death in 1969, artists and craftsmen trained by him con-tinued their work at the studio. Open Mon.-Fri., 10-4. 609-392-2207.

From W. State St. go N on Parkside Ave.

CADWALADER PARK

About 200 acres of city park featuring tennis courts, ball fields, small zoo, picnic grounds. Along the south edge runs the feeder of the Delaware and Raritan Canal.

LENOX, INC. *(china showrooms)* Prince and Meade

Walter Lenox made the first American china for the President of the United States and ever since, this has been the type of dinner service used in the White House. American Beleek made in the 1880's by Walter Lenox and other rare creations of his are in the famous Ceramics Museum of Sèvres, France, and in the Trenton showrooms too are museum pieces and commemorative china. Determined to make china tableware surpassing imports, Lenox set up his own factory but just as he was about to realize his goal, at the age of 36 he became partially blind and paralyzed. Undaunted, he worked every day for 25 years though he had to be carried into his office.

JOHN A. ROEBLING'S SONS CO.   640 S. Broad St.

Colorado Fuel and Iron Corp. Offices

First to have success in building suspension bridges with 100-foot spans, John A. Roebling flew a kite to carry the first strand of wire across Niagara's gorge, which he bridged in 1854, the first suspension bridge in history to carry a railroad train. While building the Brooklyn Bridge—which contemporaries doubted could be done—Roebling lost his life through an accident. On the same project his son, George Washington Roebling, became paralyzed from caisson disease but was able to watch the jubilant dedication by telescope.

The present-day wire and cable mills are on 417 acres at Trenton and Roebling. Tours arranged through the Director of Industrial Relations.

ASSUNPINK PARK   5 mi. E of Trenton; S of

Princeton Mercerville-Quakerbridge Rd.

A 200-acre lake to be created by a Federal dam on Assunpink Creek will be the heart of 3000 acres of parkland, a 25-year project.

PRINCETON: A BATTLE AND
AN EDUCATION

Princeton
Princeton Battlefield
Princeton University
Kingston
Rockingham Manor

Hopewell Museum
John Hart Homestead
Pennington
Lawrenceville
Rider College

PRINCETON

Home of a world-renowned university and center for
explorations within the atom and in outer space, through
such institutions as the Forrestal Research Center and
the Sarnoff Research Laboratories, Princeton yet man-
ages to retain the air of a leisurely Colonial town, a
living proof that history and progress are compatible.
Offering not only numerous historic sites, attractive
shops, good restaurants and inns but also many concerts,
plays, and lectures, Princeton, as in Washington's stay
here, is a cultural center for the State. The town's delightful setting makes a good base for exploring nearby
points of interest such as Trenton and Washington
Crossing. Student guides in the Orange Key Office, just
west of Nassau Hall, conduct free tours of the campus,
weekdays from 9 to 5. Phone Orange Key through the
university switchboard. Free maps from the Chamber
of Commerce, 55 Palmer Square W. Occasional open-
house tours of many of Princeton's historic residences.

PRINCETON BATTLE MONUMENT 1922
   W end of Nassau St., at Mercer and Stockton Sts.
   Commemorating the victory which opened the year
1777 for the Americans, this 50-foot marble sculpture in
high relief depicts Washington leading his troops and
Gen. Hugh Mercer mortally stabbed as he refused to
surrender. Designed by Thomas Hastings, sculptured
by Frederick MacMonnies.

THE BATTLE OF PRINCETON

Of rare historic value, this painting is by the deaf-mute son of General Hugh Mercer who died of bayonet wounds in the fight for Princeton. The battlefield is now a memorial park, and Stony Brook Meetinghouse, shown in the painting, still stands. Painted by William Mercer.

Stockton St., first house on right . . .

MORVEN 1701

OFFICIAL RESIDENCE OF NEW JERSEY'S GOVERNORS

Much history has flowed by and through Morven, for the road it faces was once the Assunpink Trail of the Lenni Lenape, later the Old Dutch Trail, then King's Highway. The present street bears the name of the rich Quaker Richard Stockton who came here from New Amsterdam in 1691 and, having bought some 6000 acres from William Penn, built this splendid mansion and fathered a famous family who owned it until 1945. In 1954 Governor Walter E. Edge presented the house, now beautifully restored, to the people of New Jersey to be used as the Governor's Mansion.

Stockton's grandson Richard, loyal friend of Washington and a Signer of the Declaration, when he heard that the British were on their way to seize Princeton, fled with his family to Monmouth County. But instead of finding refuge he was imprisoned, brutally treated, then informed that he would be freed if he signed a loyalty oath. The "Signer" signed, but came home in disgrace and sadly set about restoring Morven, its loss through British looting and burning then estimated at £5000.

Before the war ended Richard Stockton had succumbed to cancer and, because of other staunch patriots in the family, his recantation was soon glossed over. When the Dutch minister brought news of peace, Stockton's beautiful widow, Annis Boudinot Stockton, whom students called the Duchess, and her brother Elias entertained with a state dinner at Morven, the Washingtons heading the guest list of victorious Revolutionaries.

Catalpas near the gate and many other fine old trees were planted by the Stocktons. Early May when dogwood and wisteria are likely to be blooming is an ideal time to see Morven. Mansion open Tuesdays, 2-4, by appointment.

Continue on Stockton, take first right, to Library Pl.
WOODROW WILSON'S HOMES *(private)* 72 and 82 Library Pl.

As professor of political science on the Princeton faculty, Dr. Wilson lived at No. 72, a house built in 1836 by architect Charles Steadman, who designed many Princeton mansions. Later as the university's president, Woodrow Wilson resided on campus at "Prospect" *(see below)*. When he became New Jersey's governor, just before he went to the White House as President in World War I, he lived at 25 Cleveland Lane.

Go S on Library Pl., turn right at Mercer Rd.
ALBERT EINSTEIN'S HOME *(private)* 112 Mercer Rd.

The world-famous physicist, often called the 20th century's greatest mind, lived in this modest house while he was associated with the Institute for Advanced Study from 1933 until his death here in 1955.

Continue W out Mercer Rd. 1.2 mi. to Princeton Battlefield, marked, a 40-acre State park.
PRINCETON BATTLEFIELD

In the south half of the park a pyramid of cannonballs marks the spot where Gen. Hugh Mercer fell fatally wounded, near the tree now called the Mercer Oak. In the north park a group of classic columns leads to a memorial to British and American soldiers. Panic seized Mercer's weary brigade, sent ahead on the night march from Trenton to destroy Stony Brook Bridge, when at dawn they were attacked by Col. Mawhood's fresh troops just west of Quaker Road. The rout was turned to victory with the arrival of Washington and the main body of soldiers, and cannonades from Moulder's battery. An outnumbered crack British brigade was dispersed, and Washington seized Nassau Hall and Princeton for a few hours.

Continue W to next left, Quaker Rd. Near Mercer Rd. is sign of . . .

STONY BROOK MEETING HOUSE 1760

Bloody hand-to-hand fighting took place all around this stone structure in the Battle of Princeton, as it was along Quaker Road that the Americans came marching to Princeton. Richard Stockton, the Signer, is buried in this stone-walled cemetery, in an unmarked grave, according to early Quaker custom.

Return to Princeton via Mercer; at Maxwell La., go right to oval (Olden La.). Large bldg. on right is . . .

INSTITUTE FOR ADVANCED STUDY 1930

Founded to offer scholars uninterrupted study free from teaching or other official duties, the Institute is perhaps most renowned for individuals who were pioneers in atomic fission, particularly Albert Einstein, Robert M. Oppenheimer, and John Von Neumann, but researchers in other fields, like political scientist and ambassador George F. Kennan, also pursue their investigations here. The Institute has had 8 Nobel Prize winners.

Return to Mercer, en route toward Princeton ctr., left at Edgehill St.

THE BARRACKS *(private)* 32 Edgehill St.

One of the oldest houses in Princeton this stone structure was erected by the Stocktons before they built Morven in 1701. A troop barracks in the Revolution.

Continue via Stockton to Nassau St.

BAINBRIDGE HOUSE 158 Nassau St.

HISTORICAL SOCIETY OF PRINCETON

Com. William Bainbridge who commanded the U.S.S. *Constitution,* "Old Ironsides," in the War of 1812 was born in this 18th-century house built by the Stocktons. British Gen. Howe's headquarters in the fall of 1776. The Historical Society of Princeton has beautifully restored this former public library with choice antiques in period rooms, including a portrait of Commodore Bainbridge. Free guided tours. 609-921-6748.

NASSAU HALL   1756   Nassau St. on Princeton campus

"From a little obscure village we have become the capital of America." So wrote Ashbel Green in 1783, then a student at the College of New Jersey (Princeton) and later its president. Threatened in June by a mutiny of Pennsylvania recruits, the Continental Congress hurriedly fled Philadelphia for Princeton and set up government in Nassau Hall. Feeling need for advice and reassurance, Congress invited General Washington to visit Princeton. Deferred to as if he were already President, Washington stayed for three months at nearby Rocky Hill. A portrait of him painted at this time by Charles Willson Peale still hangs in Nassau Hall. It replaced one of George II, which was decapitated by a cannonball from Alexander Hamilton's battery.

Opened on Nov. 13, 1756, by Princeton's second president, the Rev. Aaron Burr, Sr., Nassau Hall was once New Jersey's capitol as well: it was here in 1776 that the State Constitution was adopted and the first governor elected.

Pillaged by the British, burned in 1803 and in 1855, the original walls still stand, and the structure is now a National Monument. An Orange Key guide will open the Faculty Room and describe the many interesting portraits.

PRINCETON CHAPEL   1928

A Gothic design by Ralph Adams Cram, the chapel, seating 1800, has some of the finest stained-glass windows in the western hemisphere, and over a thousand individual memorials. Exceptionally beautiful is the carved oaken pulpit, 16th-century French. Nondenominational services Sundays at 11 A.M. during college year.

HARVEY S. FIRESTONE LIBRARY   1948

With over two million volumes, from among the many rarities such as incunabula, illuminated manuscripts, Egyptian papyri, early American books, manuscripts of Woodrow Wilson, John Foster Dulles, William Faulkner, F. Scott Fitzgerald, and other Americans, frequently changing displays are on public view. On permament exhibit is a room depicting the College of New Jersey's library in 1760, furnished with the Rev. John Witherspoon's desk, chairs once owned by James Madison, and other rare antiques. Open daily during college year; Sundays at 2 P.M.

THE DEAN'S HOUSE   1756 *(private)*   Just west of Nassau Hall

Home of Princeton's presidents until 1879, this yellow-washed brick residence by Robert C. Smith has been host to George Washington, John Adams, Henry Clay, and Andrew Jackson. At the entrance, two giant trees are part of a group planted in 1766 and early known as the Stamp Act Sycamores.

PROSPECT   1849
FACULTY CLUB

On campus, southeast of Nassau Hall, this Tuscan villa was designed by John Notman. Many unusual old trees. Flower garden at the rear is open to the public.

FIRST PRESBYTERIAN CHURCH   1836   61 Nassau St.

A masterpiece of the Classic Revival, by Charles Steadman, the church is within the campus, and the university, originally founded for the training of Presbyterian clergymen, retains the right to hold commencement exercises here.

Nassau to Bayard Lane (Rte. 206 N. West of this street is one of the finest historical residential areas.)

Take Rte. 27 NE for 3 mi.
KINGSTON

Marching from Princeton, Washington and his generals paused here to debate strategy. Should they gamble all in a raid on New Brunswick with its abundant stores and British gold? The grievous answer was no, because the soldiers were almost dead on their feet. Instead the army was allowed to rest at Millstone, and later Washington set up winter quarters at Morristown. A tiny building at right of the bridge over the Delaware and Raritan Canal in Kingston is an early telegraph office *(see Delaware-Raritan Tour)*. Facing canal is lock-keeper's house. Stone bridge was built in 1798.

Continue on Rte. 27. At Rte. 518 left for 2 mi. to . . .
ROCKINGHAM   *(State historic site)*
WASHINGTON'S HEADQUARTERS, AUG.–NOV., 1783

While the Continental Congress was in session at Nassau Hall and everyone awaited the treaty of peace, George Washington and his wife held court here, with many a gay dinner party under a "marquis" on the lawn. As delegate, David Howell of Rhode Island wrote about the general: ". . . the contracted pensive phiz, betokening deep thought and much care, which I noticed on Prospect Hill, in 1775, is done away, and a pleasant smile . . . succeeds." In this affable mood Washington had his portrait painted by Peale and submitted to a covering of wet plaster for a life-mask, which the nervous sculptor broke. Amid all the festivities Washington did not forget his needy friends. Thomas Paine whose words had urged Americans to continue to fight in the dark years was then living in penury in Bordentown. Urging him to visit Rocky Hill, Washington wrote: "Your presence may remind Congress of your past Services to this Country . . ."

The jubilant news of the end of the war was announced in Nassau Hall on October 31, and by November 2 Washington had issued his "Farewell Orders to the Armies," a moving document written in the Blue Room of this house. From Rockingham Washington bade farewell to his guard of honor: "Men who have so bravely defended their country will likewise in their peaceable retirements contribute their best endeavors to confirm that happy Union of the States and its citizens . . ."

Once a 20-room mansion owned by Judge John Berrien who drowned himself in the Millstone River, Rockingham, originally in the valley below and twice moved to avoid damage by quarry blasting, has been restored and refurbished.

Continue W on Rte. 518, through early village of Rocky Hill; 1.5 mi. W of Rte. 206, note . . .

WASHINGTON WELL FARM c. 1750 *(private)*
The well opposite was drained dry, say local records, by thirsty soldiers guarding Washington on his ride from Newburgh, N.Y., to Rocky Hill in 1783.

Continue on Rte. 518 to Hopewell.

HOPEWELL

HOPEWELL MUSEUM   26 E. Broad St.
Lavish costumes, dating as far back as 1788, unusual tools of early craftsmen, Colonial weapons, and early china, of an excellence not usually found in small-town museums. Mon., Wed., Sat., 2-5. Free.

JOHN HART FARMSTEAD *(private)* 60 Hart Ave.
Why only John Hart of the five New Jersey Signers of the Declaration of Independence had a price on his head, alive or dead, is not clear. Facts about his life are tantalizingly meager, although his many public honors are well documented. In August of 1776 as an outspoken patriot he was named Speaker of New Jersey's Provincial Congress, yet he was soon forced to flee to the Sourland Mountains where for weeks he lived like a hunted animal, his only visitor a Negro servant. Hart's wife and children also lived in fear of reprisals from Tory neighbors, and in October Mrs. Hart died. Griefstricken and ill, Hart nevertheless reconvened the Legislature after Washington's Trenton and Princeton victories. But shock and sickness had taken such toll that John Hart, despite his great stamina, was dead two years later, before he could see victory for the cause to which he had given all he held dear.

The Hart homestead has been restored by Col. and Mrs. Cleon E. Hammond who are compiling biographical data on the Signer.

OLD SCHOOL BAPTISTS' MEETING HOUSE   1748
W. Broad St.

John Hart, a martyr to the Revolution, in 1747 gave land for this church, though not a Baptist. In 1865 his remains were brought here from the Hunt burial plot near Woodsville and the present monument erected. Soon after his ordeal of being hunted like a criminal, Hart died at his Hopewell home on May 11, 1779, not 1780 as the marker records. His birth date is unknown.

Rte. 69 and Spur 518, at NW corner of cross-roads . . .

JAMES MARSHALL HOUSE   *(private)*
Marshall's Corner

Growing up here in the 1820's in this hamlet named for his father, a wheelwright, James Marshall could have had no inkling of the Pandora's box he would one day open. He was the man who first discovered gold in California while building a flour mill for Captain John Sutter in 1848. Although others scooped up riches, James Marshall died nearly broke, in California's Kelsey County Hospital. But in his 75 years he'd had his money's worth of excitement.

Rte. 69 S to Pennington.
PENNINGTON

Once called Queenstown, then Penny Town, this pioneer settlement of Hunterdon County even now, with its white frame houses and tree-lined streets, has much of the charm of a Colonial scene. In 1776 when Lord Cornwallis was pursuing "that gray fox" Washington to the Delaware shore, a British division was posted here, the source of many brutalities inflicted on villagers, according to old newspaper records. It was from Pennington that Cornwallis dispatched a handful of men to Basking Ridge where they pulled the fantastic coup of capturing General Charles Lee in his bed at the Widow White's Tavern.

PENNINGTON SCHOOL FOR BOYS   1838
W. Delaware Ave.

Red brick with white pilasters, this school has a pleasant garden created by Dr. Francis Harvey Green, former headmaster.

HOWELL HOUSE   *(private)*   52 E. Curlis Ave.

This early Dutch house, one of the first of the more lavish residences, was bought in 1728 by the Welling family who lived here for many years.

2 mi. W of Pennington Circle, on N side of Washington Crossing Rd. . . .

WOOLSEY HOUSE   1765 *(private)*

Built for Jeremiah Woolsey, and an excellent example of early Georgian architecture.

Rtes. 69 S, 546 E, and 206 N to . . .

LAWRENCEVILLE

Of high reputation, *Lawrenceville School* (1810) for boys was long known as a Princeton "prep" academy. During the Revolution Hessian troops are said to have compelled a captured American to preach a sermon in the *Presbyterian Church.*

RIDER COLLEGE

Founded at Trenton in 1865, Rider College celebrated its centennial with the completion of its relocation to a new 140-acre campus on the Lawrenceville Road. The accredited, coeducational college is now housed in attractive modern buildings especially designed for effective teaching, with over 2500 students enrolled full-time and about 1500 in evening classes.

Andrew Rider, the man whose endowments created the college named for him, popularized South Jersey cranberries in England by using modern advertising techniques. He showed chefs of London hotels how to use the fruit and then won even Queen Victoria's approval by sending a crate of the berries to her son, the Prince of Wales, later Edward VII. Rider revealed a real flair for publicity when he bought a race horse and named it Cranberry. The horse won England's two top racing events: the Ascot and the Derby.

Photo by Adeline Pepper

QUAKERS, BONAPARTES, HESSIANS, AND SWEDES

BORDENTOWN: HOME OF THE FAMOUS

Bonaparte Park
Clara Barton School
Gilder House
Hopkinson House

Columbus
Crosswicks
Allentown
Cranbury

BORDENTOWN

When it happened in 1816 it was the talk of all New Jersey. The deposed King of Spain and Naples, Joseph Bonaparte, brother of Napoleon the Great, in flight from his subjects, was coming to live in Bordentown. Buying 1500 acres on Crosswicks Creek he created a magnificent estate, "Point Breeze," where not only royalty but American statesmen such as John Quincy Adams, Daniel Webster, and Henry Clay gathered, the latter often gambling with Bonaparte's profligate nephew Prince Murat. Part of Point Breeze, whose residents gave New Jersey the tag of "New Spain," is still in Bordentown *(see Divine Word Seminary below)*.

Thomas Farnsworth in 1682 established Bordentown as a settlement for the much-persecuted Quakers, but a century later Bordentonians literally drove Tom Paine out of town for his unorthodox views.

Members of the State Legislature, all of Bordentown, and the Bonapartes turned out on November 12, 1831 to see New Jersey's first working railroad, the Camden and Amboy, with 6½ miles of track. Shipped unassembled from England, the engine's parts were put together by a Bordentown mechanic, Isaac Dripps, who had never seen a locomotive before. As the "John Bull" spewed black smoke and sparks, the crowd shrank back. But Caroline Fraser, a Bordentown belle who had had the courage to marry Prince Murat, stepped forward to try the new mode of transportation. Visiting dignitaries could do no less. The successful ride was followed by a restorative luncheon at Arnell's Hotel.

Its red brick, white-trimmed buildings close to the tree-lined street, Farnsworth Avenue could be the set for a Colonial movie, if a few signs were removed. One block away, Prince Street, with white clapboard, green-shuttered houses, has equal charm.

HILLTOP PARK   Farnsworth Ave. at the river.

On a wooded bluff this small park with a Southern look has a sweeping view of the river. Just below is Crosswicks Creek where Joseph Bonaparte used to embark in a 16-oar barge presented to him by Stephen Girard.

FRANCIS HOPKINSON HOUSE   1750   *(private)*
   101 Farnsworth Ave.

One of the five Jerseymen who signed the Declaration of Independence, brilliant Francis Hopkinson, frequently in the lead of his times, wrote "A Prophecy" in 1774, predicting the Revolution. A lawyer and a man of many other talents, Hopkinson designed the Great Seal of the United States and its first 13-stripe flag, and wrote lyric poetry.

In 1777, submarine-experimenter David Bushnell set afloat powder-packed kegs in the Delaware to destroy enemy ships. Physical damage proved slight but the British became so jittery that Hopkinson wrote a mocking poem, "The Battle of the Kegs," soon sung in all the taverns. As the kegs had been made in the cooperage of Col. Joseph Borden, Hopkinson's father-in-law, the British retaliated by burning the colonel's house to the ground. The invaders dined in Hopkinson's splendid red brick house but though they took some of his possessions they did not burn the building. Hopkinson's son Joseph was the author of "Hail, Columbia."

PATIENCE LOVELL WRIGHT HOUSE *(private)*
   100 Farnsworth Ave. at W. Park St.

America's first sculptor was a Bordentown girl, Patience Lovell (1725-1786), who did not attain recognition for her artistic talents until she was 47 and the mother of four sons. Working in wax, she executed a full length statue of William Pitt the Elder in this unusual medium, which was placed in Westminster Abbey, the first American sculpture so honored. Mrs. Wright's son Joseph was a portrait painter and designed some of the first United States coins.

HOAGLAND TAVERN *(private)*   1 E. Park St.

Startlingly Spanish in design, this white-calcimined square building with high iron balcony and carved brown cornice was actually the American House, a Revolutionary tavern run by Col. Oakly Hoagland of the American Army. The striking Mediterranean look of the building no doubt reveals the Bonaparte influence of the early 19th century.

BORDEN HOUSE *(private)*   NW cor. Farnsworth Ave.
   and Park St.

This house survives as a memorial to the enduring patriotism of the Borden family. The original dwelling erected at this corner by the first Joseph Borden was burned to the ground. In retaliation for the Borden-Bushnell plan to blow up enemy ships with submerged mines, 800 men in 5 armed vessels from Philadelphia descended on Bordentown, May 7, 1778.

MURAT ROW *(private)*   47-53 E. Park St.

These interesting row-houses are remnants of Linden Hall, a girls' boarding school opened by the American wife of Prince Murat after he had squandered his fortune and hers. After the French Revolution of 1848, Louis Napoleon recalled Murat to France and later made him a prince, but American friends had to pay the traveling expenses of his family so they could join him.

BONAPARTE GALLERY   Park St. near Second St.

An antique mall and restaurant occupy "Old Main," formerly the main building of Bordentovn Military Institute, which closed in 1972. The left side of the building was once the residence of Louis Maillard, secretary to Joseph Bonaparte. Fri. 12-9; Sat., Sun., 9-9.

Continue on Park St. to Divine Word Seminary . . .

BONAPARTE PARK   N side of E. Park St.
Divine Word Seminary

Crown jewels kept in a secret room, paintings by Rubens, David, Goya, and other masters, statues of Napoleon and the entire Bonaparte family, rare Sèvres porcelain, murals of Napoleonic victories—these were some of the eye-opening sights which favored guests at Point Breeze saw while ex-King Joseph Bonaparte (alias the Count de Survilliers) lived here in luxurious exile. Known for his neighborliness and generosity, Joseph, was called locally "the *good* Mr. Bonaparte," to distinguish him from the one on St. Helena.

In 1850 Henry Beckett, a one-time British consul in Philadelphia, bought Point Breeze and about 250 acres. When he promptly demolished the royal mansion, Bordentonians dubbed him Beckett the Destroyer. The house he built was remodeled about 1912 by millionaire Harris Hammond who tried to revive the splendor of Bonaparte Park, but in the Depression the property was bought by the mortgagor for $200.

Bonaparte Park is now a Catholic seminary for boys, with the Beckett-Hammond House as administration building. Here one can see an exquisite mantel of antiqued mirrors that was once part of Point Breeze. The great trees and ancient boxwood hint of the former idyllic landscape depicted in watercolors by Karl Bodmer. The gatehouse lodge, though covered with modern siding, retains the original form of a Bonaparte house. Of exceptional interest at the steep river bank is the entrance to a brick-lined tunnel. The underground passage formerly led to two Bonaparte mansions and, while the tunnels were convenient for moving goods from ships to the dwellings, the more vital function was to afford escape from much-feared Spanish and British spies or assassins.

At the opposite end of the campus are mysteriously attractive grottoes and piles of gray-white rock brought in at great expense by Harris Hammond.

Visitors are welcome at the Divine Word Seminary, but permission to see the campus should first be obtained at the administration building.

CLARA BARTON'S SCHOOL   142 Crosswicks St. at E. Burlington St.

Before she became founder and first president of the American Red Cross, Clara Barton, a crusading young woman of 31 persuaded Bordentown city fathers to open a free public school in 1853 and donated her services as teacher for three months to prove that the poor would welcome free education. Without detracting from Clara Barton's many achievements, it is inaccurate to claim that this was New Jersey's first free school. Allaire Village, for one, had a free school as early as 1834, and probably 1822, attended often by as many as 100 pupils. The one-room school is open by appointment; Bordentown Historical Society.

GILDER HOUSE *(municipal site)*   Crosswicks St. opp. Union St.

Four Gilder brothers and their sister who lived here in the 1880's made names for themselves in the arts and science: Richard Watson, as editor of *The Century*; William, as geographer-explorer; John, as a composer; Joseph and Jeannette, as editors of *The Critic*. Some of the furnishings in the Colonial house are said to have come from the Bonapartes' Point Breeze estate. Free, weekdays; inquire of superintendent. Group tours through Bordentown Historical Society. Nearby community center with picnic facilities.

Go S on Rte. 206 and follow Columbus Exit at right to top of hill and Main St. Large brick house to left of Railroad Ave. . . .

PRINCE MURAT HOUSE *(private)* 32 Main St., Columbus

Palatial compared to the usual white clapboard house in Columbus, this hilltop dwelling in the 1820's was the home of royalty in exile, the profligate Prince Lucien Murat whose father was Joachim, King of the Two Sicilies, and whose uncle was ex-king Joseph Bonaparte, then living at Point Breeze on the Delaware. It was Prince Murat who eloped with beautiful Caroline Fraser of Bordentown and squandered her inheritance before returning to France.

Cross bridge over Rte. 206 and take Exit 206 N. At Rte. 130 above Bordentown keep to right; turn off at large sign: Ward Ave. Crosswicks. Follow to center of Crosswicks.

CROSSWICKS

The change from Route 130, with trucks thundering down through a forest of signs, to Crosswicks' main street is an agreeable shock. Far better than any synthetic "restoration," this Quaker settlement of the 1680's summons up a vision of Colonial life. Main Street still has the S-curve of the earlier Indian path and old houses crowd close upon it as if their owners did not want to miss anything. As the old custom was to plant a buttonwood tree in front of and at each end of a new dwelling, the village has many large sycamores.

CHESTERFIELD MEETING HOUSE 1773

Church and Front Sts.

In a Revolutionary War skirmish close by, on June 23, 1778, several cannonballs hit the new-built house of worship and one is still embedded in the north wall. The earliest Crosswicks meetinghouse dates back to 1693. The present 2-story one with white shutters is of red brick laid in Flemish bond pattern typical of many handsome residences on the byroads of Crosswicks. In the meetinghouse yard is the venerable *Crosswicks White Oak*, 17½ feet in girth at its base, over 80 feet high, and about 300 years old.

ORTHODOX FRIENDS MEETING HOUSE 1853
    Main St.
The first church here was built in 1831 after the Hicksite-Orthodox split among the Quakers in 1827.

HILLTOP INN   Main St. and Chesterfield Rd.
A tavern in 1776, this building is still used as an inn and is well preserved, albeit with many alterations.

UNION FIRE COMPANY 1882   Main St.
An old hand-pumper engine here was built in 1774 and originally owned by the Union Fire Company of Philadelphia.

JOSEPH HENDRICKSON HOUSE   1750 *(private)* Buttonwood St.
This oldest house in Crosswicks was used by English troops in the Revolution.

ALLENTOWN

Quite different in character from Crosswicks, Allentown, its white houses set back on green lawns, also has an air of early times. One of the village's most famous residents was Molly Pitcher, born October 13, 1754, on a nearby farm owned by her father John Ludwig. At the age of 15 Molly went as a servant to Carlisle, Pa., where she met and married John Caspar Hays, a true love-match judging from her devotion. Her husband enlisted in the First Pennsylvania Regiment of Artillery, and, while he was engaged in many of the New Jersey skirmishes, Molly returned to Allentown to be near him and her parents. And that was how she chanced to be carrying pitchers of water to her husband and other soldiers on scorching Monmouth Battlefield.

GOVERNOR NEWELL HOUSE *(church property)*   Main and High Sts.

Three times elected to Congress, Dr. William A. Newell used those years with the indefatigable purpose of creating a United States Life-Saving Service on the New Jersey coast, an accomplished fact in 1848. A rocket lifeline which he devised for use with an egg-shaped lifeboat developed by Joseph Francis saved 200 passengers stranded in the barque *Ayreshire* off Squan Beach in 1850. Pioneering also as a physician, his early practice in Imlaystown, Dr. Newell performed one of the first skin grafts, that of forming a new eyelid. When he was elected Governor in 1857, the doctor walked in a snowfall from his house in Allentown to the inauguration in Trenton.

PRESBYTERIAN CHURCH   1809   High St.

A splendid landmark and house of worship, the church had one of the first Sunday Schools and temperance societies in America. Governor Newell is buried here.

IMLAY HOUSE   1790 *(private)*   26 S. Main St.

A fine bit of architecture well preserved from an early day.

CRANBURY

FIRST PRESBYTERIAN CHURCH   S. Main St.

Early 19th century, the white church with two fluted columns sets the New England atmosphere of Cranbury.

BRAINERD LAKE

Named for David and John Brainerd, missionaries who often preached to the Indians under one of Cranbury's elms. Flood-lighted ice-skating to music. Fishing and boating in summer.

CRANBURY INN
Still serving travelers as it did in 1780. Among the famous guests then were George Washington and Alexander Hamilton.

METHODIST CHURCH N. Main St.
Another charming 19th-century structure.

CURTIN HOUSE N. Main St.
In this frame house Aaron Burr spent a harried night as he fled from New York to Philadelphia after shooting Alexander Hamilton in their duel at Weehawken.

PERRINE'S AZALEA GARDENS Pleasant Hill Rd., 2 mi. NE of Cranbury
Acres of azaleas, rhododendron, and dogwood, their height of bloom from May 1 to mid-June. Free.

BURLINGTON AND MOUNT HOLLY

Burlington	Haddonfield
Mount Holly	Medford Lakes
Rancocas	Lebanon State Forest
Rancocas State Park	

Exit 5 of New Jersey Tpke.; or Rte. 130 from Bordentown or Camden to . . .

BURLINGTON

On the day in 1677 that a boatload of William Penn's Quaker colonists set sail to found the city that would become the capital of West Jersey, they received the blessing of no less a person than King Charles II from his barge on the Thames. Finding safe harbor and fertile land, the Quakers prospered, and John Crips wrote home, "The Indians are very loving to us . . ."
With the partitioning of Nova Caesarea, by which William Penn and other trustees received the westerly half, Burlington in 1681 became the capital of West New Jersey and so continued until Jerseymen ousted the last Royal Governor, William Franklin, natural son

of Benjamin. The governor was actually held prisoner for a time in his residence down by the waterfront.

With many significant as well as charming early structures still standing, Burlington offers a rare chance to study at first hand the setting of important events. The blocks from Broad Street to the river, between High Street and the bridge provide a delightful walking tour.

LORDS PROPRIETORS' OFFICE   1914   West Broad St. nr. High St.

This tiny red-brick building is a treasure chest of history, for in it are kept some of the earliest records of land grants in the Province of West Jersey. This is the office of one of the two oldest corporations in the United States—the Lords Proprietors of West Jersey. Its counterpart, for the Lords of East Jersey, is in Perth Amboy.

The Concessions and Agreement of 1677, crackling parchment signed by the 151 original Lords Proprietors, is far more than a record of property rights. Written from the painful memories of England's persecution of the Quakers, this document guaranteed such fundamental freedoms as the secret ballot, trial by jury, and absolute religious toleration. The General Council of the Proprietors still meets at this office once a year in May, its only functions now being to dispose of any unclaimed land discovered west of the Province Line and to issue warrants for land surveys. Open by application to the Council of Proprietors, Burlington.

PROPRIETORS' SIDEWALK MEETINGS

Every April 10 since 1688 the Proprietors of West Jersey have met outdoors at the spot marked by a plaque on the bank at High and Broad Streets; their purpose: to elect 5 members of the General Council. Requirements for membership in the corporation are 1/32 of a share and hereditary descent from an original signer.

J. FENIMORE COOPER HOUSE   c. 1780 *(museum)*   457
High St.

That prolific chronicler of historical romances, James Fenimore Cooper, was born here in 1789. The Burlington County Historical Society has on display a portion of the manuscript of *The Spy,* the hero of which is said to have been modeled after John Honeyman, a spy for George Washington *(see Griggstown).* Genealogical library. Many Revolutionary and Civil War items. Sun. 2-4; also by appointment. 609-386-4773. Donation.

JAMES LAWRENCE HOUSE   1742, 1820 *(State historic site)*   459 High St.

"Don't give up the ship!" This motto of the U.S. Navy, was the command of dying James Lawrence, who was born in this house on October 1, 1781 and lived 17 of his short years here. When Lawrence, in the war with Tripoli, boarded and burned the captured *Philadelphia* under enemy guns, Admiral Lord Nelson called it "the most brilliant deed of the age." But Lawrence's shining future was blacked out in the War of 1812, when he with his ship *Chesapeake* accepted a challenge to a sea duel with the British frigate *Shannon.* Inferior to her in guns and size and with a green crew, the *Chesapeake,* part of her rigging shot away, collided with the enemy vessel. In the bloody hand-to-hand fighting that ensued, Captain Lawrence was mortally wounded. His *very* last words were, "Blow her up!"

Of 5 ships named for the daring Lawrence, the last was a guided missile destroyer, launched in 1960. A document signed by Lawrence and some furniture belonging to his family are among the memorabilia in this historic house. 25¢.

GOVERNOR BLOOMFIELD HOUSE   *(private)*   SE cor.
High and Library Sts.

This was the residence of Joseph Bloomfield who was Mayor of Burlington from 1795 to 1800 and Governor of New Jersey from 1801 to 1812. He gained prominence when he successfully defended the young men of Greenwich who burned a cargo of British tea on the night of Dec. 22, 1774. A captain in the Revolution and a brigadier general in the War of 1812, he died in 1823 and is buried in St. Mary's churchyard.

FRIENDS MEETING HOUSE 1784 High St. near Broad St.

Unusual for its high wall and heavy iron gate, this meetinghouse replaced one which had already seen a century of service. At the rear of the building, under the boughs of a huge sycamore is the grave of Indian chief, Ockanickon. The marker is inscribed with his last words: "Be Plain and Fair to All, Both Indians and Christian, as I have Been."

THOMAS REVELL HOUSE 1685 *(private)* Adj. 217 Wood St., originally at 8 E. Pearl St.

Oldest house in the county, this was the office of Thomas Revell, Registrar of the Proprietors of West Jersey and Clerk of the Provincial Assembly from 1696 to 1699. Tradition holds that Ben Franklin en route to Philadelphia stopped here and was given a piece of gingerbread by an old woman. Next door to the High Street Synagogue is the site where Franklin set up the first copper-plate press in America and printed the first currency for the Province. In the same printshop Isaac Collins published the first newspaper in the Province, the *New Jersey Gazette,* on Dec. 5, 1777. Collins also printed the first quarto Bible in America, one of which can be seen in the Trenton Masonic Museum.

BURLINGTON ISLAND Foot of High St.

As early as 1624 Swedish colonists set up a post on Matinicunck Island for trade with the Indians. In 1682 the island was ceded to the City of Burlington, with the stipulation that all revenue be used for local schools, the oldest educational trust in the Nation.

OLD ST. MARY'S CHURCH 1703   W. Broad and
   Wood Sts.

Gray stucco with white trim, this Georgian Colonial church is the oldest Episcopal house of worship in West Jersey. The congregation possesses a silver communion service presented by Queen Anne. A National Historic site.

ST. MARY'S CHURCH 1854

The impressive Gothic building now used for Episcopalian services was designed by Richard Upjohn, architect of Trinity Church in New York City.

BOUDINOT HOUSE 1804 *(private)* 207 and 209 W.
   Broad St.

Elias Boudinot, the man whom the Revolutionists chose as President of the Continental Congress, built this house and for about half a century it was maintained as a splendid mansion. Boudinot's daughter, Mrs. William Bradford, wife of the nation's first attorney general, resided here to the end of her life.

GENERAL GRANT HOUSE *(private)* 309 Wood St.

The family of Ulysses S. Grant lived here while he was leading the Union Army in the Civil War. It is said that the general was here the night Lincoln was shot.

From Burlington take Rte. 541 SE to Mount Holly.

MOUNT HOLLY

Settled by Quakers about 1700, Mount Holly has preserved much of its 18th-century heritage, not only early houses but public buildings as well. The courthouse and jail, in fact, are the nation's largest group of such early county buildings in continuous use. When Mount Holly was the State Capital for two months of 1779, Governor William Livingston issued a proclamation declaring December 9 of that year as New Jersey's Thanksgiving Day, a decade ahead of the national one advocated by Elias Boudinot.

Mount Holly's most interesting historic buildings can be seen on an easy walking tour. Parking lot on Washington St., near Main St.

COURTHOUSE 1796   Main St. between Garden and Union Sts.

Samuel Lewis, designer of Congress Hall in Philadelphia, was the architect for this charming yellow brick building with arched doorway and windows. Regarded as one of the most noteworthy examples of Colonial architecture in the country, the courthouse is flanked by harmonizing buildings, the Surrogate's Office and the Administration Office, both erected in 1807. The sycamore trees were planted in 1805. Mon.-Fri., 9-4:30.

COUNTY JAIL 1810   Next to courthouse

In use as a prison for over 155 years, this one was built by Robert Mills, the architect who designed the wings of Independence Hall and who studied with Thomas Jefferson. In presenting his drawings, Mills included a brief which offered suggestions on the management and reform of prisoners. An inscription above the doorway reads: "Justice, Which While It Punishes Would Endeavor to Reform the Offender."

ST. ANDREWS CHURCH 1846   Main St.

The church, whose congregation received its original grant from King George III in 1765, has been beautifully restored in recent years, with jewel-like windows added.

FRIENDS MEETING HOUSE 1775, 1850   Main and Garden Sts.

This simple red brick structure was the capitol of New Jersey in November and December of 1779. Two legislative sessions were held here when it was feared that the British would invade Trenton. In 1778, when Hessians camped in Mount Holly, the church was used as a commissary and slaughterhouse. Benches still show the marks of butchers' cleavers.

BRAINERD SCHOOL   1759   35 Brainerd St.

Oldest school in the state, its name honors the Rev. John Brainerd, who taught here in 1767 and who founded the New Jersey settlement of Brotherton (now Indian Mills), the Nation's earliest Indian reservation. Mon.-Fri., 9-4:30.

STEPHEN GIRARD HOUSE *(private)*   211 Mill St.

In the basement of this house Stephen Girard in 1777 opened a shop where he sold rum, tobacco, sugar, and molasses. From this modest start he branched into foreign trade in Philadelphia and acquired a fortune with which he helped the Government finance the War of 1812. He established Girard College in Philadelphia as a school for orphan boys.

THREE TUN TAVERN   1723   67 Mill St.

In Colonial times inns were sometimes rated as to size by tuns, the measure of a hogshead of liquor. A 3-tun tavern perhaps was needed to accommodate the ironworkers of Mount Holly furnace established in 1730.

RELIEF FIRE COMPANY   15 Pine St.

This volunteer fire company, dating back to July 9, 1752, is believed to be the oldest active one in the United States. Old-style leather buckets bearing the date 1752 and the company's original name of Britannia are on display here.

JOHN WOOLMAN MEMORIAL   1783 *(museum)*   99 Branch St.

Now regarded as one of the noblest Quakers of all time, John Woolman, born near Rancocas, settled in Mount Holly at the age of 20 and soon became a successful merchant. But in later life he devoted his energies to traveling among the Quakers and persuading them not only to liberate their own slaves but to work for the abolition of all slavery. His published *Journal* has become a classic, both for its style and its creed of universal love. The 2-story brick house built on his land is now a Quaker Center. Memorabilia of Woolman are on display here in a delightful 18th-century setting which includes an old-fashioned garden. Weekdays, 9-5; Sun., 1-5. Groups by reservation: 609-AM 7-3226.

MOUNT HOLLY PARK   N end of High St.

The park surrounds the hill, Mount Holly, which rises 183 feet and gives the town its name.

Take county rd. W to . . .
RANCOCAS

Early colonists of the 17th century lived in caves along Rancocas Creek before they built their village, but when their descendants constructed a town, they made it to last, of red brick, white trimmed. Some of the Rancocas buildings date from pre-Revolutionary times, while others were constructed in the early and middle 19th century, yet all blend to create a charming village. On the main street, surveyed in 1771, is the Friends Meeting House, built a year later. The Friends School dates from 1822. In the surrounding countryside are numerous early plantation houses. Rancocas Creek, remote and secluded though it meanders near highways, has great appeal for canoeists, who favor launching at Brown's Mills for a trip down to Mount Holly. Canoes can be rented there and at Pemberton. Rancocas State Park: see Supplement.

Take Bridge St. S to Haddonfield via Rte. 537, then Rte. 41.
HADDONFIELD

A young Quaker maid of 20, Elizabeth Haddon, left her prosperous family in London to go to the wilds of West Jersey in 1701. As a child she had heard John Estaugh, a missionary, and the great William Penn talk so convincingly about new lands opened for Quakers that her father bought 500 acres. However, it was not he but Elizabeth who went to colonize the plantation of Haddon Fields. There she again met John Estaugh and, according to Longfellow's "Theologian's Tale," she proposed to the Quaker missionary. After 40 years of marriage, when John fell ill and died in the West Indies, Elizabeth wrote: "Few, if any in a married state, ever lived in sweeter harmony than we did . . ." Their lives were devoted to ministering to the Indians and in making converts to the Society of Friends.

Haddonfield's main street, lined with buttonwoods and once the great road from Burlington to Salem, has a distinctive historic flavor and some of its early dwellings have been successfully restored as shops and offices.

INDIAN KING TAVERN   1750 *(State historic site)*
     233 E. King's Hwy.
This hospitable-looking brick tavern was such a hub of Colonial traffic that the Provincial Assembly held several sessions here. When New Jersey's legislature met here in 1777 they approved Francis Hopkinson's design for the Great Seal of New Jersey. At one period Dolley Madison, who forsook subdued Quaker ways to become one of the gayest of Presidents' wives, was a frequent visitor, when the innkeeper was Hugh Creighton, her uncle. Besides the bed in which Dolley slept, the inn has many other authentic furnishings, a delightful collection of dolls and toys, and ceramics from Wingenders' pottery established in Haddonfield in 1888. One-hour guided tours. 25¢.

GREENFIELD HALL   1841 *(museum)*   343 King's Hwy.
Now the home of the Haddonfield Historical Society, this brick dwelling was built by John Gill IV, whose first ancestor here was a contemporary of Elizabeth Haddon and who built a house on this site in 1714. Tues., Thurs., 2-4:30. Free. The historical society offers a map and walking-tour directions for Haddonfield.

HOPKINS HOUSE   1742 *(private)*   23 Ellis St.

This small house, formerly on King's Highway, was the home of Elizabeth Haddon's sister Sarah and her husband Ebenezer Hopkins.

Rte. 70 E, then 541 S to Medford and Medford Lakes.
MEDFORD LAKES

The community center for residents around a chain of finger lakes with dwarf pine woodlands. Most of the shores are privately owned but the region has some pleasant drives and spots for roadside picnicking. In Colonial days, the site of Charles Read's Etna Furnace.

Return to Rte. 70; go E to . . .
LEBANON STATE FOREST

Some of the unique place names of New Jersey are clustered around this 22,216-acre forest of pines and cedars: Ong's Hat, Mt. Misery and Stop-the-Jade Run, their origin varying according to the oldtimer one talks to.

Five-acre Pakim Pond has a sand beach, bathhouse, and rustic cabins, while at Deep Hollow Pond there are shady groves for family camping. Much of the forest rises from a bed of sand, one reason for the start of the Lebanon Glass Works here in 1862. Scientific reforestation has brought back woodland destroyed for glasshouse fuel. The thousands of acres away from the campsites are among the most sequestered in all of New Jersey forests, and deer roam undisturbed except for one week's hunting in December.

VICTORY AT RED BANK

Woodbury	Swedesboro
Red Bank Battlefield	Woodstown
Ann Whitall House	Malaga
Finnish Log House	Glassboro
Camden	

FERRY TRAVELING FROM PHILADELPHIA TO CAMDEN, 1850's
The steamboat is seen about to enter a canal through Smith's Island.
Barber and Howe, Historical Collections of New Jersey

WOODBURY

Now nearly engulfed by expressways, Woodbury's Broad Street, once part of the Colonial Great Road to Salem, still has many two-century-old buildings in use. County seat of "Old Gloucester" as early as 1788, Woodbury began as a Quaker settlement in 1683 when John and Alice Wood came here from Bury, England. On October 22, 1777, the neutral Quakers found themselves in the midst of a ferocious battle at Red Bank on the Delaware when 300 Hessians were slaughtered in an American cannonade. In 1793 all of Woodbury became skywatchers when Jean-Pierre Blanchard floated in a balloon over the Delaware and landed nearby, the first airborne man in America.

The Soldiers' Memorial was designed by R. Tait McKenzie.

FRIENDS MEETING HOUSE   1716   120 N. Broad St.

Bricks for this Quaker church were burned right in Woodbury "on the side of the Creek." Still in use, the building was converted to a hospital after the Red Bank Battle. Two noted people are buried here in nameless graves: Ann Whitall, mistress of Whitall Mansion, who sat spinning as the battle raged just outside her door; and her brother John Cooper, Revolutionary patriot, whose house is still at 16 North Broad Street.

HOTEL PAUL   1720   N. Broad, opp. Meeting House
WILKINS INN

Thomas Wilkins paid ten shillings for his tavern license here in 1732. Built from surplus bricks left from the Quaker meetinghouse, the inn was later named "The American Defeating the Hessian," after the Red Bank victory of October 2, 1777.

GENERAL DAVENPORT HOUSE   1760 *(private)*   67 N. Broad St.

Considered Woodbury's most distinguished citizen, General Franklin Davenport fought in the battles of

Trenton and Princeton, helped put down the Whiskey Rebellion, was president and co-founder of Woodbury Academy, a leading Abolitionist, first surrogate of Gloucester County, and a member of the illustrious Gloucester County Fox Hunting Club.

HUNTER-LAWRENCE HOUSE 1765 *(museum)* 58 N. Broad St.

A desk once owned by Elizabeth Haddon, founder of Haddonfield, an Indian dugout canoe, old Quaker dresses, an early wooden bathtub, and rare coins are just a sampling of thousands of antiquities in this varied museum, home of Gloucester County Historical Society and patriotic organizations. Free. Wed., and by reservation. TI 5-5500.

Andrew Hunter, who was one of the "Indians" in the Greenwich tea-burning of 1774 and later a chaplain in the Continental Army, lived here when he was principal of Woodbury Academy. While a student at Woodbury Academy, James Lawrence who became one of America's great naval heroes, lived here in the house of his brother John. *(See Burlington.)*

LOW-FRANKLIN HOUSE c. 1740 *(private)* 44 N. Broad

An early log house covered by clapboard.

FRIENDSHIP FIRE HOUSE 40 Delaware St.

A rare treasure is the hand-pumped fire engine bought in 1799 for the Friendship Fire Company organized that year.

N on Broad St. to Colonial Ave.; left at Lafayette St.

CANDOR HALL 1688 1337 Lafayette Ave.

Thought to be the oldest brick house in Gloucester County, this was built by Quaker John Ladd who surveyed and plotted the city of Philadelphia. Ladd was expelled from Woodbury Meeting because as a court officer he married couples outside the Quaker faith. Ladd's Castle, as it is also known, though privately owned, is open free, by reservation; phone 609-TI 5-0618.

Return to Rte. 130. At overhead sign, "National Park," go W to end of Hessian Ave. (National Park is a town, not a federal park. The community takes its name from the fact that in 1870 Congress authorized purchase of 20 acres of the Red Bank Battlefield. Fort Mercer Park is now supervised by the Gloucester County Board of Freeholders.)

FORT MERCER PARK
RED BANK BATTLEFIELD
ANN WHITALL HOUSE 1748

Perhaps not to be seen anywhere else is an original *chevaux-de-frise*, resembling a horse's mane, like the wooden fragment of this underwater stockade, almost two centuries old, at Red Bank Battlefield. From this point on the Delaware to Fort Mifflin opposite, the Americans in 1777 had set up a mile-long barrier of enormous spiked logs capped with iron, to keep supply ships from British-held Philadelphia. But after bombarding Fort Mifflin the enemy cut a 7-foot channel through the submerged stockade, then sent Count von Donop with 2500 Hessians to mop up Fort Mercer which was held by Col. Christopher Green and 400 troops, many of them Negroes and mulattoes. Camouflaging the cannon and ordering his men to hold musket fire until almost point-blank range, Col. Green simply mowed down the Hessians. In the first charge 400 were killed or wounded and in the next attack Count von Donop himself fell and was captured, mortally wounded. The 40-minute battle was an astounding victory for the Americans.

A tall column with the figure of a soldier atop is a memorial here to courageous Col. Green and nearby is a plain gray stone put up in 1829 to mark the burial place of Count von Donop whose bravery was much admired by the Continentals. Some earthworks of the old fort still remain.

James and Ann Whitall stayed in their house during the fierce battle, and a reputable historian says that when a cannonball hurtled through a wall, Mrs. Whitall, who was spinning, probably to steady her nerves, took her wheel to the cellar. At any rate the stairwall has a patched place the size of a cannonball. The residence of the caretakers, the house has two period-style rooms and many interesting structural features. Guided tours, 9-4 daily.

Take Rte. 44 S to Gibbstown. At Repaupo Rd. turn S (left). About 1 mi. below Gibbstown, on right side of Repaupo Rd. (opp. brick house) and NW of Rte. 130 viaduct, is . . .

FINNISH LOG HOUSE   c. 1640 *(private)*   Repaupo Rd.
CHARLES NOTHNAGLE FARM

Believed to be the oldest log house in the Nation, this one, attached to the side of a white 2-story frame house, was built about 1640 by a Finn, Anthony Neilson (Antti Niilompoika), who is recorded in courthouse documents as the first taxpayer in Gloucester County. That he was a property-owner is shown in the record of his range-cattle "earmarks": "both ears a half moon out on the undersides." Within the hut is an immense corner fire-place, and a trap door leads to a loft above. Often called Swedish, the cabin is now said to be of Finnish construction because of its flat, adzed logs with dove-tailed corners. An object of much study by architects and historians, the house is often shown to visitors by the Nothnagles, whose ancestors have lived here for over 150 years.

Continue S on same rd. to . . .
REPAUPO

Now a crossroads village with an Indian name, Repaupo was long described as the most Swedish settlement remaining in New Jersey, but it no longer warrants this label. The whole Delaware region south and east of here was being explored and settled by Scandinavians well before the official Swedish expedition of 1638. Without blood-letting but with 7 ships and 700 men Peter Stuyvesant took over such posts as Fort Elfsborg *(see Finns Point)* on the Delaware and put an end to New Sweden in 1655.

Continue S to Swedesboro.

SWEDESBORO

Early known as Raccoon, this was a major settlement of the Swedes, who were colonizing the Delaware Valley long before the English take-over of New Jersey in 1664. The Swedish village established here about 1642 became an important stop on the Camden-Salem stageline.

OLD SWEDE'S CHURCH   1784   King's Highway at Church St.

On special occasions in this beautiful pink-brick church the communion service of beaten silver that was purchased by the first congregation is displayed. The silver is inscribed "Trinity Church att Rackoon 1731" and at that date was used in a log building. Originally Lutheran, the congregation, succumbing to the all-pervasive English influence of the 18th century, became Episcopalian. As the most important congregation in New Sweden after the one at Wilmington, Del., Raccoon's church had such celebrated pastors as the naturalist Peter Kalm, who lived in Swedesboro for one winter, and Nicholas Collin (1770-1786), the last clergyman sent to America by the King of Sweden. Through Collin's efforts the present handsome church was built. Still with the original pews and gallery and handblown window panes, Old Swedes' is almost unaltered except for a tower added in 1838. The congregation has the original deed for 100 acres, a plot now reduced to a brick-walled yard mellowed by ancient boxwood. Among old sycamores, barely legible markers of Swedish colonists are intermingled with tombstones of such Revolutionary leaders as Colonel Thomas Heston and Colonel Boddo Otto. Church is usually open daily; inquire at rectory, 208 King's Highway.

Take King's Highway (Rte. 551) S from Swedesboro

to fork. Where 551 curves left, take unmarked *blacktop road S. Church on right, 3 mi. from Swedesboro ctr.*

MORAVIAN CHURCH   1789   Sharptown Rd. S of Swedesboro

Followers of Jan Huss, the Moravians, coming to Pennsylvania in 1740, built the town of Bethlehem. One of their missionary outposts was this simple red brick structure, with separate doorways for the brethren and the sisters. Pastor Schmidt, preacher in the earlier log church here, wrote in his diary that on Oct. 22, 1777, the cannonading at the Red Bank Battle could be heard here, nearly 20 miles away. *(See also Hope, a Moravian village in Warren County.)*

Go S to . . .

WOODSTOWN

FRIENDS MEETING HOUSE   1785   North Main St.

Less austere than some New Jersey meetinghouses this church still has a saddle-high door for graceful dismounting from horseback.

OAKHOLM *(private)*   164 East Ave.

Choice collections of Jerseyana sometimes exhibited in Salem open-house tours.

GARDEN COUNTIES

For miles around here, as far south as Salem and Bridgeton and east beyond Vineland, this is great peach-growing country, an exquisite sight in April when the leafless trees are masses of salmon-colored blossoms. Topping others in vegetable production, Cumberland and Gloucester counties alone warrant New Jersey's name of the Garden State. The millions of bushels of asparagus, tomatoes, and sweet potatoes keep the State's major processors of canned and frozen foods at peak operation. Tourists who visit here at well-timed seasons come away with fresh-picked fruits and vegetables at bargain prices.

Take Rte. 40 E to Elmer and Malaga at junction of Rte. 47.

MALAGA LAKE

This small clear lake with a bathing beach is one of several nearby on branches of the Maurice River: *Iona Lake* at *Porchtown; Willow Grove Lake,* south of Malaga; and *Wilson's Lake.* Handblown window panes were made in Malaga as early as 1813 by the Franklin Glass Works.

Go N on Rte. 47.

FRANKLINVILLE

Little Ease Run and the lake here are popular with fishermen. Franklinville Inn, at the crossroads, was an early stagecoach stop.

CLAYTON

When P. T. Barnum brought Jenny Lind, the Swedish Nightingale, to America for a concert tour in 1850 the nation was mad for souvenirs of the singer. Here at the Fislerville Glass Works (extinct) a famous historic flask was created, the Jenny Lind calabash bottle. Reproductions of this liquor flask, as well as other bottles and pitchers, are being blown today in Clayton at the *Clevenger Glass Works,* which was started as a one-pot furnace during the Depression.

GLASSBORO

As the Wistar Works near Alloway was the first successful glasshouse in America, so the succeeding one, that which the seven Stanger brothers opened here during the Revolution, can be said to have been the most influential of its time. These virtuoso glassblowers were among the most sought after of their day and carried their skills to the Amelung glassworks in Maryland, the New Geneva works near Pittsburgh, the Louisville works,

WHITNEY GLASSWORKS, GLASSBORO

Founded in the Revolution by the seven Stanger brothers, virtuoso glass blowers whose "South-Jersey-style" glass is now in museum collections.

Courtesy of Rutgers University

the Ellenville factory, and many others in New York and Pennsylvania. Today the free-blown "South Jersey style" ware they developed is in such great glass collections as those of the Metropolitan, Winterthur, the Philadelphia, Toledo, Newark, and Corning museums. Concentrating solely on glassmaking, the Stangers were succeeded as managers by prominent Revolutionary figures, Colonel Thomas Heston and Thomas Carpenter, and they in turn by the Whitney brothers in 1842. It was the latter who produced the popular "booze" bottle, made for a Philadelphia distiller named E. C. Booz whose product moved fast in log-cabin-shaped flasks.

FRANKLIN HOUSE *(inn)*   Five Points

From the time that glassmaker Solomon Stanger applied for a tavern license here in 1781, there has always been an inn at this corner. Opposite Franklin House a marker indicates the site of the first Stanger Glass Works. The five roads here were once paths made by glassworkers going from their homes to the furnace.

GLASSBORO STATE COLLEGE   1923

A 4-year accredited college, Glassboro's attractive campus was originally the 55-acre estate "Holly Bush," of the Whitney family. The college's collection of South Jersey glass given by the late Charles A. Philhower, archeologist and historian, is sometimes exhibited in the library building. Here also is the Frank Stewart Collection, on New Jersey history.

Glassboro was the rendezvous for an elect group, the Old Gloucester Fox Hunting Club, founded at Hugg's Tavern, Gloucester in 1766, whose members continued to ride to hounds until 1819. Whipper-in of the hounds was Jonas Cattell, a tireless 6-footer who at 50 outran an Indian in a trial of speed from Mount Holly to Woodbury, over 22 miles.

Continue N on Rtes. 47, 41, 42, and 30 to Camden.

CAMDEN

Camden has been making industrial history ever since the wood-burning *John Bull* locomotive first hauled the cars of the Camden and Amboy Railroad in 1834. With broad frontage on the Delaware, the city has been a natural for shipyards. In the 1950s and 1960s three major ones were: The RTC Shipbuilding Corporation, the John H. Mathis Company, and the New York Shipbuilding Corporation. The latter in its 70 years launched over 600 ships, the most famous of which, the N. S. *Savannah,* is the world's first atom-powered merchant vessel.

Starting a preserve factory in Camden in 1869 Joseph Campbell and Abraham Anderson made little progress until a chemist joined the firm in 1897, at $7.50 per week. He was John T. Dorrance whose method of condensing soups in tin cans brought him a fortune and the presidency of Campbell's Soup Company.

CAMPBELL MUSEUM 1970
   Campbell Soup Co., Campbell Pl., near Ben Franklin Bridge

Devoted to the theme of beautiful soup tureens dating from 500 B.C., some appraised at $25,000, this exhibit of rare soup servers, in pottery, porcelain, silver, imaginatively created in shapes from swans to ships, is having a magnetic effect. Could it be saying that man does not live by bread alone? Mon.-Fri., 9-5. Weekend guided tours by appt., 609-964-4000. Free.

   From Rte. 30 take Memorial Ave. (at Sear's center) to Kaighn Ave.; turn right at Park Ave. to . . .
POMONA HALL 1726 (*museum*)   NE cor. Euclid Ave. and Park Blvd.
CAMDEN COUNTY HISTORICAL SOCIETY

Near *Farnham Park,* this imposing Georgian mansion of Flemish-bond brick was built by Joseph Cooper, Jr., its well-preserved interior suggesting the owner's opulent life. The house is now a memorial to Charles S. Boyer, and the library contains the historian's papers as well as 9,000 volumes on New Jersey and United States history. Besides an early American kitchen and a Colonial bedroom, the excellent museum of the Camden County Historical Society has Indian artifacts, Civil War relics and Jersey glass. Cobbler, blacksmith, and harness shops. Tues.-Fri., and Sun.: 12:30-4:30. Free 1-hour tours.

WALT WHITMAN TOMB   Harleigh Cemetery, end of
Park Blvd.

Two years before his death on March 26, 1892, Walt
Whitman began planning his tomb. The inscription,
"For That of Me Which Is to Die," was written by the
poet and engraved at his request.

*Follow Park Blvd. to its opposite end at Haddon
Ave., then Seventh St. to its end at Pyne Point Park
to . . .*

JOSEPH COOPER HOUSE   c. 1700   N end of Seventh
St. at Erie St., in Pyne Point Park

Probably the oldest in the city the stone house was
built by the son of William Cooper, Quaker pioneer
whose activities gave Camden its early name of Cooper's
Ferry. In 1681 he built a house and named the tract on
which Pyne Point Park is situated.

Go E to . . .

BENJAMIN COOPER HOUSE   1734 *(private)*   NE cor.
Erie and Point Sts.

A British-Hessian outpost commanded by Colonel
Abercrombie in the Revolution, this 2-story stone and
brick house was then called The Stone Jug.

Go S on Third St. to . . .

WALT WHITMAN HOUSE   *(State historic site)*
330 Mickle St., nr. Third St.

One of America's greatest poets chose to live here in
his last eight years. After he had suffered a paralytic
stroke at the age of 53, Walt Whitman moved to Camden
to live with his brother, then later bought this house.
It was here that he prepared the final edition of *Leaves
of Grass* and wrote the poem, "Prayer of Columbus."
People in Camden bought him a horse and buggy, and
he often made trips to the shore at Absecon, Laurel
Springs, and Atlantic City. Writing at the parlor window
of this little house, he lived in a clutter of manuscripts
and personal belongings. Many of the latter are still here;
his books, his clock, his felt hat, his easy chair, his bed-
side "splashtub," and his shoes give a sense of his presence as if he had just stepped out to chat with neighbors.

TIDEWATER COUNTRY

FENWICK'S SALEM AND GREENWICH TEA-BURNERS

Fort Mott State Park
Finns Point
Salem
Elsinboro

Alloway
Hancock House
Greenwich
Roadstown

From Exit 1 of the N. J. Tpke. take Rte. 49 S, through Salem, to . . .

FORT MOTT STATE PARK
FINNS POINT NATIONAL MONUMENT
KILCOHOOK WILDLIFE REFUGE

With the advent of the missile age Fort Mott, largely intact except for armaments, becomes as great a curiosity as a colonial stockade. As early as 1837 the national government set up the Finns Point Battery which could rake shipping coming up the Delaware. Then in the Civil War Pea Patch Island, opposite Finns Point, was fortified, becoming Fort Delaware. The present elaborate complex of tunnels, gun emplacements, moat, and ordnance buildings on the mainland was begun in 1896, and the name changed to honor General Gershom Mott, Commander of the New Jersey Volunteers in the Civil War. As late as 1922 a permanent garrison was stationed in the dungeon-like fort, which can be explored. The promenade deck now offers a fine view of Delaware River ships which pass within a few hundred yards. Picnic groves and tables. Playfields. Fishing.

The expected naval war in the Delaware never came, and so Pea Patch Fort was converted to a prison for Confederate soldiers. By the close of 1863 some 12,000 prisoners were squeezed onto an island adequate for 4000. Some escaped to the Underground Railroad in Salem which was helping slaves to flee in the opposite direction. Smallpox, dysentery, and cholera took terrible toll of those on the island. Over 2400 died and were buried north of Fort Mott. In 1875 the Federal Government placed the 85-foot obelisk here on which are inscribed the names of military prisoners who died at Fort Delaware.

North of Fort Mott Park is *Kilcohook National Wildlife Refuge,* a 1500-acre sanctuary mainly for waterfowl. Hunting and trapping forbidden.

In colonizing expeditions which Sweden sent up the Delaware between 1638 and 1655 were a number of Finns, and evidence is strong that Finnish explorers were in South Jersey as early as the Dutch in the 1620's. For over 300 years the name Finns Point has clung to this cape.

Return to Rte. 49S for . . .
SALEM

Rarely has a man received such a bargain as when Major John Fenwick bought from Lord Berkeley all of West Jersey for £1000 and, as bonus, 100 beaver skins a year. After having fought for Cromwell and been converted to the Quaker faith, Major Fenwick in 1675 sailed up the Delaware to colonize his extensive kingdom. Envisioning a splendid city he called it New Salem, with a Broad Way 100 feet wide and 16-acre plots along it. Fenwick called himself the Lord Proprietor of his colony, to such effect that twice he was sent in chains to New York on charges of impersonating a royal governor. But while his Quaker colonists prospered, Fenwick's debts mounted, and 7 years after arrival he was forced to sell for trifling sums nine-tenths of his holdings, mainly to

William Penn. Embittered, accusing friends of trickery and betrayal, Fenwick died a year later; his grave is now lost. The bargain proved to be Penn's, for with his New Jersey profits he founded the city of Philadelphia.

Yet Fenwick's Salem thrived, first as a busy port, then as a glassmaking center, which it is today. Still well preserved are many historic buildings and charming "towne" houses, testament of Salem's history as first English-speaking settlement on the Delaware.

THE SALEM OAK   W. B'way. near Fourth St.

Because of its age, symmetry, splendid health, and historic associations, the great white Salem Oak in the Friends Burial Ground is one of the most distinguished American trees. Estimated to be half a millennium in age the Salem Oak is over 80 feet high and more than 30 feet in circumference. Cared for by the Society of Friends, the tree thrives and each year its acorns are collected to fill world-wide requests. John Fenwick sat beneath the tree when he bartered with the Indians for his Salem territory in 1675, and about a century later the Queen's Rangers under Maj. John Simcoe marched along Broadway past the Salem Oak.

ALEXANDER GRANT HOUSE   1721   *(museum)*
   79-83 Market St.
SALEM COUNTY HISTORICAL SOCIETY

These three connecting houses, dating from the early 18th century, have room-settings with fine Salem furniture and paneling of distinctive character. Accessories of rare china and pewter. Articles from the Wistar Glass Works, Indian artifacts, and early documents add to the interest. Wed. afternoons, except July and Aug. 75¢.

FIRST PRESBYTERIAN CHURCH 1854 Opp. Grant
House

The 184-foot spire is lighted at night. The pewter
Communion Service used in the original church of 1821
and the other historical items are frequently displayed
on the second floor.

ROBERT GIBBONS JOHNSON HOUSE 1802
90 Market St.

Salem County offices

Col. Johnson who built this impressive red brick house
became a hero in South Jersey when he stood on the
courthouse steps and ate tomatoes to prove they were not
poisonous as was commonly believed. He is also known
as Salem County's first historian. Formerly at the rear of
the house was an octagonal structure said to have been
the first brick law office in the Colonies. It is now located
at the rear of the Grant House.

FRIENDS MEETING HOUSE 1772
E. Broad, at Walnut

One of the most interesting of the many Quaker meetinghouses in Salem County, this building has handblown
window panes thought to have been made at the Wistar
Glass Works, near Alloway.

HOLMELAND 1750-1784 *(private)* Elsinboro on the
Delaware, 4 mi. S of Salem ctr.

An imposing three-wing red brick mansion erected for
Benjamin Holm, a colonel of the militia during the
Revolution. Owner of 1600 acres and a ferry which was
the terminus of the old King's Highway, Col. Holm's
house and ferry were set afire by the British at the time
of the Hancock's Bridge massacre in March, 1778. The
British carried off his grandfather clock but the doughty
colonel finally brought it back from New York and today it is still keeping time. Furnished with rare antiques,
the house is pictured in Dorothy and Richard Pratt's
Guide to Early American Homes.

ELSINBORO POINT Nr. Holmeland and school
SITE OF FORT ELFSBORG
There is not even a "land" mark at *Fort Elfsborg*, for
the Delaware tides have long since washed away all trace
of the bastion built in 1643 by Johan Printz, despotic and
able governor of New Sweden. Because mosquitoes "almost ate the people up there," the post was nicknamed
"Myggenborg" or "Fort Mosquito," but it was not insects
to which the Swedes succumbed but rather the insatiable
appetite of Peter Stuyvesant for conquest. New Sweden
was swallowed up by bloodless take-overs of the Dutch,
then the English. Today the only known record of the
Finns and Swedes in the Delaware Valley is in their
names, old documents, and a few churches.

"FLEMISH BOND" BRICKWORK

Fascinating to connoisseurs of historic houses are the
many in Salem and Cumberland counties with elab-
orately patterned brickwork. Not only are walls set in
herringbone and zigzag designs but the bricks are in
contrasting colors of red and blue, the latter, achieved
by heating the bricks until they became vitrified. Initials
of the owner and his wife as well as the date are sometimes "worked" in brick at a gable end, looking like a
cross-stitch sampler. Patterns such as these are seen in
English country houses of Kent and Sussex and have
been traced back to 15th-century France; hence the name
"English bond" or "Flemish bond." South Jersey has at
least 103 such houses, more than in all the rest of the
country. Many are to be seen in the countryside around
Salem and Greenwich and are sometimes scheduled for
open-house tours in spring.

*From Salem ctr., 3 mi. SE on Rte. 49 to Quinton,
then Rte. 581 to Alloway.*
ALLOWAY

The first successful glassworks in America was started
near here in 1739 by Caspar Wistar, a German who set-

tled in Philadelphia. Wistar's imported German blowers created forms that have come to be known as the South Jersey style which had great influence on later glass made in New York, Pennsylvania, and Ohio. No building remains of the Wistar Glass Works, which operated until the Revolution; the site, now on private land, is about two miles northeast of Alloway.

JOSIAH REEVES HOUSES *(private)* N. Greenwich St.
   These three fine houses were erected by Josiah Reeves, an Alloway ship-builder of the early 19th century. The brick dwelling on the north Reeves built for himself in 1826, the middle frame one (1817) and the other brick house (1848), for his sons.

QUINTON'S BRIDGE at Alloway Creek, Rte. 49, Quinton

Maj. John Simcoe's battalion ambushed and killed some of the rebel militia headed by Col. Benjamin Holm on March 18, 1778. The Americans were saved from further disaster when Andrew Bacon grabbed an ax and, under fire, cut away the draw section of Quinton's Bridge. Monument 200 feet south of bridge.

   *From Quinton take road SW, to Greenwich. 4 mi.
S of Salem is . . .*
HANCOCK HOUSE 1734 *(State historical museum)* Hancock's Bridge

The murderous hatred between Loyalist and Patriot Jerseymen during the Revolution reached its nadir in a massacre within this house. Events began when Washington at Valley Forge sent General Wayne to forage in Salem County for food. Eluding the English at Philadelphia, "Mad Anthony" succeeded in rounding up about 300 head of cattle, and Washington later credited the survival of his starving army to these "good offices of the people of South Jersey." In reprisal the British sent Maj. John Simcoe to Salem. At night his 300 men ambushed 30 home guards asleep in the house of Judge Hancock. Simcoe's men barricaded doors and stabbed some of the men as they slept, then drove the rest into the attic where they were savagely bayoneted. The bloodstains are still there. Judge Hancock made the mistake of returning home that night and in the darkness he was killed, too.

The 2-story house, an excellent example of diapered brickwork, bears in the gable the initials of the owners, William and Sarah Hancock.

CEDAR PLANK HOUSE

On the grounds of the Hancock property is a reconstructed plank house made of South Jersey cedar.

ALLOWAYS CREEK MEETING HOUSE   1756

Hancock's Bridge

The saddle-high door was a convenience in dismounting from a horse. This Quaker edifice is little changed from early times. Old farm implements in shed.

GREENWICH   1684

A picture-book village, Greenwich was founded, like Salem, by Maj. John Fenwick, who ordered "Ye Great Streete" to be 100 feet wide for an entire mile. Since then the maples and sycamores have arched tall over Great Street, but otherwise Greenwich clocks seem to have stopped in the 18th century (except for a gas pump). Many of the village residents, who treasure their homes filled with antiques, hope that old Greenwich will never really catch up with the space age.

Unlike placid Salem, Greenwich in Colonial days partook of Fenwick's own obstreperous nature, and in 1774 a rebellion occurred that led to a grand jury hearing. Ten nights before the event, the brig *Greyhound* snaked up Cohansey Creek with a cargo of tea that had been refused at Philadelphia. The ship's captain, learning of a sympathetic Tory, Dan Bowen, in Greenwich, unloaded the unwanted tea in his cellar. In the dark of December

22, householders were astonished to see on Great Street an enormous bonfire, 'round which Indians leapt in a war dance. Fuel for the fire was tea—the *Greyhound*'s entire cargo.

When the names of the "Indians" leaked out, the British Tea Institute insisted that the "hoodlums" be punished, but even after two tries the Chief Justice was unable to find a Tory grand jury that would bring in true bills against the tea-burners, ably defended by such patriots as Elias Boudinot and Joseph Bloomfield. When the people of Cumberland County were free to choose their own officials in July, 1776, one of their first acts was to elect a tea-burner, Joel Fithian, as high sheriff. Ringleader Ebenezer Elmer, like a number of the Greenwich and Bridgeton patriots, was active in the Revolution: regimental surgeon, brigadier general, and, later, congressman.

In 1908 the State of New Jersey erected a marble monument to the tea-burners which is inscribed with the names of 23 young men known to have joined in the war dance.

RICHARD WOOD MANSION 1795

Bacons Neck and Great Sts.

The classically simple doorway, fireplaces, and woodwork mark this as the home of a man of taste. Richard Wood was also a man of great wealth, an early entrepreneur, and owner of thousands of South Jersey acres. Peacocks once strutted in the garden when this was the summer home of Richard's son George, the physician who was co-author in 1833 of the first U.S. Dispensatory of drugs. Now owned by the Cumberland County Historical Society. Sun., 2-5. Apr. 1 to Nov. 1.

RICHARD WOOD STORE 1795   Bacons Neck St.

Built for Richard Wood this is one of the oldest retail stores in the country.

STONE TAVERN 1734 *(private)* Great St.

In 1748 several court sessions were held in this stone inn, but when Cohansey Bridge (Bridgeton) was named the county seat, local citizens, claiming the election and the courthouse had been stolen, rioted and broke the tavern's chairs and glassware.

GIBBON HOUSE 1730 *(museum)* Great St.
CUMBERLAND COUNTY HISTORICAL SOCIETY

The splendid house of Nicholas Gibbon, shipowner and merchant in this once busy port, is restored, with authentic room settings.

A noteworthy example of red and blue Flemish-bond brickwork, the 3-story house has the date on a gable plaque. Arched corner cupboards and a 9-foot fireplace are well preserved, as are the interiors of most Greenwich houses.

Important collections of Ware chairs, 19th century pottery and porcelain, a roomful of children's playthings. Frequent lectures on collectibles and history. Sat., Sun., 2-5. Apr. to Nov. 1. 25¢.

FRIENDS MEETING HOUSE 1771 Great St.

On a shady knoll surveying the length of Ye Great Streete and Cohansey Creek, this impressive meetinghouse of red brick bespeaks a prosperous congregation. First session of Cumberland County Court was held here May 31, 1748. Key can be obtained from Harding House, next to firehouse.

SHEPPARD'S FERRY HOUSE *(private)* Cohansey Wharf

John Sheppard in 1767 was granted a franchise to run a ferry from here to Fairfield for 999 years, but the boat service was abandoned after only 71 years when Cohansey Bridge was built and the new county seat became "the big town." Oldest portion of this house probably dates from about John Fenwick's time, 1686, with wings added in 1734 and 1900. It was here that the brig *Greyhound* disgorged its hateful cargo of taxed tea.

HANCOCK'S HARBOR

Downstream half a mile a marina attracts fishermen, duck-hunters, boatmen, and water-skiers.

At jog in Great St. near the Brownstone School House (1811), take rte. to Sheppard's Mill. On right side, near Great St. is white frame Fithian House.

PHILIP VICKERS FITHIAN HOUSE   c. 1750   *(private)*
Sheppard's Mill Rd., nr. Molly Wheaton Rd.

Exuberant tea-burners met at Philip Fithian's house to don Indian disguises before raiding the cellar of Tory Dan Bowen. Two years later Philip, who had been married only eleven months to his beloved Laura Beatty and had become an army chaplain, was dead. A Princeton classmate of Philip Freneau and Aaron Burr, Fithian, despite his premature death at 29, has left a testament of his keen mind in two journals published in this century, diaries which, written mainly in Virginia, give rare insight into 18th-century life in America.

Continue E to . . .

ROADSTOWN

In this crossroads village Maskell Ware about 1790 began making such excellent slat-back chairs that his sons and grandsons continued the tradition down to the present century, and now most of this fine furniture is in important collections. The corner store here dates from Maskell Ware's time.

COHANSEY BAPTIST CHURCH   1802

A country church of marked architectural distinction, its doorways patterned after Christopher Wren designs, "Old Cohansey" was opened amid tragedy. One of the congregation, Isaac Wheaton had gone to Philadelphia to select a stone for the church doorstep and took his daughter Hannah along to choose her trousseau. On their return voyage the ship was hit by a squall and capsized. Wheaton and his daughter, the captain's son, and another passenger were drowned. When the ship was righted, the stone doorstep was still aboard. It remains today at the church's south door.

HOWELL HOUSE *(private)* Rd. to Shiloh

The low white house set back from Shiloh Road (first house on left, nearest Roadstown) was the home of the Howell twins where some of the tea-burning "Indians" met before gathering by night at Philip Fithian's house. Lewis and Richard Howell were both active later in the Revolution. His taste for intrigue perhaps whetted by the tea party, Richard engaged in some secret work for George Washington. From 1792 to 1801 Richard Howell was Governor of New Jersey.

From Salem to Dennis Creek, the shore along Delaware Bay offers many public hunting and fishing grounds.

By following the highway east from Roadstown to Bridgeton, this tour connects with the Bridgeton-Millville-Vineland Tour.

GLASSBLOWERS AND GARDENERS

Bridgeton	Vineland
Port Norris—Bivalve	Parvin State Park
Millville	Centerton Inn
Holly Grove	Seabrook

The triangle formed by Bridgeton, Millville, and Vineland encompasses one of the greatest glassmaking centers in the United States, a reputation the area has enjoyed ever since the War of 1812, when adolescent American industry came of age. Today, thanks to these three towns, Cumberland outranks all New Jersey counties in glassmaking, in which the State is the Nation's sixth top producer. Because coastal South Jersey was a sea floor some 50 million years ago, the land has furnished a seemingly inexhaustible source of fine silica sand, so desirable for making clear glass. In some sections along the Delaware River these deposits are estimated to be 300 feet deep.

Fruitful above ground as well, this region has bountiful harvests of strawberries, peaches, blueberries, apples, and cranberries.

BRIDGETON

Richard Hancock, John Fenwick's surveyor who plotted the towns of Salem and Greenwich, built the first mill here at Cohansey Bridge. But Scotch Presbyterians from New England, rather than Quakers, put a more lasting stamp on Bridgeton. Today it has a decidedly Southern flavor, from wisteria in the gardens to crab cakes on restaurant menus.

LIBERTY BELL Cumberland County Court House, Broad St.

Bridgetonians like to say that the only difference between their Liberty Bell and the one in Independence Hall is that theirs isn't cracked. Bought in 1763 by citizens of Cohansey Bridge this bell too rang out the stirring news when Independence from Britain was declared. Rebellion rose up two years earlier when youths from Bridgeton were ringleaders in the tea-burning "Indian" war dance at Greenwich. The Liberty Bell is on view weekdays in the main corridor of the courthouse.

POTTER'S TAVERN *(city historic site)* 49 W. Broad St., opp. Court House

A popular gathering spot for patriotic hotspurs prior to the Revolution, this tavern was where a New Jersey weekly news sheet, *The Plain Dealer,* was written and displayed, an incitement to independence from the Crown. Restored, the building was opened as a museum in 1973.

BRIDGETON PARK Commerce St.

Over a thousand acres of wooded hilly terrain with two lakes and a winding millrace a mile and a half long comprise a lovely city park, rife with laurel, azalea, dogwood, and rhododendron. In midsummer Egyptian lotuses bloom in profusion on the raceway, a romantic spot for canoeists. A man and his two sons are said to have dug the raceway by hand in 1814, a year's work at the rate of 50 cents a day. Sunset Lake has a small beach and there is bathing at Tumbling Dam as well. The zoo has swans, peacocks, deer, and monkeys. Canoe rentals at 68 Franklin Drive.

THE NAIL HOUSE MUSEUM 1815 Antiquarian League of Bridgeton W. Commerce and Atlantic Sts., just within entrance of Bridgeton Park.

No exhibit of old nails, this! Instead, a handsomely displayed, choice collection of toys, antique banks, lighting devices, dolls, Jersey glass and ceramics. Carefully restored by the Bridgeton Antiquarian League, the tree-shaded, white clapboard house was once the paymaster's office at the early nail factory employing 500 workers. Frequent exhibits from private collections. Thurs., Fri. 1-4; Sun. 2-5. Free.

OLD BROAD STREET CHURCH 1792 Broad St. at West Ave.

Little known, yet one of the most beautiful Georgian churches in the United States, this is the pride of all Bridgeton and, though no longer used for regular services, is carefully preserved. On a 2-acre plot donated by Quaker Mark Miller after the Revolution, this Presbyterian edifice is of great size for its time. Vine-draped, the brick exterior is well proportioned but it is the pristine white interior with superb architectural detail that catches attention: the high pulpit lighted by an oil lamp, and overhead the Seeing Eye, tall multi-paned Gothic windows letting in floods of light upon boxed pews, the gallery on three sides. Seeming anachronisms are two black cast-iron stoves set in brick-paved aisles, but the stoves are fully as historic as the church. They bear the stamp "Jacob Downing, Atzion Furnace," one of New Jersey's most important early ironworks (*see Wharton State Forest*).

After £600 had been raised for the church and yet more funds were needed, a lottery was authorized by General Ebenezer Elmer, member of the Assembly. The lottery produced $1500, but despite all the records connected with it, the creator of the architectural treasure is still a mystery.

Once the church was the scene of a murder trial, conducted there to accommodate the crowd. A sailor, John

Patterson, convicted of killing his captain, was sentenced to death and broke into a frenzy, then later committed suicide.

A service to which all are welcome is held at 10:00 A.M. on Thanksgiving. At other times, apply to caretaker.

GENERAL JAMES GILES HOUSE 1792 *(private)* 143 Broad St.

A New York artillery officer under Lafayette's command, Gen. James Giles received a sword from the French marquis. On his triumphal return in 1824, the sword was handsomely remounted and worn by him at the reception tendered by the New Jersey Society of the Cincinnati.

About 0.5 mi. on Port Norris Rd., at New England Crossroads . . .

OLD STONE CHURCH 1780 South Ave.

The sturdy sandstone building of the Presbyterians has such early features as bricked-in aisles and a high aloof pulpit.

From Bridgeton: Rte. 49 to Millville; or take side trip via Rte. 533 S to . . .

PORT NORRIS AND BIVALVE
MAURICETOWN
PORT ELIZABETH

In this tidewater country one can still catch unexpected glimpses of the past: along byways to the Delaware beaches salt hay is being harvested just as it was in Colonial times.

Rightly named, Bivalve not long ago shipped out mountains of mollusks, as did Port Norris, until a blight hit the oyster beds here. Now under the scientific care of Rutgers University and the State Department of Environmental Protection, bivalves are multiplying again. Harbor life connected with them makes for much interest, not to mention good photos.

On the east shore of the Maurice River, Dorchester and Leesburg have built boats since the days of the clippers, skills later applied to wartime vessels and now to pleasure craft.

Half a century before the English took over the Delaware, Swedes were in this region, not merely as navigators and explorers but so well settled that by 1637 they had built a church at Port Elizabeth. Today the only trace of their pioneering is in such Scandinavian names as Peterson and Vanaman, and an occasional 2-story house of cedar boards weathered to old pewter. James Lee, founder of industrial Millville, had a windowglass factory in Port Elizabeth as early as 1800, when most folks were still using oiled paper for panes.

Rte. 47 to Millville.

MILLVILLE

Heirs of Col. Joseph Buck, Revolutionary officer, were selling for a song the lots he laid out in 1795 for a prospective village here. Not until a Belfast Irishman, James Lee, came to open a glass factory in Millville in 1806 did it begin to show signs of life. From then on Millville has never been without a glass factory and now has two of the nation's largest.

Another catalyst like Lee was David C. Wood of Greenwich who, buying into the Union Company in 1814, put it into the bog-iron business, with a smelter at nearby Cumberland and a Millville foundry that made waterpipes, fences, lampposts, and tons of firebacks and stove plates stamped "Cumberland." When bog iron and wood fuel grew scarce, the company, in 1854, switched to textiles and continued as the Millville Manufacturing Company. Because it diversified this is the only one of all the early ironworks in South Jersey which has survived.

WOOD MANSION 1804 Columbia Ave. nr. W. Green St.

Enlarged since it was built by David C. Wood, the ironmaster, this attractive house now has 20 rooms. Unusual in early South Jersey architecture are its ornamental iron pillars. Made of ironstone, mined near

Cumberland, the house, formerly headquarters of the Millville Historical Society, has been converted to offices.

WOLF'S HOLLY GROVE   Rte. 49, 4 mi. E of Millville
Just before Christmas in 1926 Clarence Wolf thought it would be nice to send packs of South Jersey holly to his customers. The response was so enthusiastic that Mr. Wolf began raising holly. One thing led to another until he became the owner of this 16-acre holly grove and president of the Holly Society of America. Through Mr. Wolf's gifts many local lawns now have holly trees and Millville has been designated "the Holly City of America." Berries from this grove with over 11,000 trees of 16 different varieties have probably appeared on more magazine covers than any other kind. Amid the grove is a 135-year-old farmhouse, restored in Williamsburg style, which has the largest collection of holly-decorated antique china in the country. One room is furnished completely with holly wood. Mon.-Sat. 8-4:30.

Rte. 47 N to Vineland.
VINELAND
When Charles K. Landis, a Philadelphia lawyer, bought 32,000 acres of flat, swampy, and fireswept real estate here in 1861, even the sellers, the Richard Woods family of Millville, doubted his good sense. He was even more suspect when he announced that the main street in this wasteland would be an avenue 100 feet wide and that around a square-mile section would be other 100-foot avenues all lined with double rows of shade trees. Years later Landis was able to say, "I rightly expected that this would make one of the most beautiful places in the country and that the lack of natural scenery would be made up by the labor of art." Vineland's residences, set back as Landis ordered, have lush plantings, among them azalea and wisteria which thrive in South Jersey's mild climate.

Gazing at his cutover land the pioneer city planner conjured up vineyards, and for its first quarter century Vineland's principal income derived from grapes, for the culture of which many Italians were brought here. In 1869 a local dentist, Dr. Thomas B. Welch, originated a method for preventing fermentation of grape juice. Developed originally for church Communion services, Welch's grape juice zoomed to national popularity.

For all this liquid refreshment there had to be containers, and Vineland obliged with hundreds of hand-blown glass ones from 20-gallon demijohns to half-pint flasks. A Vineland tinsmith, John L. Mason, in the 1850's invented the first fruit jar with a screw-top tight enough to preserve foods for months. The simple-appearing device revolutionized not only home-canning methods but eating habits and nutrition. Clayton Parker of Bridgeton is credited with blowing the first workable Mason jar, at the Crowleytown glassworks. The first successful glass linings for vacuum jugs were hand-blown at Vineland.

Not only utility glass but beautifully designed tableware was created in Vineland, particularly in the 1920's at Victor Durand's Flint Glass Company. Both master blower and designer here, Swedish-born Emil J. Larson left a heritage of free-blown glass remarkable for beauty of color and form.

VINELAND HISTORICAL SOCIETY   S. Seventh and Elmer Sts.

A large collection of Indian artifacts, also shells and minerals. The Charles K. Landis Room has a life-size portrait and a marble bust of the founder of Vineland, as well as his diary and family memorabilia. Among the interesting exhibits is one of the large hand-blown glass cylinders or rollers from which window panes were cut, a process made obsolete by automation about 1918. An addition for a museum of Jersey glass is under way. Various American antiques and a sizable library, Sat., 1-4.

6 mi. W of Vineland, Rte. 540 nr. Centerton is . . .

PARVIN STATE PARK

This is a beautiful woodland park of 1025 acres with abundant flora and bird life. Parvin Lake, nearly 100 acres, formed by damming Muddy Run which once powered sawmills and gristmills here, offers good fishing. Campsites here, and attractive rustic cabins at Thundergust Pond. Swimming and picnicking. Boats and canoes for rent.

YE OLDE CENTERTON INN   Jctn. of Rtes. 540 and 533

In Colonial days this was a coaching inn on the "Grate Egg Harbor" Road and a relay point intersecting the busy stage route between Port Greenwich and Philadelphia. The white clapboard inn is now a restaurant with red-vested waiters and old-time atmosphere. A country store, coach house, and stables. Buggy rides an extra attraction in summer.

HIKING TRAILS

As a labor of love for the joys of walking in the wilds, a federation of hiking clubs known as the New York–New Jersey Trail Conference maintains nearly 500 miles of footpaths in northern New Jersey and southern New York. More than 60 different trails in wooded and wilderness areas are marked and kept open, most of them interconnected to offer a well-planned network. Among the most famous is the Appalachian Trail running atop Sussex County's Kittatinny Mountains into New York. The Trail Conference has even placed lean-tos at strategic locations here. About 50 miles of such trails lie in New Jersey's Wyanokie region (Norvin Green State Forest), and on Bearfort Mountain in the Abram S. Hewitt State Forest another outstanding series of paths have been cut through. The Trail Conference also has responsibility for maintaining almost 200 miles of marked trails in Palisades Interstate Park. Information on club addresses and publications can be obtained by sending 10¢ to the New York–New Jersey Trail Conference, G.P.O. 2250, New York City. Regional trail maps, 25¢ each.

STATE PARKS AND HISTORIC SITES *

New Jersey state parks and forests are open year 'round, and many have not only scenic attractions but a host of facilities for recreation. Entrance to most of the parks is free. Leaflets on charges for day and night facilities supplied free by the New Jersey Department of Environmental Protection, Box 1390, Trenton, N.J.

Most of the State-owned historic sites are open daily except Mondays and major holidays. Hours are usually from 10 to 12 and 2-5; Sun. 2-5. Fees usually 25¢. Advance appointments are required for group tours (*see chart for addresses*). Descriptive folders for each park or site can also be had at the individual localities.

* The following chart is reproduced through the courtesy of the New Jersey Environmental Protection Department.

NEW JERSEY STATE FORESTS, PARKS & RECREATION AREAS	Map Locations	Acreage	Bathhouse	Bathing	Small Boat Launching (With or Without Motors)	Small Boat Launching (No Motors)	Boat and/or Canoe Rentals	Cabins	Camping (Family)	Camping (Group)
Abram S. Hewitt Forest	B-6	1,890								
* Allaire Park	F-7	2,029							•	•
* Barnegat Lighthouse Park	H-7	31	•	•						
* Bass River Forest	H-6	9,100	•	•		•	•	•	•	•
* Belleplain Forest	K-5	11,223	•	•		•			•	•
Bull's Island Rec. Area	E-4	80			•				•	
* Cheesequake Park	E-7	1,001	•	•					•	•
* Edison Park	D-6	36								
* Fort Mott Park	H-2	104			•					
* Hacklebarney Park	C-5	569								
* High Point Park	A-5	12,396	•	•		•		•	•	•
* Hopatcong Park	C-5	108	•	•						
* Island Beach Park	G-7	3,002	•	•						
* Jenny Jump Forest	C-4	1,118						•	•	•
* Lebanon Forest	G-6	26,996	•	•				•	•	•
Norvin Green Forest	B-6	2,296								
* Parvin Park	J-4	1,125	•	•		•	•	•	•	
* Penn Forest	H-6	3,366	•	•		•				
Rancocas Park	G-5	1,056			•					
Ringwood Park	B-7	3,112	•	•		•	•			•
* Ringwood Manor	B-7	579								
* Shepherd Lake	B-7	541	•	•		•	•			
Skylands	B-7	1,117								
* Round Valley Rec. Area	D-5	4,000			•				•	
* Sandy Hook Park	E-8	795	•	•						
* Spruce Run Rec. Area	D-4	1,863	•	•	•					
* Stephens-Saxton Falls Park	C-5	222		•					•	
* Stokes Forest	A-5	14,843	•	•		•		•	•	•
* Swartswood Park	B-5	1,253	•	•		•	•		•	•
* Voorhees Park	D-5	437							•	
* Washington Crossing Park	E-5	785								
Washington Rock Park	D-6	36								
Wawayanda Park	A-6	6,025				•	•			•
* Wharton Forest	H-5	99,639		•	•			•	•	•
* Worthington Forest	B-4	5,830			•				•	•

HISTORIC SITES

	Map Locations
Absecon Lighthouse	J-6
* Allaire Village	F-7
* Barnegat Lighthouse	H-7
* Batsto Village	H-5
* Boxwood Hall	D-7
* Cleveland Birthplace	C-7
* Fort Mott	H-2
* Hancock House	J-3
* Indian King Tavern	G-4
* Lawrence House	F-5
* McKonkey Ferry House	E-5
* Old Dutch Parsonage	D-5
Ringwood Manor House	B-7
* Rockingham	E-5
Somers Mansion	K-5
Trenton Battle Mon.	F-5
Twin Lights	E-8
Von Steuben House	C-7
* Wallace House	D-5
Walt Whitman House	G-4

LODGE RENTAL (BELLEPLAIN)
LODGE ROOMS (HIGH POINT)
RESTAURANT (SHEPHERD LAKE)

TRAP AND SKEET SHOOT (SHEPHERD LAKE)
ANTIQUE TRAIN RIDES (ALLAIRE)
GARDENS (RINGWOOD MANOR
AND SHEPHERD LAKE)

Children's Playground	Fishing	Hiking	Horseback Trails	Hunting	Manor House	Historic House Museum	Nature Area	Naturalist Service	Observation Tower or Lookout	Picnicking	Refreshments	*Folders for individual Forests, Parks, Recreation Areas and Historic Sites are available upon request. Mailing Address
		●	●						●			c/o Ringwood State Park
●	●	●	●			●	●	●		●	●	Box 218, Farmingdale 07727
	●								●			c/o Island Beach State Park
●	●	●	●	●			●	●		●	●	New Gretna 08224
●	●	●	●	●			●			●	●	R.D. 2, Woodbine 08270
	●						●			●		R.D. 2, Box 242, Stockton 08559
●	●	●					●			●	●	Matawan 07747
					●							Edison 08817
●	●								●	●		R.D. 3, Salem 08079
●	●						●			●	●	R.R. 2, Long Valley 07853
●	●	●					●	●	●	●	●	Sussex 07461
●	●									●	●	Landing 07850
	●						●	●		●	●	Seaside Park 08752
●		●		●			●		●	●		Box 150, Hope 07844
		●	●	●				●		●		New Lisbon 08064
		●	●						●			c/o Ringwood State Park
●	●	●					●	●		●	●	R.D. 1, Elmer 08318
●	●	●	●	●						●		c/o Bass River State Forest
	●		●				●	●				Box 69, Rancocas 08073
●	●	●		●	●		●	●	●	●	●	R.D., Box 1304, Ringwood 07456
●	●	●		●			●	●		●	●	c/o Ringwood State Park
●	●	●							●	●	●	c/o Ringwood State Park
	●	●	●	●								c/o Ringwood State Park
	●	●	●						●			c/o Spruce Run Rec. Area
	●						●	●		●	●	Box 417, Highlands 07732
	●	●	●						●			R.D. 2, Clinton 08809
●	●	●								●	●	Hackettstown, 07840
●	●	●	●				●	●	●	●	●	R.R. 2, Branchville 07826
●	●		●				●	●		●	●	R.R. 5, Box 548, Newton 07860
	●	●	●				●		●	●		R.D., Glen Gardner 08826
●	●	●				●	●	●		●	●	R.D. 1, Titusville 08560
									●	●		Green Brook 08812
	●	●	●				●					Box 198, Highland Lks. 07422
●	●	●	●	●	●	●	●	●		●	●	Batsto, R.D. 1, Hammonton 08037
	●	●	●				●		●	●		c/o Stokes State Forest
						●		●				c/o Wharton State Forest
						●					●	c/o Allaire State Park
								●				c/o Island Beach State Park
					●	●					●	Batsto R.D. 1, Hammonton 08215
						●						Elizabeth 07201
						●						Caldwell 07006
								●				c/o Fort Mott State Park
						●						Hancock's Bridge 08038
						●						Haddonfield 08034
						●						Burlington 08016
						●						c/o Washington Crossing St. Pk.
						●						Somerville 08876
					●							c/o Ringwood State Park
						●						Rocky Hill 08553
						●						Somers Point 08244
Elevator Service									●			207 Old Rose St., Trenton 08618
						●		●				c/o Sandy Hook State Park
						●						River Edge 07661
						●						Somerville 08876
						●						Camden 08103

No reservations for facilities are handled by the Trenton Office. Reservations should be made through the Area Office. Rate lists and application forms may be obtained by writing to the mailing address listed above.

SUPPLEMENT

BERNARDSVILLE

From Bernardsville ctr., take 202 W and turn left at second traffic light. Continue to small intersection, at Hardscrabble Rd. About 1 mi. from here is . . .

SCHERMAN WILDLIFE SANCTUARY   100 acres

NEW JERSEY AUDUBON SOCIETY

An estimated 300 varieties of plants grow in this wooded preserve coursed by Indian Grove Brook, once part of the Harry Scherman country estate and now a restful haven for visitors and wildlife. The stone house is thought to have been built in the early 19th century. Walks are laid out for nature study and there is also a small teaching museum. Group classes for children and adults. Tues. through Sat., 9-5. Free. Children under 15 must be accompanied by an adult. 201-766-5787.

BURLINGTON

Entrance to following 3 buildings of Burlington County Historical Society through their Cooper House, 457 High St., see p. 203. Donations welcomed. Sun. 1-4; Groups: 609-386-4773.

PEARSON-HOW HOUSE   ca. 1705-1725   455 High St.

Great minds tend to have many facets. Isaac Pearson's was such a mind. He was one of three founders of the famous Mt. Holly ironworks constructed there about 1730. During the Revolution Pearson's iron smelter was the source of cannon and ammunition for the patriots, a fact that enraged the British. Their raiders effectively wrecked Mt. Holly furnace. Today Isaac Pearson is almost forgotten as an ironmaster but is famed as New Jersey's first silversmith. Also a fine clockmaker, he was first in the Colonies to make both the works and the cases of "grandfather" clocks.

This house where Pearson lived from about 1710 to 1749 now has one of his treasured signed clocks. Restored both inside and out, this dwelling contains some rare 18th-century furnishings.

Samuel How, owner of the house from 1782 to at least 1839, was a Burlington County judge.

ALINE WOLCOTT MUSEUM

Antique lighting devices and early kitchen and farm equipment are noteworthy in the 500-piece Wolcott collection. A surprising item is a jinricksha made for export by the James H. Birch carriage factory of Burlington in the 1860s. Charming collections of children's treasures.

DELIA BIDDLE PUGH LIBRARY

Scarce source material, out-of-print books, maps and deeds relating to the history of Burlington County and New Jersey. Also photographs by historians Nathanael Ewan and George DeCou.

CHESTER TWP.

BLACK RIVER PARK   240 acres
MORRIS CO. PARK COMMISSION

Rte. 24. W of Chester and rd. near Milltown leading S to Hacklebarney Park.

More of the fascinating terrain of Black River is preserved in this park restricted to hiking and fishing. An old mill will be restored and opened to the public.

DOVER

HEDDEN PARK   210 acres
MORRIS CO. PARK COMMISSION

Entrances from Reservoir Ave. or Concord Rd.

This ruggedly beautiful park with Indian Falls and several rock outcroppings is in the midst of Dover. Jackson and Wallace brooks flow through the park which has an abundance of wildlife, laurel and large oaks. Picnic sites, hiking trails, parking, a softball field. Free.

FAR HILLS
Rte. 512, Liberty Corner Rd.

UNITED STATES GOLF ASSOCIATION, HDQS.

American golfing's Hall of Fame is now luxuriously situated at the 60-acre estate and 3-story Georgian-style mansion formerly owned by the W. J. Sloane family. Among the memorabilia in the organization's 78-year history: the Bob Jones room containing his 13 national championship medals; clubs used by Presidents Taft, Wilson, Franklin Roosevelt, Harding, Eisenhower and Kennedy; a photograph gallery including such rare ones as Franklin Roosevelt swinging a club. A golfing library of 5,000 volumes. The building's architect was John Russell Pope who also designed the Jefferson Memorial and the National Gallery of Art. Free, Mon.-Fri., 9-5.

FLEMINGTON

BLACK RIVER & WESTERN RAILROAD Turntable Junction, Inc.   2 Church St.

A 12-mile ride through the hills of Hunterdon County from Flemington to Ringoes is the delight of children and adults. This is a full-size train, with standard-gauge tracks. The coaches and stations of Black River & Western Railroad are furnished in nostalgia: oil lamps, pot-bellied stoves, green plush seats, and sun-bonneted hostesses. About 9 round trips daily, $2.00, and $1.00 for children.

Although fired up with steam for tourists from April through November, the BR&W is diesel-powered in winter, for the line hauls some 600 freight cars a year. So popular are the summer excursions that groups now make reservations for caboose trips on the diesel freight. 201-782-6622, or P.O. Box 83, Ringoes, N.J. 08551.

TURNTABLE JUNCTION, INC. Church St. just W of Main

Next to the BR&W depot is this re-created early 19th-century village with about 30 shops, craft studios and food shops such as the Lunch Bell with country school atmosphere. On a siding in the center of the village is a quaint early caboose and the Patriots' Dining Car. Hub of the village is the openair turntable beside the Spread Eagle Inne offering meals and lodging. Particular attention is paid to groups who are often given an entire day's program devoted to their special tastes, whether cookery, antiques or history. Phone 201-782-8550. Free admission. Open year 'round.

LIBERTY VILLAGE   Church St. opp. Turntable Junction.

First-rate museums and professional craftsmen at work can be viewed in the individual buildings.

Vandermark Glasshouse   In Colonial costume, two young men with fast reflexes create handblown glass in the early Jersey style, even the famed lilypad pitcher.

Swan Museum of the Revolution   Kels Swan, collector of this fabulous assemblage of documents and relics of the Revolution, is usually on hand to enlighten visitors. First floor has some unusual 17th century furnishings.

Viviane Beck Ertell Button Collection   Far from utility buttons, these are exquisite objets d'art, jeweled, enameled, sculptured. Also a collection of antique glass and silver.

Boehm's Birds   An entire house, furnished in antiques, is devoted to displays of Edward Marshall Boehm's ceramics which are made in New Jersey and early American silver.

Gunsmith Shop   One of only 3 such in the nation, where antique firearms are re-created from maple boards into finely detailed collectors' guns.

Charles Palmer Woodworking Tools, William Titfoot Forge, candle-dipping, weaving.

Guides on hand at each house. $2.00 and $1.25. 10:30-5:30 daily.

RAGGEDY ANN ANTIQUE DOLL AND TOY MUSEUM   171 Main St. at Church St.

An entrancing collection of dolls of many lands and quaint toys. 75¢ and 50¢. 201-782-1243.

GREEN BANK

At Rtes. 542 and 563, take latter N for 7 mi. to settlement of Jenkins Neck, then marked right road for 2 mi. to . . .

PENN STATE FOREST   3,318 acres

Seasoned Jersey canoeists know well this woodland of loblolly pines, chiefly because Lake Oswego here leads to the Oswego wilderness stream, to the ghost-town site of Harrisville, thence to Wading River, and on out to tidewater Mullica. Penn State Forest is a living memorial to young men of the Civilian Conservation Corps created in the great Depression of the 1930s. Nearly incredible today, the good roads that extend for miles through this forest were built by hand, without road machinery, by teenagers of the vicinity. They also raised the dam which formed Lake Oswego, and along which one can drive to New Gretna. The attractive bathhouse and a picnic shelter a few miles beyond it are structures also built by the CCC men. Blueberry bushes, fishing, swimming in a small clean lake with hard bottom are other attractions. Lifeguards in summer. No camping, but see nearby Absegami Forest. Cranberry bogs on two sides of Lake Oswego. Canoe rentals at Jenkins.

HACKENSACK

WORLD WAR II SUBMARINE, THE *LING*

Hackensack River at Hackensack

The *Ling,* only surviving high-speed submarine of the U.S. fleet from World War II, has been presented to the State of New Jersey and is now moored in the Hackensack River. The 312-foot vessel is a memorial to the 3,505 American submariners who died in that war. Members of the Submarine Memorial Association of Hackensack have taken title to the historic craft in order to restore for opening to the public.

ROSELAND-LIVINGSTON

Follow Eagle Rock Ave. to Roseland Center. Continue on Eagle Rock for 1.7 mi. to Locust Ave. on left, **BECKER TRACT** (Essex Co. Park Commission) 1969

Left naturally wild, these 146 acres with brooks and fine white oak trees have much appeal for birdwatchers and other naturalists. Walking trails on easy terrain.

HIGHLANDS

FORT HANCOCK, Sandy Hook peninsula

Relatively few tourists have ever trod the northern tip of Sandy Hook, on which the U.S. Army's Fort Hancock has been located since 1807. But now individuals as well as groups are welcome to view the grounds of this once top-secret missile base. Applications should be sent to the Deputy Post Commander, Fort Hancock, attention of Operations Officer, Highlands, N.J. 07732. On Saturdays the museum is likely to be open from 11 to 4. Besides seeing a panorama of the New Jersey-New York harbor, visitors can also view one of the largest cannons ever built and get a close-up of venerable Sandy Hook beacon, now supervised by the U.S. Coast Guard. This oldest continuously operated lighthouse in the nation has a fixed light visible for 19 miles (see also p. 89).

Before the U.S. Bicentennial of 1976, the upper three-fourths of Sandy Hook will become part of the 26,142-acre National Gateway Recreational Area, ringing this most historic Federal harbor.

HOLMDEL

GARDEN STATE ARTS CENTER

At Telegraph Hill Park, Garden State Pkwy., Exit 116

This popular center for the performing arts in an attractive setting at historic Telegraph Hill features national stars in symphony, ballet, musicals and light opera, jazz and rock, as well as noted entertainers. Programs announced in New Jersey and New York newspapers. Fri. and Sat., 9 P.M.; other nights, 8:30. $3.50 to $7.50 at box office or by mail to Box 116, Holmdel, N.J. 07733. Season usually June through Sept. Nonprofit, sponsored by the New Jersey Highway Authority. A variety of afternoon programs, mostly for special-interest groups. 201-264-9200.

LAMBERTVILLE

JAMES MARSHALL HOUSE *(State historic site)*
    60 Bridge St.

In 1964, New Jersey's Tercentenary year, this house was scheduled to be torn down for a parking lot. Since then the home of James Marshall, first man to discover gold in California, was purchased by the State and has been attractively restored, a monumental refutation to Alistair Cooke's statement that the discovery of gold at Sutter's Mill was made by a Scotsman named Marshall. As yet, no gold nuggets are on exhibit. The house is now the office of the Lambertville Historical Society. See p. 146.

MATAWAN

THOMAS WARNE MUSEUM AND LIBRARY From
    Rte. 9, take 516 E about 3 mi., toward Matawan.
MADISON TOWNSHIP HISTORICAL SOCIETY

In this one-room Cedar Grove School House, ca. 1885, two of New Jersey's famous early potters, Warne & Letts, partners at South Amboy, are honored by examples of their pioneering stoneware. Here too are local fossils and Indian artifacts, early farm tools and Colonial primitives from a richly historic area neglected in modern times. Wed. 9:30-12 N. Also first Wed. eve. of month, 7:30-8:30.

MILFORD

From Bulls Island State Park it's enjoyable to travel north on Rte. 29 and visit quaint Frenchtown on the Delaware, and thence take Rte. 32 to Milford. From there travel Rte. 519 NW toward Warren Glen. About halfway, in Holland township, is the entrance to . . .

MUSCONETCONG GORGE NATURE PRESERVE 353
acres bisected by Rte. 519, nr. Dennis Rd., N of Oak
Hill golf course.

HUNTERDON COUNTY PARK COMMISSION

Saved in 1973 by County and State funds these forested
hilly acres will, hopefully, always stay wild. Nearby are
the meandering Musconetcong and the swift-flowing
Delaware, while roundabout are long vistas of early
American farmlands.

West of Rte. 519 are a series of roads dipping sharply
to the Delaware. At Spring Mills Farm, a yellowstone
and white clapboard farmhouse on a rich scale, Spring
Mills road wends to a way that should be preserved as a
relic of the Delaware frontier: green meadows full of fat
sheep in spring, sagging 200-year-old farmhouses, filled
corncribs, stone barns, placid cattle, and at the bottom
of the hill, the tiny Holland church.

South of Spring Mills Farm is Spring Garden road,
still wild, and north is Andersen road where modern
householders are beginning to build, but with feeling for
this lovely country.

Out of Milford, from Rte. 519 N, turn left on Ander-
sen Rd. At dead end, follow slight jog, which becomes
Adamic Hill Rd., to . . .

OLD DUTCH WINDMILL   (private but open to public)

A startling sight in modern Jersey is this full size
Dutch windmill, yet it is singularly appropriate because
Netherlanders were among the first white settlers here
along the Delaware in the mid-1600s. This authentic
mill for grinding grain into flour is the dedicated construction of Poul Jorgensen who remembered with nostalgia such a mill when he was a boy in Denmark during
World War I. The millstones, weighing over 4,000
pounds, were hand-hewn in the Marne Valley, France.
With sails flying, the octagonal mill rises to 90 feet. Mr.
and Mrs. Jorgensen act as guides, from April through
November. Daily, except Tues., 10-6. Donations welcomed.

MILLVILLE

WHEATON VICTORIAN VILLAGE

Entering from N via Rte. 555, turn left at Coombs Rd. or G St. and follow signs marked with a glass flask.

A fresh approach in re-created "villages," this one is Victoriana in the light Cape May style. As the village is maintained by a foundation of the Wheaton Company, whose forebears and descendants are glassmakers, this community is the first large-scale tribute to Jersey glassmen, American pioneers in the art. Quite sensational is the full-size replica of a flaming furnace like that built for Dr. T. C. Wheaton in the 1880s. Seasoned glass gaffers are at work here producing their handmade objects in the old-time manner. A museum of glassmakers' tools in conjunction. In a separate building a large museum of many types of glass from hand-made to pressed. Museum, $1.00. An old-fashioned general store, gift shops, a Victorian ice-cream plaza. Weekdays, 9:30-5.

MORRISTOWN

On Morris St. just E of railroad trestle, turn left on Ridgedale; at East Hanover Ave. go right for about 2 mi. to Morris County Library; entrance opposite is . . .

FRELINGHUYSEN ARBORETUM 125 acres
MORRIS COUNTY PARK SYSTEM

A rose garden, plantings of some 20,000 tulips and other bulbs, trails of azaleas and rhododendrons, and flowering trees are among delights on this former country estate. Library of over 700 volumes on horticulture. Special lectures on gardening, $1. Grounds and house free. From April through Nov., daily 9-5; other months, except 2 in midwinter, open Mon.-Fri. 201-285-6166.

MORRIS MUSEUM OF ARTS AND SCIENCES

Normandy Heights and Columbia Rds.

One of the elite group of nationally accredited educational museums, the Morris on busy weekends fairly throbs with the enthusiasm of families examining dinosaur bones and tracks, katchinka dolls, the Heiser portrait dolls, rare American Indian costumes, fluorescent minerals, operating exhibits on electricity, sound and color, art shows, and much more. An auditorium for concerts, films, puppet shows, and the astronomical and mineralogical societies. Numerous workshops. 10-5 weekdays; 2-5 Sun. Closed Sun. and Mon. July and Aug. Book tours 3 weeks ahead: 201-538-0454, or Box 125, Convent, N.J. 07961. Free; most tours, 25¢ per person.

ACORN HALL 1853 68 Morris Ave., next to Gov. Morris Hotel
MORRIS COUNTY HISTORICAL SOCIETY (headquarters)
A Victorian Italianate house scarcely changed, except for electricity and plumbing, since it was built by Morristown architect Ira Lindsley, this was the home from 1853 to 1971 of four related and prominent New York families stemming from Dr. John Schermerhorn, John Hone III, Augustus Crane and Dr. J. Leonard Corning. Among equally notable wives was Jane Perry, daughter of Com. Matthew C. Perry. In this house are lacquered tables and Japanese vases presented by the Emperor of Japan to Commodore Perry after the 1854 Treaty of Kanagawa, which he negotiated, opening Japan to the West for the first time in two centuries.

Remarkably, much of the furnishings in Acorn Hall— ceiling decor, woven carpets, wallpaper, draperies, lace curtains, Victorian furniture—is original. This living museum, the milieu of a group of well-to-do American families, was presented in 1971 by a descendant, Miss Mary Crane Hone, to the Morris County Historical Society. Open by appt. only: 201-539-5517.

ALFRED VAIL MILL AND VILLAGE 333 Speedwell
A cluster of Morristown residents and a descendant of the Vails have rescued this historic mill whence Alfred Vail and Samuel Morse sent the first telegraph message, on Jan. 10, 1838. In 1973 the giant iron waterwheel, 24 feet in diameter, began turning again, the refurbished

Vail homestead was opened with exhibits, and wooden patterns made at the Speedwell Iron Works were put on display. Three early houses about to be destroyed by new highways have been moved in and nestle as closely to the slopes as if they'd been there for 150 years. Tues., Thurs., 10-4. Sun. 2-5. Adults, 50¢. See also p. 50.

THE YESTERYEAR MUSEUM 300 Mendham Rd., 3½ mi. W of Morristown on Rte. 24, at Mendham Cultural Ctr., large building at crest of hill.

What Edison wrought, soon after he captured the secret of recording human voices and musical instruments, is the essence of this assemblage of musical nostalgia: music boxes, antique phonographs and records, pianolas, even a calliophone, all in playing order. But much more, for here is the collection of Charles Edison, a son of Thomas Alva, who was a Governor of New Jersey. Already popular, this could well become the most entertaining of musical Victoriana museums. Informative free guided tour. Weekends, 2-6 except in hot months, July-Sept. Groups by appt., midweek: 201-540-1890. Donations appreciated.

MT. HOLLY

Appr. 4 mi. from Mt. Holly on Rte. 626 . . .

RANCOCAS STATE PARK

In the nick of time, these thousand acres preserve a lovely stretch of the north and south branches of Rancocas Creek, historic Indian waters now favored by today's canoeists for tranquil cruising. Close by are historic towns like Mt. Holly, offering supplies as well. Canoe rentals at Pemberton. A ranger and a naturalist are on hand.

NEW BRUNSWICK

UNIVERSITY ART GALLERY Voorhees Hall, Hamilton Street bet. George and College Ave.

The former Voorhees Library, now an imposing home for some 3,500 paintings, prints, sculptures in rotating

displays. Art Library. Series of gallery talks and concerts.
Mon.-Sat., 10-4:30. Sun., 1:30-4:30. Free.

OCEAN CITY

OCEAN CITY HISTORICAL MUSEUM   409 Wesley Ave.

Life in an Ocean City Victorian home takes on delightful reality here in authentic room settings with wax models, including children, wearing appropriate costumes. The latter range from some as lavish as those in the film "Gone with the Wind," to amusing Gay Nineties bathing suits.

A splendid 4-masted bark, the *Sindia* left Japan in July, 1901, to sail the 10,000 miles around Cape Horn with a valuable cargo for New York. In a violent December storm the vessel foundered on the sands off Ocean City and could not be saved. Ever since, people have been collecting relics and bits of cargo such as Japanese porcelains. The *Sindia* room here tells the full story, even contains the ship's figurehead.

Excellent collections of dolls, shells, Indian artifacts, early postcards, maps, stamps, decoys, and mounted birds. Summer: Mon.-Sat., 10-4; winter: Tues.-Sat., 1-4. Free. Groups by appt. 609-399-1801.

CULTURAL ARTS CENTER OF OCEAN CITY
409 Wesley Ave.

Townsfolk and tourists commingle happily at the center which has gallery exhibits changed monthly, free films on second Tuesday nights of the month, popular classes taught by experts in painting, sculpture, drama, ballet, fencing, as well as special concerts and lectures. Schedule of events available at center. Open year round. Tues.-Sat., 10-4. Tues., Wed., Thurs., 7-10 P.M. 609-399-7628, Ext. 80.

PARAMUS

BERGEN COMMUNITY MUSEUM   Ridgewood and Far
View Aves.

The skeleton of the Hackensack mastodon uncovered on a highway site in recent years is the magnet in the

Science Hall that has many other attractions as well. For other visitors, the B. Spencer Newman art gallery with changing exhibits every 6 weeks ranks in quality with metropolitan art exhibits. Altogether, a top-rated museum for activists: demonstrations, lectures, craft classes. Exhibits free. Wed.-Sat., 1-5. Sun., 2-6.

PRINCETON

PRINCETON UNIVERSITY MUSEUM OF ART

On campus

The subtle interior design of this building has created so congenial an atmosphere for fine art that great collections seem to be magnetized here, to wit, the 1973 show of treasures from the Norton Simon Foundation. On entering, the impression is one of uplift to splendor, yet almost subliminally there is a glimpse of more riches below. Extensive collections from Western Europe, the United States, East Asia, and the early Mediterranean. Tues.-Sat., 10-4; Sun. in academic year, 1-5; summer, 2-4.

RAMSAY

From Rte. 17 N take Spring St., overpass to Island Rd., location of . . .

THE OLD STONE HOUSE ca. 1709 (State owned)

RAMSAY HISTORICAL ASSOCIATION (museum)

Saved by the historical society from highway destruction in 1965, this Dutch Colonial cottage seems rockbound against the centuries. Known also as the Benjamin Westervelt house, for its first owner, the hip-roofed dwelling has been carefully restored and furnished chiefly with Colonial Dutch antiques, including a rare *kas* or cupboard. Sun. 2-4:30, Apr. to Nov. 25¢ and 10¢. From Wyckoff a pleasant route to Ramsay is Wyckoff Ave. In Ramsay on W. Main, turn left at N. Central Ave. and Island Rd. for about 1 mi., to dead end at Spring St.

RAVEN ROCK

BULL'S ISLAND STATE PARK

Today Bull's Island, 78 lushly wooded acres opposite the tiny settlement of Raven Rock below a limestone escarpment, is a haven for quiet campers and fishermen who catch bass, pickerel and shad in the fast-flowing Delaware. One enters the park over a bridge atop the original canal locks. North tip of the island offers a boat ramp; no rentals, no lifeguards. From a suspension foot-bridge leading to Lumberville, Pa., there is a stirring view of the Delaware, one of the great historic rivers of the United States.

RINGWOOD

SKYLANDS MANOR AND GARDENS   1920s
   (State historic site)
   A section of Ringwood State Park (see pp. 11-13). From Ringwood Park entrance go south 0.2 mi. and turn left at Morris Ave.

This 44-room English Jacobean mansion on a thousand acres of flowering wooded land with mountain vistas was created for financier McKenzie Lewis. With richly carved paneling and mantels, mullioned and stained-glass windows, the interior, even though not furnished, is as impressive as an English castle. The grounds are a lovely sight from May through September when there are colorful displays of spring flowers, crab-apple trees, rhododendrons and chrysanthemums. 9:30-4:30. Grounds, free; guided tour of manor, 25¢. The thickly wooded, hilly estate has 15 miles of equestrian trails.

SOMERS POINT

ATLANTIC COUNTY HISTORICAL SOCIETY *(museum)*
   907 Shore Rd. nr. Circle

Devoted and generous volunteers in historical conservation have graduated to their own 3-story brick building housing a museum of Jerseyana and Victoriana, especially that of The Shore, and an excellent library. The society is continuing to contribute period furnishings to the nearby Somers mansion. Exhibit-teas held second Sundays of summer and fall months, 1-4. Lectures (admission fee) on first Monday evenings in winter months. Museum and library open Tues. through Sat., 10-4.

Castle-like Skylands Manor has old-English fireplaces, paneled walls hand-carved, lovely gardens, splendid vistas. See Supplement.

Photo by Adeline Pepper

SOMERVILLE

Rte. 206 S of Somerville Circle; at Dukes Pkwy. and traffic light, turn right to Duke Farms for . . .

EXHIBITION OF SOUTHEAST ASIAN ART AND CULTURE 1972

Scores of antique Thai and Burmese art objects, many of them gilded or inlaid with semiprecious stones, mirrors and mother-of-pearl, create a glittering display against walls hung with rich Thai silks. The unique collection ranges from 12th century Burmese stone portraits to 18th century hand-carved altars and monks' beds. Sculptured bronze temple birds, grotesque masks worn by Thai dancers, ancient musical instruments, and Oriental paintings are just a few of the many rare objects described on a guided tour. Admission $2.50. Tues.-Sat., 1-5. Advance reservations required; phone 201-722-3700. Closed July and Aug.

WALLACE HOUSE 38 Washington Pl.

After undergoing major historical restoration, this house, where Washington stayed longer than at any other during the Revolution, was re-opened in 1972 and is now furnished with rooms of the period, which include fascinating possessions of the general. See p. 74.

SUMMIT

SUMMIT ART CENTER 68 Elm St.

With over 1,000 members and 400 students, this non-profit organization founded in 1933 expanded in 1973 to handsome new quarters with numerous studios and a mezzanine gallery offering frequent exhibits. 201-273-9121.

TUCKERTON

Rte. 9 about midway between Tuckerton and New Gretna . . .

THE UGLY DUCKLING
DORFEE GLASS WORKS

In a cluster of quavery buildings reminiscent of drawings by Ronald Searle, Dr. Suess and Maurice Sendak,

Life-size Buddha in gilded, jewel-encrusted costume is one of hundreds of Oriental treasures from the Exhibition of Southeast Asian Art and Culture on the Duke estate at Somerville.

Courtesy of Duke Farms

some true craftsmen are at work, in the Jersey tradition. The Ugly Duckling specializes in decorative aquatic birds, carved and painted on the premises.

Next door is Dorfee Glass Works with its Company Store and a ramshackle house where one can watch molten glass being formed into realistic objects: fragile spiders, zodiac symbols, imitations of early Jersey wineglasses. This is not glassblowing in the early Jersey style with 5-foot iron blowpipes. Nor is it fussy "lampwork," which are souvenir items, usually. A glassmaking graduate of the Salem Vocational Institute, Michael Dorofee is creating some originals. Daily, 10-5. Free.

WAYNE TOWNSHIP

From Franklin Lakes Tpke. drive west on Rte. 502 (Berdan Ave.) to Point View Reservoir adjacent to . . .

VAN RIPER-HOPPER HOUSE   1786

WAYNE MUSEUM (Wayne Historical Commission)

Six fireplaces, pine-planked floors and great hand-hewn beams attest the antiquity of this hospitable Dutch farmhouse, a choice example of the homes of Jersey's earliest European settlers. In 1786 Uriah Van Riper built this solid fieldstone house when he married Polly Berdan. Decades later, "Yurrie's" great-granddaughter, Mary Ann Van Riper, married Andrew Hopper, and the generations continued . . . until 1928. In Dutch tradition, the main hearth fire was never allowed to die until New Year's day when a new flame was set on the clean bricks. Still today there is a cozy hearth in the kitchen, as well as other rooms furnished in antiques. Picnic tables beside an herb garden. Mon., Tues., Fri., Sat., Sun., 1-5. Free. Groups: 201-694-7192.

RAMAPO VALLEY COUNTY RESERVATION

624 acres

Bergen County Park Commission

Take Rte. 23, then 202 NE to Oakland. At edge of town, 202 becomes Ramapo Valley Rd. Follow about 7 mi. to Immaculate Conception Seminary. Entrance on left . . .

A microcosm of the Ramapo mountains, which still retain their brooding mystery, this wilderness preserve is covered by tall forests beneath which are masses of boulders and thick growth of shrubs. Here too is a portion of the Ramapo river, open to canoeists (bring your own), as well as several mountain streams with lovely waterfalls. A steep rocky climb of about a mile ends at a beautiful spring-fed lake, McMillan reservoir. Another trail leads to a lookout from which Manhattan towers can be seen. On low ground is a deep pond where fishing is allowed and around which are picnic and tent sites. Some firm rules: positively no swimming, and no vehicles allowed except at the entrance parking lot. Free. Rangers on duty.

About .2 mi. N of Ramapo Valley Park, at Darlington Ave., turn right to signs for . . .

DARLINGTON COUNTY PARK   180 acres

Bergen County Park Commission

A wooded, green-lawn park with three spring-fed lakes, two for swimming, the other for fishing and boating, is for people who enjoy people. This well-run park offers sand beaches, bathhouses, lifeguards, snack bars, game courts, and an 18-hole golf course planned for 1973. Free, except for swimming season of Memorial Day to Labor Day, when rates are $1.00 to $3.00. 201-327-3500. Or write Bergen County Park Commission, Hackensack, N.J. 07601. Closed Dec. through March.

Turning west for .2 mi. toward Rte. 202, take left turn to

CAMP GAW MOUNTAIN RESERVATION 1351 acres

Bergen County Park Commission

Although a hilly terrain with fine stands of trees, Camp Gaw Mountain is far less rugged than Ramapo Park and

A genuine stagecoach that ran in the 19th century between Absecon and Long-a-Coming now offers excitement for children at Batsto Village.

Photo by Adeline Pepper

"Rockingham" at Rocky Hill, where General Washington wrote his "Farewell to the Armies of the United States," Nov. 2, 1783. See p. 188.

Photo by Adeline Pepper

provides less demanding trails. Wooded picnic groves and secluded camp sites (by permit), some with tent platforms. The 4½ miles of bridle trails are being supplemented with a riding center offering instruction and horses for hire. A ski area with a 1500-foot main slope has two chair lifts and machine-made snow. Flanking side trails depend on natural snow. Also 1600-foot toboggan chutes. In warm weather the ski lodge becomes a nature center offering a small museum and special programs for groups.

In the American Revolution *Ramapo Valley Road* was one of the few routes passable by military forces in this mountain wilderness of north Jersey. Near Oakland, at the juncture of Ramapo Valley Road and Franklin Ave., is an old stone house, the *Hendrick Van Allan* homestead, where Washington and his troops rested on July 14 and 15, 1777.

WESTFIELD

Appr. 1 mi. N of E. Broad St. Accessible also from Route 22.

MILLER-CORY HOUSE c. 1740. **614 Mountain Ave.**
WESTFIELD HISTORICAL SOCIETY FOUNDATION

Surrounded by Colonial-style houses where there may be microwave ovens, this genuine Colonial farmhouse of white clapboard has recently been the scene where dried-apple pies were baked at the hearth, just one of many craft demonstrations that has caused visitors to stand in line on Sunday afternoons to see the inside of the farmhouse built by Samuel Miller, then lived in by Joseph Cory and his descendants from the 1780s to 1921. Rescued and preserved by dollars and devoted labor from hundreds of people in the Westfield area, even beyond, this dwelling, within 6 months of opening in September, 1972, became a living museum. Weekday group tours: 201-232-5788. Sun., 2-5. 50¢ and 25¢.

WHIPPANY

At Whippany station of Morris County Central Railroad . . .

THE PINE HILL EXPRESS

"The Great Train Robbery," one of the first movies, was filmed in New Jersey, so what could be more fitting than a bandit holdup of an 8-mile excursion on this bona fide railroad? Passengers are furnished with "funny money" for the "robbery." Interesting rolling stock for buffs of all ages. Hourly weekend trips, 1-4. Daily schedule, July and Aug. Adults, $2; children 3 to 11, $1.

INDEX OF PRINCIPAL
PLACE NAMES

Places starred (★) are open to the public at certain times.
Towns are in italics.

Note: The Supplement, which supplies new information on tour sites, is not indexed, but places of interest can be readily located through the following alphabetical list of towns: Bernardsville, Burlington, Chester Twp., Dover, Far Hills, Flemington, Hackensack, Highlands, Holmdel, Lambertville, Matawan, Milford, Millville, Morristown, Mt. Holly, New Brunswick, Ocean City, Paramus, Princeton, Ramsay, Ringwood, Somers Point, Somerville, Tuckerton, Summit, Wayne Township, Westfield, Whippany.

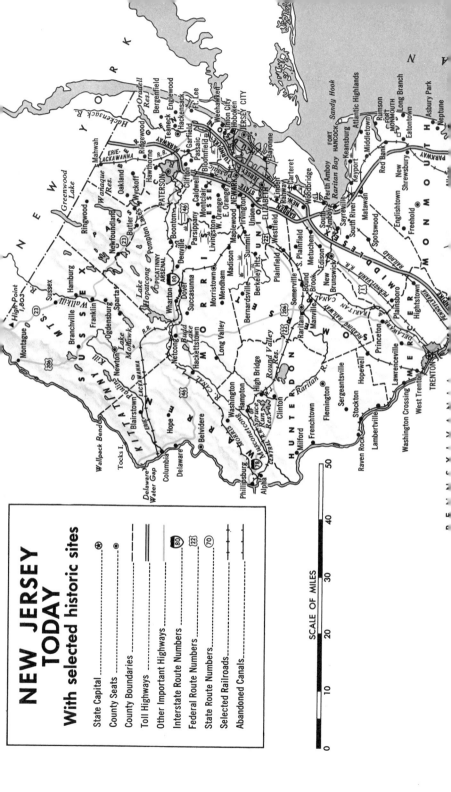

NEW JERSEY TODAY
With selected historic sites

State Capital	⊛
County Seats	◉
County Boundaries	
Toll Highways	
Other Important Highways	
Interstate Route Numbers	80
Federal Route Numbers	22
State Route Numbers	70
Selected Railroads	
Abandoned Canals	

SCALE OF MILES

0   10   20   30   40   50

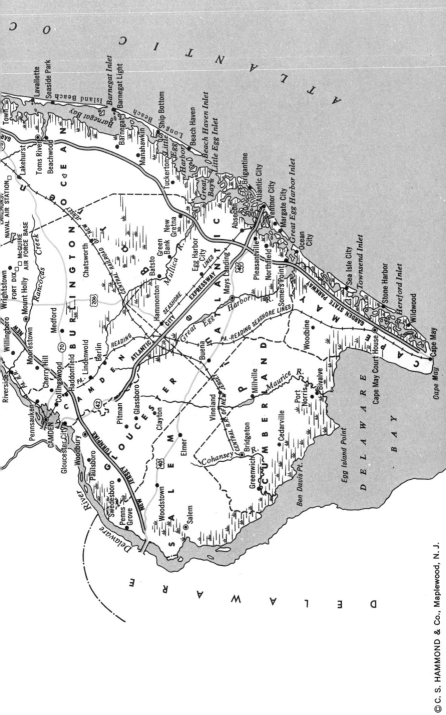